175

THE UNEXPECTED YEARS

Laurence Housman.

THE
UNEXPECTED
YEARS

By LAURENCE HOUSMAN

ILLUSTRATED

THE BOBBS-MERRILL COMPANY
PUBLISHERS
INDIANAPOLIS   NEW YORK

Printed in the United States of America

PREFACE

IF A man intends or expects to live to the age of seventy, he should not publish his reminiscences before. Reminiscences, to be in their right place, should come—like grace after meat—at the end, not in the middle of the meal; still less should they be trotted out (as has happened too often of late years) as an apéritif for the career which is to follow. For who, indeed, knows till the meal is over how much he has to be thankful for? A dessert of sour grapes may spoil everything. So long as a man feels that he has still much waiting for him to do, or to endure, or is still adventurously inclined, he would do well to postpone not perhaps the writing but the publication of his reminiscences.

I began writing my own a little before date, having no confident hope or wish to live beyond seventy. It had, in fact, always been my intention to die at sixty-seven, which I had come to regard as my lucky number. But when I reached that age I had no definite reason for wishing to part from life; and having now "passed on," in the sense of exceeding the time I had set myself, I have employed these last few unexpected years in putting on record memories of a life which to me at any rate, has been interesting, and of associations which I may reasonably hope will prove interesting to others.

"Was there ever," said my brother Alfred, on one occasion while recalling childish memories; "was there ever such an interesting family as we were?" There were probably many, but none, I daresay, more interested in itself, and for the shaping of that interest in all sorts of ingenious ways, he was largely responsible. At any rate, now that these reminiscences are finished, I find that the most interesting to me are its earliest chapters, to which distance in time has lent the proverbial enchantment.

As for the rest—the sixty years that came after—I look back on a life which has not, in the ordinary sense, been adventurous. Even such domestic adventures as marriage, paternity, divorce, bitter bereavement, have stayed beyond the range of my experience; I have not had to face either the misery of poverty or the anxieties of wealth; I have escaped the penalties of the law, and the terrorising influences of the theology which afflicted my youth. I have made and I have lost friends, with a residuum to the good. I have had pleasures and disappointments; but though the disappointments are perhaps more numerous and present to my recollection than the pleasures, I continue to find life worth having; its first ten years were the happiest, its next ten the least happy; after that, every decade has, so far as my personal experience is concerned, brought me increasing ease and contentment; and it seems to me now that if in age one can retain one's health, age is the likeliest time for getting on good terms with one's self and one's neighbours.

So much then, for the life I still have in hand, and to the brief prospect which lies ahead. Looking back on that which is passed, I see its ups and downs like an evenly disposed landscape of an arable rather than of a rugged and romantic character. In my fortunes there has been no steep rise or decline, no chasm has at any point opened under my feet; no torrent, without bridge or plank to provide a crossing, has turned me from the course to which my daily footsteps have led; looking back I see quite clearly the comparative uneventfulness of my life. Why, then, should I wish to tell of it, or expect it to have interest for others?

The main reason—for my own interest at any rate—is that it has been so unexpected, so extraordinarily unlike anything I had ever imagined that it could be—not merely in my childhood, when romantic dreams of an unrealizable kind were natural; but from then onward, in every decade that has followed, the unexpected has always happened—not sensationally or drastically, or even noticeably from an outward view, but in a vast multiplicity of small ways, mounting up into something that has always been fresh and spontaneous in its appearance, generally so ordinary that I could never have imagined what interest it would have for me.

What then, has this life of unexpected years done to me—given to me in such an unlooked-for degree as to make the ordinary so interesting? In the pages that follow I have reviewed in a measure the contacts, intimacies, estrangements, experiments, losings and findings, extending over more than half a century of the world's life, and in it this little spot of life which I thought my own.

That is the mistake one makes very early; and the violent intrusions of nurses, parents, relations, does nothing to lessen the illusion—rather the other way. When my nurse laid me across her knee and spanked me for things that I have now forgotten, in the midst of my helplessness I belonged desperately to myself, and if my mind to me was not exactly a kingdom under such circumstances, it was a rebellion against kings. And in my subsequent attitude there was more conformity than allegience towards the powers which ruled my life. That difference has, perhaps, continued. I have given more conformity than allegiance to the powers that be, and the conventions which impose themselves. But however little it conforms or tenders allegiance, no life worth living can be isolated from the lives of others. Even the rebel forms part of the general scheme of things, and if the scheme becomes a bloody entanglement, he belongs to it all the more. And that, I think, is what makes life so interesting: whether one wills it or no, one has to belong.

CONTENTS

ILLUSTRATIONS

THE UNEXPECTED YEARS

THE UNEXPECTED YEARS

CHAPTER I

"THE HOUSE WHERE I WAS BORN"

THE life of our first parents began in a garden; so, during its short stage of innocence, did mine, though I was born in a house. The house, with its thick coat of ivy and its sham Gothic windows, had its share in the upbringing of the family of seven in which I came last but one. But I think the garden, as a protector of our liberties and a field for individual development, was of more moral importance. There—as could not so easily be done within doors—we were able to get out of sight and hearing of our elders, and do very much as we liked, and there were many things we liked doing, which we preferred that our elders should not know.

" 'Tis very sure God walks in mine" wrote the poet, T. E. Brown, when singing his praise of gardens; and I, too, am sure, as I look back, that a God walked also in ours; but not the God of the Scriptures—not the God to whom we were made to say cold prayers, morning and evening, asking to be made good boys and girls, and be blessed, along with father, mother, brothers, and sisters ("all kind friends" were left out: our prayers for blessing were strictly family prayers). Our Garden-God was a very enjoyable God, but a God whom morals did not concern; and under his guidance we did things which were not wicked, only "naughty"—that is to say, natural. And the fact that the garden was nearly two acres in extent, and for the most part beautifully screened from the house, gave us—in those most important years of our family life—two acres of freedom from supervision for three or four hours daily.

15

House and garden lay at the foot of a small hill, at the top of which, less than two hundred yards away, stood Bromsgrove Church. Seen from our front lawn, it rose over a high bank of trees beginning with yew, laurel, birch and laburnum, and ending with the lime trees which made a ring around the churchyard. At the crowning point of all came the leaning lines of the spire, with its full-breasted weathercock, which, in later years, two of my sharpshooter brothers used as a target for practising with air rifles; and they would tell delightedly how they could hear the "ping" of their pellets, when with a lucky shot they got the Bird! Forty years later, when the weathercock was brought down for repair and regilding, perforations were discovered in it, and though no names were mentioned, the wanton damage was properly castigated in the local press.

That spire, whose serene beauty was a presiding presence through the early years of our childhood, and again in our later youth, attracted us in more ways than one. When peals were rung, we could see its top actually waggling with the vibration; the stone shaft seemed to bend as it swung on its axis; and in spite of our love for it, we longed to see it break and fall; for hungry curiosity is with the young a stronger force than affection.

One day, I remember, we came upon a spider's thread sloping down from the upper air to the lawn; and by the direction of its glint as it passed upwards, we saw that—if it had any attachment at all—it must be to the tower itself, or possibly even to the spire—so high, clear of the trees, was its drift.

One day, from that tower, I heard a man ring his own death knell. At half-past seven on a Saturday night, came a short sharp stroke of the small treble bell which we called the "ting-tang," and the next morning we heard that the sexton, crossing the belfry in the dark, had fallen through the trap door set open to clear the church from the fumes of its heating apparatus, and catching at the bell-rope in his descent, had broken it—but not sufficiently his fall; and on the floor below had been found dying by his nephew, who, a few minutes later, had remembered the open trap, and come running to warn him.

Living in a house thus close to the church, our childhood was timed very consciously to the sound of bells; peal, clock-stroke, and chime gave a decorative color to the passing hours, and the difference between weekdays and Sundays. The church clock and the clock on the stairs kept rival times; we heard them both equally; and so that they might serve a double use, we set our clock to a domestic time a quarter of an hour ahead—a useful reminder beforehand for the most important events of the day: breakfast at eight, school at nine, dinner at one, tea at five, and the late dinner of our parents at six—gradually thereafter shifting to seven, but never so far on as eight; for at ten even the grown-ups of the family had gone to bed; and when told of neighbors who sat up till eleven, we thought such an hour unreasonably late.

Our church bells had a ritual of their own, which I have never quite fathomed; for I did not inquire as to their meaning at a time when explanation might have been given; and now, I suppose, not only the ritual but all memory of it has gone. The curfew was rung regularly, and always with some record of days and dates in the changing sequence of its bells—the day of the week, the day of the month, the month, and I think also the year were consecutively numbered on a change of bells. A similar ringing took place on Sundays at seven in the morning, when there was no service to account for it; and then other numbers would be added, belonging to the Church Calendar. At one o'clock on Sundays a bell was again rung—why, I cannot imagine; but to that ringing we gave a domestic name and meaning of our own— "the Yorkshire-pudding bell" we called it; Yorkshire pudding being, on three Sundays out of five, or thereabouts, the most popular feature of the midday meal. Beef in some form or another, boiled or stewed, we might have on a weekday, but Yorkshire pudding never; contrary to the ways of manna, it came to us from Heaven only on the day of rest.

For church service, morning and evening, the bells rang a full half-hour; beginning small on two or three bells only, they mounted gradually to the full eight. The final crescendo took place at ten minutes to; this was our signal for a rush from happier engagements to get ready for church; and because it was a rush, we called them "the dreadful bells," while in the scant time left we got into our newest pairs of boots (never shoes), brushed hair, washed hands, cleaned nails, and then for a finishing touch—boys as well as girls—put on gloves. In those days it was not respectable to go to church with ungloved hands. Some years later, it became a mark of "high-church ways" to take gloves off during service, but in our family this was never done.

By the time the "dreadful bells" had ended, we were all assembled with our governess in charge, ready to start. Last of all, at five minutes to the hour, came the "ting-tang," a small cheerful wind-up on the treble bell; and as it began, forth we all sallied, crossed the road, went up the hill which was "Adams Hill," and were in our places beautifully to time.

I am sure that so long as we were at Bromsgrove, during those early years, we enjoyed church as much as was reasonable for young things. But when in my seventh year we changed home to Fockbury two miles away, with Catshill as our parish, church became a desolation and also something of a mockery. For the Vicar, poor man, had a dull mind and a heavy drawl. He was spiritually lazy, I think; and under his ministry the bread of the gospel turned to stone. And Fockbury itself, though beautiful and with special attractions of its own, was never as intimately our home as Perry Hall had been. It had been our father's in his childhood, when our grandfather was first incumbent of the newly formed parish of Catshill, and when it fell vacant soon after our mother's death, he inclined to the change, from which—after a five years' experiment—we reverted gladly, and came back to the old home.

Perry Hall had belonged to John Adams, a great-uncle of my father, and the church hill had been named after him. He had been, like Wordsworth in his later years, a controller or custodian of stamps; and the house used then to contain many thousand pounds' worth of government property, in a form so easily portable that it might well have attracted thieves; for which reason ponderous fittings had been provided in all directions against burglary: office windows heavily barred, a back door three inches thick, studded with nails, and with a huge lock that turned twice, shutters in the living rooms which rose up from the bowels of the earth, and were locked into place by an elaborate combination of crossbars and screws, swing bells on passage doors, and up on the roof an alarm bell waiting to be rung. And though, in our day, the place no longer contained property of much value, the ritual of shutter-closing still went on, and a big hefty job it was for the maids, filling the house each evening with the rumblings of an earthquake.

In its cover of ivy, and its enclosure of big trees, the house looked older than it was, and it had in its back premises all the appurtenances of a day when households did much more for themselves than now: a double kitchen, two cellars, two coppers, a bread oven, a large jack, two or three grinding-mills, a closed-up plate warmer of vast dimensions, and out in the yard a "beer cooler," left over from the day when home-brewing was done.

The garden was divided into three main sections: the ornamental, comprising lawns, flower beds, and shrubbery; a well-screened fruit and vegetable garden beyond; and to one side the "rubbish garden" (our own name for it) which, having nothing in it of importance, was largely left to take care of itself. In it were two large apple trees which bore a crop very sweet and small in kind, so numerous and negligible for dessert purposes that we took and ate them without sense of sin. There were also damson trees, exuding deliciously sticky gum, black currants, which in their raw state did not tempt us, and a "clay-hill" of which we made a fortress for our games, and thereon fought miniature battles.

In connection with these, Alfred, the eldest of us, and always our leader, invented three new instruments of war—the Bath Bridge, the Martin Luther, and the Flying Torpedo; outwardly quite homely objects of garden use, but imaginatively endowed with terrific powers of destruction. The Bath Bridge, a mere drainpipe to look at, was designed to swallow lighted tallow candles at one end, and send them rushing out in fire at the other. We got some candle-ends, and tried the experiment; but only a melting mess and no fire came of it. The Martin Luther was a species of gatling gun which never gatled, being nothing more than a semicircle of wood with a ground-stake, for the running of bird-lines; the Flying Torpedo was a stump of wood which he threw. But if they failed to do much execution, the names made us happy; for Alfred was always able to make us believe that his word-inventions had a meaning, and that the meaning was good.

Recalling now these influences of early years, which formed so large a part of our education, for the shaping of character and the knitting of family relations, I doubt whether any were more valuable than that old garden, into which we plunged daily out of sight and sound of our elders, and there found liberty.

Over the books we read, we were often questioned—especially over our Sunday books—but over what we did in the garden we were left beautifully free; and so long as we did not noticeably steal the fruit, or tread on the borders, or break the flowers, we were allowed to amuse ourselves in our own way without question. And how we did!

We stood compact and pugnaciously united—seven against the rest of the world. How we loved; how we hated; how we fought, divided, and were reconciled again! How we trained, and educated ourselves; and developed a taste in literature and in the writing of it, in which, until years later, our elders had no part, and with which school hours had little to do!

Certain trees in the garden became our climbing-trees, and while some (those easiest to climb, and affording a sufficient number of perches) were common territory in which we fought and played, others remained special to each; and there we sat and read, and presently composed; but that was later.

And so, looking a few years on, I remember a day when Alfred came up into my climbing-tree, and told me I was to write a sonnet. I did not then know what a sonnet was; but he having one to give away (for I think that was the explanation) I was to write one, and take over by thought-transference his as mine. He had a tough task, stuffing it down my throat and getting it out again; for the rudiments of poetic diction had not then come to

me; and when he tried to get from me some water-bird suitable
for the opening of a sonnet, I gave him first a duck, and then
(when he asked for something larger) a goose; and only finally
a swan, which enabled me to think that the first line which ran:
"The swan is sleeping on the river's breast" was really and truly
my own. It was not, I am sure, "love's divine self-abnegation"
which made him hand over to me, hard bit by bit, that poem of his
own composition to be signed as mine. He had written a poem
which he did not think good enough for himself; but he did not
want it to be lost; and so my first sonnet was written for me; and
being still in the age of innocence, I did not know how it had come
about.

Somewhere about this time, my sister Clemence was sitting up
in her climbing-tree writing a poem on the story of Perseus and
Medusa, of which I can only remember one couplet, which still
seems to me rather magnificent as the unaided composition of a
child of nine:

"Her brows were knit in everlasting pain,
Hers were the lips that never smiled again."

But I don't think the poem was ever finished; few of our poems
were. The old garden, though it stimulated our imaginations, provided us with more beginnings than ends.

It is curious that, of my garden-memories during those early
years, I cannot once remember rain, except for the terror of a
great thunderstorm coming in the night, when—by the servants'
account—a ball of fire came in through the kitchen window, ran
up the cook's arm, and disappeared up the chimney. But I do
remember snow!

Never, in my encounter of it, did snow enter and fall so deeply
and wonderfully, as into that garden. I think that, during those
years, there must have been a run of deep-snowing winters; it may
also be that to small children snowladen boughs look more over-
hanging and terrific, and snow underfoot deeper than when they
have grown to a larger scale themselves. But there was also a
solemn and dramatic arrangement of the trees, and especially of

the evergreens, which enhanced the effect. Yew, juniper, and Lawson-cypress hold up snow in bigger mass than do the kinds which shed their leaves; and the mounting bank of trees, topped by the church spire, had then a loveliness, which, through the poignancy of memory, has entered the blood and become a part of life in the unexpected years that have followed.

Through the wooden slats of the belfry, choked up with snow, the striking of the hours came softly, and the Christmas bells rang a muffled peal. And as our eyes caught the accentuated beauty of the ribbed spire, and the emphasis of the carvings on niche and parapet outlined in snow, we acquired an added interest and love for the already familiar beauty of that thing of stone; and so, while in three of us at least our love of architecture grew and grew, the old garden was the setting.

The grant of so much outdoor liberty made our elders a welcome diversion, for we did not see too much of them; and at our father's call down the garden of "Grubs, grubs, grubs!" we all came running delighted to see him—not alone because that call meant that he had fruit for us. He was a pleasant person to deal with, easy and good-natured; and he had a sealskin waistcoat in winter, against which it was my delight to snuggle. Up to my seventh or eighth year, I never remember his punishing me, and in the ten years after, only lightly and seldom. If he heard an outcry in the nursery while we were having tea, he would come and without inquiry put sugar on our bread and butter; or if he was not in the habit of doing so, he did it often enough for me to remember. At other times, when we heard him going downstairs, we would run out and thrust our legs through the banisters—three or four pairs of them—to have our toes pulled as he passed below.

They were very delectable stairs; we loved them. They were so placed that we could sit halfway down, and watch unnoticed the elders going in to dinner; which, when there was a party, or when relatives had arrived to give the event an added interest, we generally did—dinner in those days being at the comfortable hour of six, and bedtime not till nearly an hour later. The lighted hall had a stone floor and bare walls, which sent up a pleasant resonance of sound to the cosy darkness above; and there, on the half-landing at our backs, its ivory face looped with garlands of gold, ticked the old family clock, which by happy circumstance is still with me.

That large and friendly house, so characteristic in its way, had an almost personal relation to my growing mind, feeding itself daily on those fantastic loves and fears of infancy, which are too secret to be told to anyone. I loved all of it—some parts not without dread. The back stairs were dark, twisted and steep, with no window but an opaque square, which drew up a glimmer of light from the kitchen below. There were deep fixed cupboards in bedrooms and on landings, which I loved to look into by day, but which at night became full of burglars—or sometimes of bears. In the night-nursery were hot-water pipes which crackled horribly on their way up to the bathroom; someday, I expected they would burst, and flood the whole room with boiling water, in which I should drown agonizingly. There was also a little room which I visited daily—stealthily, fearing for my entry or exit to be seen by anyone except my mother or my nurse. There, at the pull of a plug, a horrible black chasm opened, and a deluge of water, descending I knew not whence, swirled soundingly through the orifice which opened to receive it.

From that daily horror, after giving the bidden pull, I would fly precipitately, unable to stay and watch the completion of a process which had in it something of the terrors of the Last Judgment, and having once in my panic flight left the plug on the up-pull, I fairly emptied the cistern before the continued outflow was discovered. And because I never told my fears, they were never explained away for me, as they might have been.

Some years later, when I heard of a burning coal mine, I cherished a scared wonder how long that underground conflagration would take before reaching to where I was, and drawing me down into its fiery embrace. Clearly, in relation to the unknown or the unexplained, I had not a nice mind. What child has?

But, in spite of fears, the house was in the main friendly, and so also were those in it. At certain times of the year there was a delicious hour before bedtime: dim gaslight burned on the landing, and turned low in the bedrooms, curtained to a firelight glow. The maids moved companionably about, "doing the rooms" for the night, and, while our parents dined, we had the free run of them for hide-and-seek, or any other game that occurred to us. In those days, when late dinner was at six, we would go down to the dining room for dessert, and be given a biscuit or a fruit, and half a glass of wine, before bidding our parents good-night.

It occurred to me one day, how much it would please and amuse them, when the time came for us to be summoned, if, instead of entering by the door, I came up from under the table. The thing was easily done; at five minutes to six I crept down to the dining room, and under the table sat myself down among a ring of chair-legs, and waited. In those days, I loved all my elders with a childish devotion—even their feet were beautiful to me. And that night I sat contemplating three beautiful pairs of feet; two pairs were female—an aunt's and a cousin's—the other pair was my father's. I was entirely contented and absorbed, paying no attention to the conversation which went on above me; but keeping count of the courses, I knew when dessert was on the table; and when word went up to the nursery for the family to descend, out I scrambled.

I looked gleefully for my joke to be shared, and beheld wrath and consternation. Questioned, I explained that I had been under the table all the time—waiting; and as I did so, I became vaguely aware that, in my innocence, I had done a deed of guilt, for not only were my beloved elders shocked and annoyed, they were also unexplainedly frightened. Of course I know now that conversation had gone on about things entirely unsuitable for my ears—family secrets, perhaps, possibly stories of an unedifying character about uncles who were better not named; and they could not understand that I had not attended to a word, or been in the least interested—so much more had I been interested in the beauty of their feet, and the shadows of legs and dresses, cast by the firelight over the carpeted gloom of my hiding-place.

I think my innocence of evil intent must have been so obvious that I was not punished for it; but I was told sharply never to do such a thing again. And I never did. All the gusto of it had gone in that stare of horrified eyes, which ever since I have remembered. Yes, how well I remember it all. I remember which side of the table I crept out from; I remember just where I stood for the inquisition, sharp and short, which I had to face. But except for that, memory has fainted dead away, and I remember no more: not the entrance of the others, or my glass of wine (perhaps that night, as a corrective, I went without), or my good-night, or my going up to bed. Those habitual things have all gone from my memory; only the unhabitual, the exceptional—the new experience of having unintentionally *not* pleased where I had so wished to please—only that remains.

We were seven in family almost as long as I can remember—not quite. My brother Herbert came three years after me; and the fact that his birthday was the day after mine always puzzled me; it presented a mathematical problem that I could not solve. I remember seeing him for the first time, lying in his cradle; and then a little later watching with distaste the screaming exposure of his gums during a paroxysm of teething. But one or two incidents in those first three years of my life, when I was sixth and last, come back to me like the momentary memories of a dream. Being lifted over a railing I could not climb, into a field of nurses and children, must, I think, have been one of them; rather later perhaps was an early attempt to drown in six inches of running water, from which I was rescued by my brother Robert. Of that I have a memory of lying face downward in the brook, and seeing strange weeds swaying under me—not conscious that I was in any danger; and then of screaming violently when restored to dry land and the discomfort of feeling myself very wet.

My second birthday I remember because of my first sight, on that day, of the birthday present which I then received, and kept thereafter as one of my dearest possessions—a cardboard box containing two tiny wax babes sunk in a bed of gold tissue, paper flowers, and silver leaves. I was told to go to a corner cupboard and look in; and crawling over the nursery floor, I pushed open the bottom door, and there found beauty awaiting me. Was it then that the love of doubtful art (which took twenty-five years to eradicate) was born in me? I know now that, for the next twelve at least, nearly every ornament and picture that I sincerely admired was not at all what it should be. In the church stained-glass windows, mostly rank bad; in the drawing room florid Victorian ornaments, heavy Victorian furniture, and gaudy gasoliers; in the nursery carpet, wallpaper, and pictures all ranged from indifferent to something much worse; and yet, from association, though their artistic merit has departed, I love them still; and one—a needlework landscape sweetly greyed by age, I still have and admire, and am powerless in the grip of association to regard as other than beautiful. So, even now, my education is not complete; nor do I wish it to be.

Seven years later an additional impulse was given to my evil taste in art. Up till then there were in the house a few old articles of furniture, beautiful, and some of them quite valuable. But when my father married for a second time, there came into the house a fine assortment of things born under the influence of the Great Exhibition of 1851; and to make room for the furniture of Queen Victoria, the furniture of Queen Anne and Queen Elizabeth was relegated to back bedrooms and attics. One—the most valuable of all—a cabinet of tortoiseshell, ebony, and ivory—was actually put up into the roof, till, on my departure from home in my eighteenth year, with a dawning sense of its beauty I asked if I might have it: and was very willingly told to "take the old thing away."

Another thing of beauty—a large chest of drawers, Dutch, seventeenth or eighteenth century, inlaid with floral designs—was put into the bathroom, and its top presently battered and burned to destruction from general rough usage, and from the habit some of us had of going to the bath with candle-ends but no candlesticks—melting a pool of grease for them to stand in, and then letting them burn down till the inlay beneath scorched or took fire. This article also survives, and is now well cared for, with a plain top substituted for that which we destroyed.

The articles of beauty and curiosity were in the dressing-up-box of which I remember chiefly a very lovely blue silk dress, about a hundred years old, brocaded with flowers all done by hand, a "Nuremburg Egg" watch, a white beaver hat of baby-size, and an Indian hunting-pouch. All these have long since disappeared: the Nuremburg Egg stolen, I fancy, by someone who had a better appreciation of its value than we had, and therefore a better right to it. Along with these was a piece of woolwork, incredibly small and dainty in the elaboration of its floral patterns—an unfinished masterpiece of the days when footstools, sofa cushions, and chairbacks formed the lifetime labor of ladies who would have been shocked to receive payment for anything they did. And I wonder would their ghosts be shocked to know that those products of their well-employed leisure now command quite a handsome price in the market, and do occasionally deserve it?

Some of that old furniture I have mentioned traces back to a previous owner, one of whose exploits is worth telling. My mother's father, Doctor Williams, had been Rector of Woodchester, and coming to a dilapidated Rectory, had taken over furniture, in lieu of repairs from the estate of the previous incumbent, an old bachelor, Doctor Hawkins. Now while Doctor Hawkins was Rector, gravediggers had brought up to the surface indubitable fragments of Roman mosaic; and Doctor Hawkins became convinced that there, waiting to be discovered, lay a Roman pavement. Anxious to bring it to light, his problem was how to do so without a faculty, and in the face of local opposition to the disturbance of bones whose descendants still lived in the parish. What he did was very bold, and very simple. He imported from a distance workmen vowed to secrecy, whom he paid well, and (supplied with food and drink) hid in a Rectory attic during the day. And when at night he brought them forth to their nefarious job of circumventing pious prejudices, he himself played ghost, and standing on the churchyard-wall in a sheet frightened intruders away.

And that is how the mosaic of Orpheus and the Beasts (a sample portion of which is now in the British Museum) came to be unearthed. I suppose that eventually, when the value of the find was established, a faculty was obtained for its permanent preservation, and in that way the Rector's illegal action regularized. As to that I know nothing; I only tell the story as it came into our family along with the old furniture.

CHAPTER II

FAMILY PRAYERS

NOTHING in this world is less meek than a child bent upon getting its own way; and if the Kingdom of Heaven really is composed of such material, it can only be because, while according to Scripture, the meek shall possess the *Earth,* the Kingdom of Heaven suffers violence, and the violent take it by force.

The earliest family quarrel that I can remember was over the things of Heaven, which we were trying to take from each other by force. It was a winter's dawn; a quarter of a mile away the high-raised roof of Bromsgrove School, with its small bell-cot, stood out in silhouette against one of those lovely variegated dawns which, ranging from green to gold, and from gold to pale rose and crimson, belong more especially to the season of late sun-risings. Four of us stood on a seat by the night-nursery window, disputing violently as to which of those clouds of glory should be ours. Probably we all wanted the same colours, and what each decided to be his or hers could not be shared by another. Our mother came and caught us at it, and we were sharply forbidden ever again to take, as our own, things so much belonging to Heaven.

My mother's scoldings must have had a virtue about them—perhaps because of their rareness—which other scoldings lacked, for I did, from that incident, carry away an uncomfortable sense of foolish behaviour—the beginning, maybe, of a feeling that beauty was holy, and for that reason not to be quarrelled about. Beauty, indeed—or what I took to be beauty—was already becoming one of my daily and most lively interests, though the things which I admired most were indifferently bad. It began with pat-

29

terns—the patterns of wallpapers, of carpets, of costumes, of glass, of chandeliers. Everything in my home which was put there as ornament, I accepted as beautiful, without question.

In the drawing room was a gas chandelier of tawdry gilt, with a white vase at its centre, and supporting—probably because of past breakages—three gas globes of different design. And I remember, on the occasion of a dinner party, when I had gone down to be on show in my white frock and blue silk sash, discussing earnestly with one of the guests the rival merits of the three patterns—wishing very much to know which she thought the most beautiful.

At that time the most beautiful thing in the world for me was a small porcelain eggshell, with two white mice running around it. One day I broke it; and I don't think I was punished; but without any remembrance of punishment, I remember my grief at the breakage.

A few other things of bright particular beauty stand out from my memories of those early years. One was an evening dress of my mother, a soft brown muslin, dotted with silken disks in two different shades; the other a silk dress of emerald green, with an embossed lozenge pattern, worn by our governess on Sundays. I suspect now that the former was beautiful, and that the other was not; but I made no such distinction then.

In those days my mother used often to wear day-dresses with hanging sleeves, and it must have been one of these which, as she was helping the Christmas pudding in its bed of flaming brandy, caught fire; and my father ran round the table and slapped it out with his hands. Word of this was brought up to the nursery, where I was still having my meals, but so real and exciting was the description of the incident, that I seemed actually to have seen it; and without the corrective knowledge, could swear that I had done so. From which fact deduce a moral—that though I "remember" all these things which I am now telling, they may not actually have so happened.

Other things do, of course, sing out because of their exceptional character as definite incidents. I remember going once into church

with my hat on, and Miss Milward, our governess, after we had
got to our pew, snatching it off so violently that the elastic snapped
off under my chin. I remember leaning against the cellar door
to stick out my tongue at the cook's back when she had turned me
out of the kitchen, and—the door being off the latch—falling
headlong down a flight of stone stairs, and picking myself up half-
dead at the bottom, but not uttering a sound, because it had served
me so right, and I did not want cook to know. I remember coming out very shyly after scarlet fever, to meet my brothers and
sisters for the first time on a front lawn covered with snow; and,
being still a little deaf, holding my head on one side to hear what
was said to me. I remember one particular whipping that my
nurse gave me, though not the cause of it; and the horrible extempore prayer which she prayed over me afterwards. It had fiery
angels in it, and the flames of hell; and it frightened me, as no
doubt it was intended to do.

Extempore prayer was not a recognized practice in our family;
it sounded strange in our ears, for with us prayer was like ritual,
and had a fixed form. In its fixity lay its virtue. The earliest
prayer I can remember saying—and I said it for years—ran as
follows:

"Cargo bress my dear father and mother, my brothers and
sisters, and make me a good boy, for Jesus Christ's sake.
Amen."

"Cargo bress" was my infantile pronunciation of "Pray God
bless." I cannot now remember whether to me it meant, "Pray
God bless," or was only an invocative abracadabra—preliminary
flourish to the statement that I was a family child, and that I
wished my family well; but I am pretty sure that I continued to
say, "Cargo bress" long after I could have said the words, "Pray
God bless" quite plainly; and that I continued to do so because
the meaning of the phrase was quite unimportant to me at that
time. The gist—the real substance of my prayer—was composed
not of God, but of father, mother, brothers and sisters, with a side

reference to the Hero of the only storybook I then knew, which had
coloured pictures, and was therefore my favourite one.

But in spite of God being the unimportant element in it, it was
not a bad prayer as a child's prayers go. In that "grace before
bed" and after, I rehearsed the names of the people whom I most
cared about, or who most mattered to me; and in that vital connection I wished myself "a good boy" for the sake of my favourite storybook. Can a small child's mind go much further in a spiritual direction, until he has had a real and personal experience of what "God"
stands for, and what "for Jesus Christ's sake" really means? And
what exactly is the value of bringing God into it at all, except to
establish an association which will afterwards become valuable,
between what a child knows and loves, and what—so far—he does
not know or love? Most certainly at the time when I made that
prayer a daily habit—or when the habit was made for me by
others—I did love my father and mother devotedly and continuously, and my brothers and sisters with breaks and reservations—
on their good days, that is to say. On their other days (or on my
other days) love was a virtue that went out of us, and we hated
and fought, as the English and French hated and fought each
other all through the Napoleonic Wars, and if their history books
did not blame them for it, why should our governess blame us?
But she did, most unhistorically, without a proper notion of how
nations and families have to grow up and come to years and
policies of discretion, and find out that quarrelling and fighting are
uncomfortable and unprofitable. But you have to find it out for
yourself, not merely be told so.

In that respect my prayer made a truthful distinction: it called
my father and mother "dear," it did not call my brothers and sisters
"dear." And they were *not,* or not often enough to have the epithet
generically applied to them; they had got to earn it. And so, also,
had God Himself to earn or to win the love which was then lacking in me. I am quite sure that during those early years, while
my family love was growing, my love for God was nonexistent,
and my love for Jesus Christ not much more than my love for
Robinson Crusoe. And is not that the natural order of things,

and only what one should expect, seeing that in normal natures birth, vaccination, and teething come first, and religious experience only second—and very often a bad second at that? It is true that the Roman Church tells us of certain saints who from their very birth have refused the breast every Friday as an act of pious self-denial; but those religious monstrosities do not occur in the Church of England, since there they are not expected to occur; and though such freaks of infantile ritual may please the professional hagiologists, one wonders if they can possibly be pleasing to God—to any God conceivable by reasonable minds.

As years went on, religion in our Victorian family took two widely differing forms—each having its own proper time and place. The dining room was the place for the one, the bedroom for the other. In its open expression it was rigidly formal and regular—entirely empty of spirituality, almost of meaning; in its private form it was as secret and surreptitious as our daily fulfilment of the needs of nature. For any of us to have been caught praying by anyone else would have been an indecency—we should have felt exposed and uncomfortable for the rest of the day. But when family prayers were being said there was no such bashfulness—to that sort of "mixed bathing" we were hardened, and we knelt about the room, each in his selected place, and endured with stony indifference while the infliction lasted.

Prayers preceded breakfast; to be late for prayers was to lose one's bacon, and have only porridge and dry bread. A minute after the ringing of the breakfast-bell, the maids were summoned from the kitchen. They came—one bearing a large tray which was set down on the sideboard; they stood facing us in a row before it. When my father had invoked the Trinity, they whisked round and knelt towards the tray while prayers were being said. Prayers lasted three or four minutes; they included the Lord's Prayer, in which we all joined. For that there was no fixed place; and I recall one or two occasions in later days when my father, forgetting whether he had said it or not, began saying it again. It was then my peculiar joy to keep him at it—though after the first sentence, becoming aware that he had said it before, he would want to stop; but as he could not stop *me,* he had to go on, and we ran it as a duet, the rest of the family keeping a disapproving silence. They had said it once; they were not going to say it again—it was a waste of words. At that time I was becoming the religious one of the family—which does not mean that I was becoming good: far from it! But a love for ritualistic observance had got hold of me; and since in the church service the Lord's Prayer was repeated twice, and even thrice, why not domestically also? So, if my father chose to begin it a second time, I made him go on with it.

A much earlier instance of the exceeding uselessness of family prayer for the cleansing of hearts, and allaying of hatred and malice, must have dated somewhere about when I was seven. I had been having a tussle with my brother Basil for the possession of a favourite chair; and just on the entry of the servants at the call of prayers, he had hit me last. From that unfinished conflict our governess had snatched me away to kneel beside her, as I then always did. We prayed, we confessed our sins, we asked forgiveness, we recited the Lord's Prayer. The moment the "Grace of our Lord" had been said, I leapt to my feet, and gave Basil the return smack that was his due. For that I was sent out to have breakfast in the schoolroom—with no bacon to it.

I felt that it was not fair. Basil had hit me first, and had also hit me last. Neither prayer nor punishment did me any good. And yet with this demonstration before their eyes that prayer meant nothing to me, my elders made no attempt to give it reality.

In the whole of my early life, I can remember only one incident when anything like a religious experience came to me. I had been guilty of a careless act of selfishness towards my youngest brother. My mother had sent me out of the room for it; and afterwards, taking me into a room by ourselves (it was dusk, I remember, and I could scarcely see her face) had talked to me seriously about it. I was touched, and I was sorry. I think it was the only time when I was really, altruistically sorry; though, of course, I was always sorry for myself when I was punished. On that occasion I was not punished. Is it for that reason that the incident has remained with me to this day, as one of the important landmarks of my early life?

I cannot remember my mother being present at family prayers. After about my fifth year, she had become an invalid; and a cousin had come to take over the household duties. But the conventions of family prayers must have been of long standing, when I, then youngest but one of a large family, was brought within their stupefying influence. I can remember still how odd it seemed to me when any of those conventions were broken. We knelt against the seats of chairs, which we pulled out from the table, and reversed for use; and if any visitor, unaware of the ritual, chose to kneel against the back of a chair instead of against the seat, it seemed to me a little funny. And when once a clergyman visitor, coming in a moment late, knelt down straightway against nothing at all, and prayed without a chair to support him—I remember how very odd it seemed to me; and I believe its oddness struck me largely because to him prayer was real, and there I saw reality joining in prayer in an atmosphere from which all reality of prayer was absent.

One hears often nowadays of the great loss to religious life among the young which has come about from the discontinuance of family prayers. Yet I believe that, in our own family, it did us more harm than good, and when, in my first years of adolescence religion became more real to me, family prayers were a most painful ordeal, from which I would gladly have escaped if I could, because of their unreality. It was much the same with grace before meat; it did not inculcate the thankful spirit. What we were about to receive were very often the shortcomings of the cook, and we were *not* thankful for them. Complaint was immediate and loud.

Years later, when I had come to London with my elder sister, a relative visiting us found, to her grave disapproval, that we had ceased to say grace, and asked why. I replied, a little restively perhaps, "In order to try to cultivate a more thankful spirit than the saying of grace ever produced at home." It was, of course, an annoying thing to say, and perhaps it was meant to be; but one found it hard sometimes not to exact vengeance, when our time came for freedom and free speech, for the afflictions of our youth.

Yet in many ways we were a happy family; and our affections for each other ran strongly—in streaks. But though our domestic life was on the whole well blended, our religious life was not. Where it was real it hid itself as a shameful thing; where it was unreal, exposure did not matter—it was clothed and unashamed.

I remember once coming down to breakfast on a Sunday morning in a new pair of trousers; and, being new and the first time on, they came under the inspection of domestic authority. All at once some sign of use caught her eye. "Have you been *kneeling* in them?" she exclaimed reproachfully. Very much annoyed by the question, I replied, "Yes, I have!" Embarrassment came on her; she understood—it was as though I had said, "I have been to the W. C." A few minutes later we knelt down to family prayers; but *that* was different.

Sometimes—at long intervals—family prayers did bring us compensation of a kind. Once, I remember the cat climbed up my father's back while he was reading prayers, and sat on his shoulder for the Grace. The descent of the Holy Dove could not have pleased us more; and he—easy-going, good-natured man—was pleased too, in a way. In fact everybody was pleased more or less; the cat had made family prayers a success.

Once something even better happened. That was when our stepmother, whom we called the "Mater," was in domestic command. One morning, not feeling well, she had told my father that she would not be down for breakfast; and as she was always the one who rang the loud-sounding breakfast bell which stood in the hall, no bell was rung. We had all come down; the servants were brought in, and prayers began. Suddenly outside came a loud clanging of the bell; the door opened, in came the Mater; she had recovered from her indisposition, but had not sent word of it. At sight of us all on our knees, "Lor!" she exclaimed, and backed out. If family prayers started without *her*, she was not going to participate. My father continued to pray without trouble—not seeing the humor of the situation. We agonized through the Lord's Prayer somehow without actual disaster; but when all was over we squealed with laughter; and the Mater coming in at the end, took it all in good part.

Why is it that quite small things happening in church or during prayers, which should not happen, are so irresistibly funny? They ought to be painful; but in youth, at any rate, they give us an unholy joy.

Once at Bromsgrove Church, during morning service, a strange clergyman got up into the pulpit to preach. But no sooner had he uttered the invocation than up leapt two or three members of the congregation, and rushed out; and two choir men, racing into the vestry, threw off their surplices and scampered after them. The poor man stared aghast. What upsetting thing had he done to cause so violent a demonstration? Nothing. But down in the marketplace, the soft, husky bell of the town clock had been heard tolling—*not* at the hour; and to the ears of the congregation that meant "Fire!" It was only the members of the fire brigade who had run out on duty bound, while the rest of the congregation sat and wondered uncomfortably which of them had a house burning behind his back, about which word might presently come. And so during that sermon there was much searching of hearts, but little attention, I fear; and as soon as things were over a very quick dispersal of the congregation took place, each running to see whether the conflagration was true.

On another prayerful occasion it was not fire but "cease fire" which caused the upset and the exodus. That incident we only had on hearsay; it happened before we were born to an elder branch of the family living in London—an old widow lady and her three grown-up daughters. One evening she, a little hard of hearing, was slowly and reverently reading family prayers. They were long; and she took her time over them, and did not notice how, under spiritual compulsion, three pairs of crinolined knees were wriggling with impatience to be up and away. No sooner had the last "Amen" been said than the room was emptied of its occupants all except herself. They had heard; she had not; and they did not stop to explain. Away in Hyde Park, guns were booming to celebrate the victory of the Crimean War—doubtfully won—and the declaration of peace.

They could, of course, have listened to the guns almost as well, and with attentions almost as undivided, while prayers were being said. But their patriotic instinct was to rush to an upstairs window, open it, lean out—and *count*. Only if they counted did they take their proper share in the national rejoicing.

In our own family grace was not said at meals that were without meat or potatoes; and at dinner parties evening prayer was left out. But two of those London sisters once went to dine at a house where the religious rule was more strictly observed. A little before they left, comforting cups of tea had been handed round; and when the tea was finished their hostess said, "And now will you join us in something better?"

"Oh, no!" one of them replied, "we never take anything of *that* sort!" But a moment later the cryptic utterance was explained; it meant family prayers.

Family prayers seem now to belong to another age. I do not know whether anyone regrets them. In some households they may have been real—and perhaps still are; in ours they were not.

But though in my childhood the inward and spiritual side of religion meant so little to me, its externals interested me greatly. The way people behaved in church—every pose, movement, gesture of the grown-ups whom I so greatly admired, attracted my imitative attention; I wanted, in order that I might be like them, to do as they did.

One day a stranger came to preach; and as he preached he moved his hand gracefully up and down. I was fascinated; I did the same; I was severely stopped, and I wondered why.

In the pew in front of us were two brothers—shopkeepers, the best-dressed members of the congregation; and one of them (with a sort of resemblance to the then Prince of Wales), in my eyes, the most beautiful. During the singing he used to put one foot on his hassock, which seemed to me to give an added distinction to his appearance. I tried doing the same. My poor little foot was pushed off; and again I wondered why what was right when done by a beautiful man, was wrong when I did it.

Another of my interests was to study the faces of grown-up people while they sang or prayed—especially when they prayed with shut eyes, which made the matter easier for me. For the most part I found myself faced by expressionless masks, but not always; sometimes character came out. Once I heard, and watched, the prayers of an old family servant, very long, and very real. That story I have told at length elsewhere.*

When we went up to Catshill, we were in a very different sort of congregation from the one at Bromsgrove—very simple and rustic, in a galleried enclosure with whitewashed walls, and with harmonium instead of organ for accompaniment. In those days, yeoman farmers and labourers came to church in the clean smocks which they would be wearing through the week; there were also a few of the old beaver hats which went with them. And it was with a new and curious interest that I would watch the hearty faces of these simple folk, as they sang hymns of spiritual yearning for a better world, or of grief for the burden of their healthy sunburnt flesh, and sorrow for their sins. Vaguely puzzled, I began gradually to be amused—and sceptical.

But I did sometimes see real prayer and striving—or what looked like it. Behind us was the vicarage pew, where I found shut eyes during prayer to be the rule; and there I remember seeing the youthful face of the present Warden of Keble (then a Bluecoat Boy) crumpled up in a strained expression which puzzled me. Was it prayer, I wondered, or was it pain?

As regards the correct conventions for the expression of various shades of religious opinion, I began to learn, at this time, that to bow the head at the name of Jesus, was evangelical and permissible, though usually only done during the saying of the Creed; but to curtsey at the Gloria was High-church, and undesirable. For after my seventh year Low-church had become the prevailing rule for all members of the family but one, and on Sunday after-

*A Modern Antaeus, Chapter VIII, pages 82-84.

noons an awful *Life of Luther,* in two big volumes, translated from the German, was being read to us—as a corrective, possibly to earlier tendencies, when we had been given holidays on Saints'-days, with church as an accompaniment. How we came to be deprived of that pious indulgence was our own fault. Watch was kept, and one day, during the school holidays, having no one to remind us, we forgot all about the Saints'-days, and did not go to church. After that, when school was resumed, the Saints'-days holidays were knocked off. Low-church had triumphed over High-church; and I suppose it served us right.

CHAPTER III

POLITICAL UPBRINGING

POLITICS began for us at an early date. Our father was a hot Tory, and his politics were ours. I remember his telling us that he was born in the year of England's great disaster—the passing of the first Reform Bill; and the earliest general election I can recall was that which followed the second Reform Bill of 1867.

I remember it for two reasons: one was that my father went to the poll armed with a "life-preserver"—a word which stuck vividly in my imagination—the other that our gardener got badly kicked on election day, merely for being in my father's employ. But I think it must have been over a bye-election somewhat later that an incident occurred in which I am told that I took part, though my own memory of it has gone.

When politics were to the fore, it was my father's custom, over the sip of wine which we took with him after dinner, to call a toast; and to the shout of "Up with the Tories, and down with the Radicals!" we all drank it together. It had become a pious ritual that we should not take our sips till the toast was given.

One evening we went in, and there found a stranger. We were given our wine as usual, but not the toast; our father in conversation with his guest appeared to have forgotten us. For a while we held our glasses, and waited; but still the call did not come. And so, after exchanging interrogative looks and affirmative nods, we followed a lead and gave it ourselves in loud chorus: "Up with the Tories; down with the Radicals!" and, as we set our glasses down, heard our father making polite apology to his Radical guest for the uncalled-for demonstration. But secretly our outbreak had pleased him; there was a twinkle in his eye; he was proud of us.

41

From that seedbed of reactionary politics we grew up, for the most part, as our father would have wished us to grow, and remained good Conservatives, all of us, for the next quarter of a century. After that—well, after that, so far as he was concerned defection did not matter. He was never to have the deep satisfaction of hearing either of Gladstone's death, or even of his final retirement from politics; while the notion of Labour ever becoming an independent party, and attaining power, had not begun to be a dream during his lifetime.

In many other respects my early life made me what I am now; but in politics, at all events, the child was not the final father of the man. Yet only when I was pulled into political agitation thirty years later, did my conservatism begin to ooze out of me, and continue to ooze till now none of it is left. But I think I am glad that I did start life as a Conservative, for so I acquired a joyous admiration for the personality of Disraeli, whose consummate artistry in politics has for me remained quite unaffected by the ultimate frustration of his foreign diplomacy, which the "military necessity" of our alliance with Tzarist Russia against Turkey in the last war brought down into the dust.

That toast-drinking incident must have come early in the '70's; but it was not till 1880 that I attended my first political meeting; and then it was a Liberal one. I went to it not with conviction, or any wish to be converted, but only for curiosity.

Our East Worcestershire division was a double constituency; and at the general election of that year Mr. Gladstone's eldest son was one of the Liberal candidates; and I was curious to see if the son was at all like his father, also to hear what strange things were said at Liberal meetings; prejudice forbade me to think that I should hear anything sensible.

I was then a day boy at Bromsgrove School; it was term time, and I ought by rights to have been at home, doing my evening work. But at seven o'clock I "stole out unbeknown," and arriving early at the Corn Exchange chose a seat against the wall halfway up the room.

Presently the place began to fill, and became packed with work people, nailers and factory hands; for in those days Liberalism was the accepted home of Labour, except in constituencies where Joseph Arch had begun to sow the seeds of doubt and discontent. I sat squeezed against the wall, in an atmosphere redolent of corduroys and tobacco. We were on benches without backs, placed closely together so as to provide the double accommodation which the occasion required. Presently Chairman, candidates, and prominent local supporters arrived, and mounted the platform amid cheers from the audience; and among them to my horror I saw my headmaster. It had escaped my calculations that he, being a Liberal of sorts, might be there; and though as a day boy I had more liberty than was allowed to boarders, I was at that hour flagrantly out of bounds.

So, making myself as small as I could, I bowed my head behind the backs in front of me, and prayed that I might escape notice. I should probably have done so; but presently from the back of the hall came an interruption—not disorderly, but provocative. Instantly (intolerant of adverse opinion, as election crowds always are), the whole meeting was on its feet and with loud shouts of "Turn him out! Turn him out!" rushed precipitately across the backless benches to the rear, where ejection was already taking place. The main body of the hall had emptied itself—of all except me. I sat alone.

The conscious nakedness of Adam after he had partaken of the forbidden fruit was no more than mine. I bowed my head; I dared not look up, but I knew that the overruling power must have detected me; and when the audience, having performed just vengeance on the intruder, settled back into place, I made no further attempt to conceal myself. But all my political appetite was turned to sickness, and I quaked over what the morrow would bring forth.

Before the end of the meeting, my headmaster was called upon to say a few words, and I can remember them to this day. He said that he had a profound pity for Mr. W. H. Gladstone, because his undoubted talents were so completely overshadowed by those of his great and glorious father; and were it not for that circumstance, he would be a very distinguished person. The speech did not go down well with his working-class audience; it was not the sort of thing they wanted to hear; but it was an unusual compliment to the party, for the Head of the School to declare himself publicly a Liberal; and when he sat down he got his proper measure of applause.

When I went into class to the Head on the third hour of the next day, I expected immediate wrath to descend on me; but nothing happened till my turn came to construe. Then he said, "Housman, where were you last night?"

A happy inspiration came on me; I looked at him without shame, as one deserving commendation. "I was at *your* meeting, sir," I said.

A faint smile twitched his face. "Then when did you do your preparation?" he inquired.

"When I got home."

"But you didn't get home till your bedtime."

"No, sir, I sat up."

It was true; I had sat up for a while; though the only lesson I had properly prepared was the one which I was to take to him. But my answer had saved me; there was no wrath in his rebuke. "I don't object," he said, "to your going to 'my' meeting; but you must not scamp your home preparation." It was one of the very few times that I received mercy at his hands; perhaps, just that once, I had pleased him.

My next political meeting (which I attended with more enthusiasm and conviction) was also a memorable one. It was in London, in the early '80's. There under the chairmanship of Sir Algernon Borthwick, I heard Lord Randolph Churchill and Sir Robert Peel the second denounce the Egyptian policy of Gladstone's government. That meeting also was a tumultuous one: at the back of the hall was a strong body of opposition, which, having only standing room, was froward and restless upon its feet. This time we sat on benches that had backs to them; but a mighty pressure from the rear drove them gradually forward, till there was no room left between legs or knees; and the seatholders were at last forced to climb and perch upon the backs of them, where—balance being imperfect—we heaved and swung like the waves of the sea, but were too tightly wedged, back and front, for a fall.

My memory of Lord Randolph is that his style was not youthful; he said violent things with an air of measured deliberation, which, I suppose, made them sound more truthful, and as though he were rather under- than overstating his case. Sir Robert Peel was delightfully amusing; he had very long cuffs, which he kept shooting out towards his audience at arm's length; and as he spoke his hands flapped and fluttered like the wings of a dove. My impression is that he said a lot of silly things, but said them so effectively, so charmingly, and with such infectious humour, that his speech pleased me better than Lord Randolph's.

The next political meeting I attended, seven years later, was one addressed by Mrs. Fawcett, on the rather academic subject of Votes for Women, twenty years before the real Suffrage agitation began; and my next, when the twenty years had elapsed, was one addressed by Mrs. Pankhurst. That meeting cost me ten shillings—and my political liberty. Thenceforth I was in bonds until the vote was won. But all that is another story, to be told later.

Those two meetings served a useful purpose for me in the after years when, during a brief period of truce over the Conciliation Bill, Lion and Lamb—Militant and Constitutional—consented to lie down and feed together. The Men's League for Women's Suffrage had provided the food, and I was put up to perform the delicate task of proposing a toast to which Mrs. Fawcett, Mrs. Despard, and Miss Christabel Pankhurst were to respond. And I told how twenty years ago I had attended my first Suffrage meeting addressed by Mrs. Fawcett, with the result that Mrs. Fawcett had made me "feel militant," and then, many years later my second—addressed by Mrs. Pankhurst. And I said that Mrs. Pankhurst had had the same unfortunate effect upon me as Mrs. Fawcett—she made me "feel militant." Thus I linked them in guilty partnership for the evil effect they had had on me; and Mrs. Fawcett, accepting the joke with kindly humour, said she wished she had known at the time that she had "such a nice little boy" in her audience. "I am very proud of my little boy!" said she, not guessing that, at the time referred to, her "little boy" was already well up in his twenties. But from that day, her "little boy" I always remained; and when I met her for the last time at the Victory Celebration in London, she remembered the story, and again called me her "little boy"; though in actual practice I had been very much more the little boy of the militant party.

If these streamlines of memory concerning my political up-bringing have carried me unduly far from the actual days of my childhood, I have the excuse that, even at the wind-up of that most disturbing interruption to my proper work as a writer, I was still something of a little boy, not having yet found my way into the political camp to which I ought all those years to have be-longed.

The winning of Women's Suffrage has, in some of its results, disappointed me; but it was not a waste of time. It pulled me up from my roots, uncomfortably, but very effectively. I was never able to set them back into their old ground. Yet the first soil of that old ground was the home garden in which my childhood was bred—the place, in all my memories, that is still most dear to me, and though now changed almost beyond recognition, the beauty of it remains.

Family life is the first kind of life that a child knows; and in happy circumstances it may be, as it was with us, very whole, and satisfying, and complete—a world to itself. Only gradually, as a thing of less importance, did we begin to take notice of and find interest in the life of the larger world. It began, I suppose, with the illustrated weeklies, of which the *Graphic,* then a newcomer, was our favourite. Through its pages we became aware of foreign countries, contemporary history, and prominent people—kings, queens, and statesmen, living, or just dead; Victor Emmanuel, with his monstrous moustache; a very human-looking Pope, Pius IX, in a charming white costume; the Prince of Wales, very hand-some, freshly recovered from the jaws of death; the Queen herself, not so handsome, but so majestically enthroned and crowned that looks did not matter; Bismarck, Gladstone, Disraeli, Cardinal

Manning—then only Archbishop. All these came to life for us, pictorially. Then came a big historical event—the Franco-Prussian War, and the siege of Paris, with Gambetta escaping precariously in a balloon. And after that something quite small and domestic—the eviction of Mrs. Girling, and her followers, the Shakers, from their holding in the New Forest, and the camp life into which it drove them. That incident had for me a strange interest which lasted for years, and resulted finally in a book called *The Sheepfold; the story of a Shepherdess and her Sheep, and how she lost them*. For though it is not the story of Mrs. Girling, it would not have been written had Mrs. Girling and her Shakers not come into being. And when, fifty years later, I was living on the borders of the New Forest, I found that I was on the very scene of the incident which had aroused my childish interest; and two miles away was Hordle churchyard in which the Mother of the Shakers lay buried; and there beside her grave, on the third day after her death, her followers had watched all night, believing that at dawn they would see her rising from the dead. Some, with the eye of faith, did so; but for the majority nothing happened; and when I went to live in the neighbourhood, only one old woman remained, aged eighty, who still believed that the thing had come to pass. She was a very simple soul, but her testimony impressed me. "The Mother told us," she said, "that we was always to have joy."

Did any Founder of a Faith ever leave to his followers a better rule than that?

Chapter IV

FAMILY HISTORY

THOUGH on my father's side we had many cousinly connections, whom we knew for the most part only slightly and met but seldom, our own family tree was a diminishing one, and we seven were the last of it. Retrospectively we had twenty-three uncles and aunts, but all except four had died before we were born, or too soon for us to become aware of them. Of the four who survived long enough for recognition, one married, but had no family; and we ourselves have continued the diminution, five having remained single, while of the two who married only one has had children. Through them there has been a check in the fall of numbers; but the marital efforts of three nephews have not yet brought the youngest generation up to seven. So, at all events in our case, the much commended Victorian family of large size has been more wasteful than productive in its monstrosity.

On my mother's side the steady mortality, which carried off in their youth all but two in a family of thirteen, may be traced to the infected and insanitary condition of old Woodchester Rectory, which, having fulfilled the will of Providence, was pulled down shortly after the Williams family vacated it.

Of my father's family, seven out of twelve managed to outlive their childhood, and five of them to reach maturity. In her declining years their old mother found it difficult to remember how many children she had actually given birth to, and had even forgotten the name shared by two who died too young to have left with her any lasting impression. One day she was counting them off on her fingers.—"And then," said an assisting daughter, "came Elizabeth."

48

"Oh, no!" protested the old lady, "I never had a child called Elizabeth."

"Indeed you had," she was told. "And when that Elizabeth died, you had another, and called her Elizabeth too." But the old lady would not believe it; so far as individuality rests on names, two of her children were as though they had never existed.

But in spite of pains and labours uselessly endured, her marriage must have been a happy one; and in her widowed age she kept certain memories warm, and would have liked them to last. "Do you think," she asked her daughter one day, "that when I'm with my old man again, we shall know each other as we used to do?"

The daughter, having a pious doubt on the matter, yet not wishing to disappoint, hesitated for an answer. But a small grandson sitting by, having no such doubt, "Why, of course, Granny!" he cried. "We shall *all* know each other!"

"*What* does he say?" inquired the old lady, puzzled at so embracing an answer.

"He doesn't understand," was the evasive reply; and he did not, the scriptural usage of the word being new to him. But it was no passing thought; and when, some years later, at the end of her long day's work, that mother of twelve lay dying, her mind was still fondly set in the same direction; and, "I do so want to get to my old man!" was the last conscious word that she uttered.

Both grandmothers I can remember well, but neither of my grandfathers. Doctor Williams I never saw; but we had a large portrait of him in gown and bands, from which a strong family likeness could be traced to some of his descendants.

A more remarkable persistence of family traits was to be seen in the portrait of an ancestor of the seventeenth century—one of the Fellows of Magdalen College Oxford whom James II expelled from their Fellowships for contumacy. There, under his big curled wig, was the very image of one of my father's sisters—and she the only member of the family in whom it all showed.

Of one interesting branch of our family tree on our mother's side we have unfortunately lost the proof—our descent, namely, from an uncle of Sir Francis Drake. All that we know is that our grandfather, Doctor Williams, was present along with other descendants at the last Drake dinner held at Plymouth in, or about, the year 1845, and having thereafter loaned his copy of the genealogy to someone by whom it was lost, he left a written statement affirming for his descendants the authenticity of the claim. There was, I believe, at one time a Drake Fund, from which impecunious descendants benefitted, but the only benefit which we personally have derived from our connection with the great pirate whom England loves to honour consists in some family plate coming from an older generation, and bearing the Drake crest. This was passed on to us by the widow of the one Williams uncle who lived long enough to marry. In his case marriage was unduly delayed, though for quite respectable reasons. Being Dean of his College (St. John's, Cambridge) he waited for a fat College living to fall vacant; when it did so, he married into it, and died shortly after. His wife was a lady with a lively sense of humour, and also a touch of mischief; and once during their long engagement, when properly chaperoned, she visited him in his College rooms and took lunch there, a group of undergraduates was seen gazing up at the Dean's bedroom window with excited interest. The reason being that when the lady had gone into the room to tidy before lunch, she had purposely hung her bonnet and veil over the Dean's looking-glass where such a feminine feature seemed highly out of place.

This uncle and my mother were very devoted to each other; but when he was dying he did her a spiritual injury, making her promise that she would never become a Roman Catholic. He had, I suppose, seen a certain tendency in that direction; and when she herself was dying a few years later, there was a struggle between her religious doubts and the promise which bound her. My father told me that a few weeks before her death she asked that she might see a Roman Catholic priest, but that a very learned High Anglican was found for her instead who was able to allay her doubts. So he told me; but sometimes I doubt it.

I was about five years old when my mother died; and certain small incidents of the day have remained curiously distinct. It was

Bromsgrove Church from Perry Hall garden.

The Garden at "Longmeadow."

a Sunday, and we were faced without explanation with a strange disturbance in the usual arrangement of things; the midday meal was transferred from the dining to the drawing room. I asked why, and was told (an incident I should not otherwise have remembered) that it was because I was late in getting ready for church that morning. The answer was of course an absurd one, and I do not suppose that I believed it. The real reason—as I came to know later—was that in the large converted bedchamber next the dining room my mother lay dying, and did actually die a few minutes after the meal had ended.

We were out on the front lawn, not playing. What my sisters were doing I do not remember; my baby brother Herbert was with them. I was walking with my nurse along the drive, by the grass-bordered flower beds. I saw our housekeeper cousin come out of the front door; she said something I could not hear. I saw my two sisters burst into tears, and throw themselves into her arms. The nurse seemed to take no notice; we walked on. "What did she say?" I asked. Nurse (who had a defective palate) with a foolish scared look on her face, mumbled something which I did not catch. I asked again; she repeated it; this time I heard. Weeping was in the air. I turned, and rushed into the house, and threw myself sobbing on to the drawing-room sofa. As I lay and wept, I found that I had destroyed something which an hour before had been dear to me. A cover for quill pens, with a label lavishly embellished in gold and red had been given me for my amusement; and I had set it in a plate of water to soak off the label—a thing of beauty—from the cardboard which I did not want. Having got it off, I had laid it to dry on a piece of paper in the corner of the sofa; and there in my wild paroxysm of grief I had irretrievably crumpled it. Weeping for the loss of my mother, I wept for that too; and thus the day of her death has always had, incongruously attached to it, a red and gold label, with a white swan in the centre, advertising the virtue of quill pens.

Of that biggest event of my early childhood I remember little else. I was taken into the death chamber, and there saw my mother lying dead, solemn and beautiful. She was in her forty-first year. At the foot of the bed, on a small table, stood a crucifix in a wooden shrine between lighted candles. I had seen it often before, for during her long illness it had kept her company; but after her death it was put away. And when my father married again a few years later, such things as crucifixes were not looked upon with favour or allowed to give colour to our religious training. Indeed the only other which I saw for a good many years after was one which hung on the watchchain of a governess who left us with a bad character.

During her stay with us she lost it while on a walk—the crucifix, I mean; her character had gone previously—and offered a reward of sixpence for its recovery. A day or two later I found it lying face upward in the mud of a lane, and received the reward.

This revived my liking for crucifixes; but it has always been a puzzle to me that my stepmother, whose discipline in things domestic and religious was somewhat fixative, should have allowed so dependent a thing as a governess to flaunt daily an object of which she must have highly disapproved.

The chronology of childhood goes in jerks, with gaps which cannot be filled. In mourning for my mother I and all the rest of us wore black stockings whose harsh texture caused such itching that I cried as I walked in them. I used also to cry in bed at night for my mother to come back to me, and believed that if I prayed faithfully enough she would do so.

Marvellous is the mind of a child. One day, as we were out walking, we were passed by a widow, stepping quickly and leading a little girl by the hand. I made up my mind that this widow was my mother in disguise, and that when we got home she would reveal herself. Who the little girl was to be I did not know.

Years later I told a pious friend how I used to pray and believe that my mother would come back to me. Apparently it was against her religious convictions to throw doubt on the possibility of the dead rising in answer to prayer. Her comment on my infant prayer which failed to get its reward was merely that God knows what is best for us, and does not always grant what we ask.

In the last year of her life my mother had been so much withdrawn from us by illness that her death made little outward change. The most noticeable one, which followed shortly after, was a change of governesses, and then about a year later, the change of house from Perry Hall to Fockbury. This was preceded by the visit of a cousin whom we had not seen before. We liked her well, and in the first walk which she and I took alone together, I proposed marriage, and telling her that I had five pounds in the savings bank, I selected the small cottage in which we were to start life together. I was too young for age to mean anything to me in that connection, and that she was older than my father mattered nothing. Nor did I know that he had already proposed marriage to her himself; and while not definitely rejecting me, she had accepted him.

In the following year, when we had settled down into the new house my father brought home the bride who should have been mine. It was an evening in late July; we were all gathered in the entrance hall to greet them and when the greetings were over, my father gave me a roguish look, which meant, I suppose, "Cut you out, my boy!" I felt shy and embarrassed, and hung my head. But my heart was not broken.

She told me afterwards, that over that first meeting with her adopted family she had felt very apprehensive and nervous; but I can remember no sign of it. She discussed with us that same evening what we were to call her. It was to be "Mamma." But as time went by we adopted the better word of "Mater." And in our grown-up years the other word fell into practical disuse. Certain names suit characters; and she was so very much more a "Mater" than a "Mamma," perhaps because of a certain Roman touch in her rule both over herself and others, but not Roman in the theological sense; quite the reverse.

CHAPTER V

COWARD CONSCIENCE

Juniper: Conscience is like a flea, Father.
Matteo: Why like a flea, Brother?
Juniper: Because it always sees a man naked—and when it gets to the weakest part of him, it bites. And there's no running away from it, is there, Father? A flea may jump only a pig's length, while the man it's on runs twenty; but it's still on him when he stops running. He may get to the other side of himself, or of the world even; turn himself inside out, or upside down—but he hasn't got rid of it yet. Jonah found that out, didn't he? And I was standing on my head for the same reason.   *The Mess of Pottage*

THE conscience with which a man gets saddled in his youth may be a help or a hindrance, a benefit or a misfortune; for it may have come to him—the chances are about equal—from the good or the evil done to him by his elders. It may have had its beginnings in an unjust spanking, or in generous but unmerited pardon; in merciful release from superstition, or in the imposition of some horrible taboo, making life a misery. It sometimes happens that what our fathers have told us, the Devil has told them; and nothing in a man's life needs more revision, more re-adjustment—sometimes of a revolutionary character—than the conscience with which others have provided him. It is far better that a man should make his own mistakes, and find that they are mistakes, than that he should make the mistakes of his ancestors, under the pious conviction that because they are inherited they must be right. Yet that is the curse under which half creation is groaning and travailing today; and of that curse, more often than not, the family is the breeding-ground.

Things which seem small to speak about are large in the life of a child; and if large, then inevitably they have had large results in after-life. That certainly applies to myself; for I can have no

54

doubt that though I am now intellectually free from the inhibitions of my early training, I still have the old fears somewhere in my blood, and am not the same man that I might have been had their weight never been laid upon me.

I look back, and in no one single person can I see the directing hand of that cruelty, which in the name of modesty imposed so much physical discomfort and mental torture upon my infant years.

To speak of this now may seem like the flogging of a dead donkey, but in the history of the human race reactions take place; and it is at least possible that from the greater freedom of the present day (though it has been blessed by an archbishop, as a better thing than that system of furtive repressions which came before it) abuses may arise and cause a re-acceptance of that Victorian code of concealment which made certain aspects of life a terror to sensitive minds. And if there be still any who think that these things should not be exposed to the light of day, the donkey is still there, and is not dead.

In our family household, composed of seven children and six or seven grown-ups—parents, governess, and servants—there were only two among the grown-ups to whom I dared speak of my natural needs or expose myself in their performance. With my nurse and mother I felt no shame, and had no modesty. In the presence of all others my modesty was overwhelming and insuperable; and that being so, it must have been inculcated, by whom I cannot tell. But I find indications. One of these was a very early sense that I must not be seen, by anyone but the two who did not matter, going to, or returning from, my morning duty. My nursery faced, across a wide landing, the red baize door which led to the inner privacy of the W. C., and every day of my life I made a frightened bolt across that strip of public way—first there and then back—in the fulfillment of a necessary duty. As a preliminary thereto, in quite early days, I had to go to my nurse for certain buttons to be undone; and I remember how one day, when the nursery was being cleaned in her absence by other servants, need came upon me of which, among those strangers to the process, I dared not speak.

Apparently some signs of my state must have shown themselves in a strained and anxious face—perhaps in inquiry as to when nurse would return; but when questioned by the maid, I stubbornly denied my need. Disaster followed, and of course I was punished for it—a wilful dereliction of my duty combined with untruthfulness being the charge. And in a sense I knew both charges to be true; and conscience told me that I had sinned, though I had been unable to do otherwise. And it was, I think, from my sense of helpless guilt in such matters, that I came early to the conviction that, if I died, hell would be my portion for ever.

A few years later, I remember, having left the schoolroom after pronouncement of the formula, "May I leave the room?"—which, though daily said by myself and others, I always found somewhat difficult—I was met at the head of the stairs by the relative who was then in domestic charge of us; and she, having some fault to find with me, found it then; and having found it, did not straightway retire to give me that right of unobserved approach which modesty required. Unable to face the terrible publicity of her presence, I returned to the schoolroom whither a few minutes later she followed me, and imputing my retreat to sulkiness over having been scolded requested that I should be punished for non-fulfillment of duty—which accordingly I was.

These are but two instances of the mental pain and disturbance which quite kind and well-meaning elders imposed on my young life. Those daily dodgings never came to an end; they were as much a part of the domestic round as family prayers, had more influence on my conduct, and laid a far greater weight upon my conscience. Every day that dawned in that single household, a dozen manœuvres of modesty had individually to be performed by each in turn behind the backs of half the rest; and when we were well up in our teens, though it terrified us less, the secretive ritual was still in operation, and was expected of us and others. When I was fourteen, a college friend of my brother came to stay with us; and though in the main he was approved by our elders, my stepmother commented severely upon the fact that, she being somewhere about, he had not observed the proper secrecy of approach. "He ought to have waited," she said. "It wasn't modest."

I am fairly sure that, with some of us, this excessive secretiveness over the natural side of things helped to produce evasion and untruthfulness on the moral side as well, and that the habit of concealment of things which were not wrong extended itself to things that were. Frankness being so much discouraged, conceal-ment and the moral sense became morbidly allied, and one grew to feel that between the individual and his social environment was a barrier which had to be defended even from those whom one loved and might naturally have trusted.

From this taboo-morality one got the idea that wrong was not so much a thing to be repented of, as a thing to be concealed; and, as I have already said, my repentances for actual wrong-doing were few and far between. But when, after punishment, the conven-tional question came, "Are you sorry?" one always answered un-truthfully, "Yes"—either because that was the easiest way out, or because one had not sufficient moral independence and honesty to tell the truth.

I remember on one occasion having been sent to my room, to repent of some misdeed in solitude; and there as I lay on my bed darkness descended, so that when my father entered, sent up on an errand of mercy to release me from my imprisonment, he went to the wrong bed, and mistaking some clothes that lay upon it for me, addressed to them his inquiry whether I was sorry. From my far corner of the room I murmured "Yes," and he did not hear me. "Very well, then you can stay where you are!" he said, and left me to a strange feeling of pride and satisfaction that by sheer accident I had not been heard saying the untruthful thing, and had not climbed down when it had been expected of me.

But though the code-conscience provided by others imposed its weight on my early years, another kind of conscience, more real and spontaneous, began to awake in me, a process of self-discovery which had no reference whatever to the judgment of others or to the fear of being found out. Two instances of that important find-ing of myself, I have used for fictional purposes in one of my books; and as the account there given is exactly as each thing happened, I cannot do better than bring them back from their fictional setting, with only the alteration of a few inessential words, as a record of two unforgotten experiences which did give me the beginnings of a conscience of my own.

I was hardly five then, and going up to the nursery from downstairs had my supper cake in my hand—only a few mouthfuls left. My small brother had been having his bath, and sitting on the nurse's knee was getting into his bedclothes, when spying me with my cake, he asked to have a share of it. I daresay it would not have been good for him, but of that I thought nothing at all; the cruel impulse took me to make one mouthful of all that was left. He watched it go without crying; but his eyes opened at me in a strange way, wondering at this sudden lesson of the hardness of a human heart. "All gone!" he said, turning toward nurse, perhaps to see if she too had a like surprise for his small intelligence. I think I have never forgiven myself that; the judging remembrance of it would, I believe, win forgiveness to him for any wrong he might now do me, so unreasonably is my brain scarred where the thought of it lies. . . .

The other thing came out of a less personal greed, and was years later. We were egg-collectors; and in the loft over one of the out-houses there was a small swallow's nest too high to be reached by any ladder we could get up there. I was intent on getting the *eggs,* and thought of no other thing that might chance; so I spread a soft fall below, and with a long pole I broke the floor of the nest. Then with a sudden stir of horror I saw soft things falling along with the clay, tiny and feathery. Two were killed by the breakage that fell with them, but one was quite alive and unhurt. I gathered up the remnants of the nest, and set it with the young one in it by the loft-window where the parent-birds might see, making clumsy strivings of pity to quiet my conscience. The parent-birds did see, soon enough: they returned—first up to the rafters, then darting round and round, and crying; then to where their little one lay helpless and exposed, hung over it with a nibbling movement of their beaks for a moment, making my miserable heart bound up with hope: then away, away, shrieking into the July sunshine. Once they came back and shrieked at the horror of it all, and fled away not to return. I remained for hours, and did what silly pity could dictate; but of course the young one died: and I—*cleared away all remains, so that nobody might see.* Since then, the poignancy of my regret, when I think of it, has never softened. The question which pride of life and love of make-believe till then had not raised in me, "Am I a God to kill and make alive?" was answered all at once by an emphatic, "No!" which I never afterwards forgot. But the grief remained all the same, that life—to teach me that blunt truth—should have had to make sacrifice in the mote-hung loft of three frail lives on a clay-altar, and bring to nothing but pain, and a last miserable dart away into the bright sunshine, the spring work of two swift-winged intelligences. Is Man, we are told to think, not worth many sparrows? Sometimes I doubt it, and would in thought give my life that those swallows in their generations might live again.

These and other findings of myself were the only religious experiences of my early life which I feel now to have had a permanent value and "God" did not come into them; God and Life were still in separate departments, and did not come together till a good many years later. But before that happened I was often actually conscious of having two minds about things—one was my own, and the other was an inculcated one, deriving from a combination of the fear, love, and respect which I had for my elders. And those being the alternatives, every single thing that I did when of two minds, at the behest of mind number one, however wrong, foolish, or useless, did nevertheless at the time seem to me—to the self-possessing part of me, that is to say—the better thing to do—sometimes the only thing. At the back of my divided mind four-and-twenty elders may have been sitting on thrones of judgment and condemning me for it; but that part of me which belonged to myself, and not to the generations which had gone before, said wholeheartedly,—smiting the four-and-twenty elders into jibbering silence—"Go in, and do it!" And sometimes— though not always—I think now that I was right, and that the four-and-twenty elders were wrong; and even in some cases, when I did foolishly make mistakes, the mistakes may have had more value in giving me experience, than would have come from my acceptance of untried precepts laid down by other experiences than my own. In a word, I think that doing wrong has sometimes a very definite value, and that unquestioning obedience, even to wise authority, does not always produce such good results as an experimental process of "trial and error" by which one acquires experience at firsthand and not through mere hearsay.

When Ruskin's mother, after due warning, allowed him to touch the hot teapot, he learned his lesson in a quicker and a better way than by a dozen preventions from discovering what touching a hot teapot was like. And a child who is allowed to fall acquires a better balance and a surer footing than one who is kept upright by artificial means for fear lest it should hurt itself.

One of the very wisest things in the Montessori system is the careful leaving of children to make their own mistakes, and only to help them out of their difficulties when they ask for it. An even more valiant exponent of that course of education was Homer Lane, whom I once met in Madame Montessori's company at the invitation of a mutual friend.

But they did not suit each other; Madame Montessori was chill, stately, and monosyllabic; Homer Lane, mischievously I think, very much the reverse. As though determined not to be taken seriously by an unsympathetic listener, he told us the story of his "Little Commonwealth"—that brave experiment with the worst and most difficult material that our reformatory authorities could provide—rather as if it were a naughty game that he had been playing on human nature; and Madame was annoyed.

I do not know whether the story, as he gave it that night, has been more soberly recorded in a published form; but here is my memory of some of the things he told us, set down, as nearly as I can remember them, in his own words.

It began, I think, in his answer to a question from our hostess: "But what is one to do if a small boy starts hacking with his knife at the leg of one's piano?"

"Put the piano out of his reach, or him out of reach of the piano; but for Heaven's sake, don't punish him, or you may spoil a good carpenter!" And then followed this account of the first day of the Little Commonwealth, which, at his own request, was started with twelve of the worst specimens with which Borstal could provide him.

"I told them," said Lane, "that we had no rules, so at present nothing was against rule; but that they would have to make rules for themselves as they went along. I said, however, that there was plenty to do, and that for my part I was going to build pigstyes. I supposed that some of them would come along with me out of curiosity and presently give a hand, but their mentality hadn't yet reached that stage. So I set to work alone. Presently I heard breakage going on; and went to see what was up. It was really quite hopeful: a sense of order had already begun—they had gathered a heap of stones and had drawn a line on the ground, and were all taking their turns to shy at a window on the other side of the yard. Directly they saw me, they all bolted. I went across, and stood looking at the broken window and the heap of stones; presently a head came round the corner to see how I was taking it. 'Here,' I said, 'what's all this for?' 'Oh, we were only throwing at the window,' I was told. 'What?' I said; 'from here? Did any of you manage to hit it?' 'Yes, some of us did.' 'Well, I wonder if I could,' I said, and I took up a stone, and began shying sparingly at the window. A lot of heads came round the corner then, they were really interested. 'Come on!' I said, 'come and take your turns!' Back they came, and we took our turns till there wasn't a pane of glass left. Then I said, 'I'm tired of this; I'm going back to my work.' That time two of the lads came with me; next day they all came. So that was the beginning of that."

A few years ago, I saw at Batcombe in Dorsetshire, a large guest house, beautiful and strong, built by these same window-breakers. The experiment had then ended in failure—not from any inherent inability of the Little Commonwealth to make good when put to the test, but because financial aid had been withdrawn. A scandalous charge had been made; and a government inspector had been sent down to inquire and to report. The charge was officially discredited; but the whole system was too revolutionary for the official mind to stomach—the sort of mind to which revolutionary success is more dangerous than failure. And so, on official recommendation, the government grant was withdrawn; and because the withdrawal followed upon inquiry into a scandal, it was generally supposed that the scandal had been true and was the cause. It was not; the Little Commonwealth had made good; but its success was too heavy an indictment of other systems—of Borstal among the rest—for its success to be welcome.

Something similar was done by Thomas Mott Osborne, at Sing Sing in America, when he started Mutual Welfare government in the prisons under his control. When I went to the States in 1916, I saw the system in full swing, happy and flourishing. Of that I shall give account later on; it was wonderful; but it was too good to last. It depended, like the Little Commonwealth, on an exceptional personality with a courage and understanding of human nature to which the present generation has not yet acclimatized itself, and of which in my young days no one in the educational world had even begun to dream.

CHAPTER VI

COUNTRY LIFE

FROM Fockbury, with its terraced garden, set on the side of a low hill, we could still see Bromsgrove spire two miles distant. Adjoining the house were the farm buildings which had once belonged to it—stable-yard, barn and rick-yard. The nearest village was half a mile away; Catshill, the parish to which we belonged, about a mile. In our grandfather's day, the house had given time to the neighbourhood, from a large clock set up on the roof, and though the clock had long since disappeared, it was still known to the villagers as the "Clock-House." Also, because a good deal of the land round about had once belonged to the family, we occasionally heard my father spoken of as the Squire—a title to which he had no claim, but which he rather enjoyed.

A few hundred yards away was the smaller house which our parents had occupied until my eldest brother was born. It was now a dame-school, run by three sisters, to whom we gave the names of "Battle, Murder, and Sudden Death"—a very suitable demoniacal possession (was it prophetic?) for the *Shropshire Lad's* place of origin. Its front was overshadowed from across the road by a large cedar which has now gone. Because of its family connection we were much interested when passing it; but as, in our time, it was always occupied, we never went in nor, I believe, have any of us been in it since.

Two miles distance from a town meant more isolation in those days than it would now; and we still lived a small and enclosed family life, though in our playtime hours we had considerable freedom and means of escape from observation in barn, rick-yard, and field. With farm labourers, and one family of poachers we

63

had friendly relations; and one beautiful yeoman farmer, named John Daffern, we loved dearly, and calling at his farm in our walks were treated now and again to draughts of milk. He had been my grandfather's tenant; but the farm, about that time, passed to other hands. At the election of 1880, he dared to vote Liberal; and my clergyman-uncle hearing of it, wrote him a reproachful letter, telling him that such conduct was disrespectful to my grandfather's memory. When I heard of it I felt that it was a shameful thing to do, for the old man had taken it to heart. "No," he said to me with a sad shake of his head, "I shan't never vote Liberal again!"

He was a good hard-working farmer, but his life's work gave no provision for his old age. Fifteen years after we had left Fockbury I went back to see him, and found him living as a poor cottage-pensioner, uncomplaining, and lovely as ever. "The doctor came to see me the other day," he said, "and gave me a shilling. I was very thankful for it."

It was about this time, or a little later, that the class-distinctions to which we were bred began to attract my attention, but not till some years after did they trouble my conscience. As regards work and wages, the servants got decent treatment, but very little liberty; and on some occasions their natural human needs were cruelly overruled. We had a married cook, whose husband had work at such a distance that they could see each other but seldom. One day he came, and his wife asked leave to stay out with him for the night. It was refused and when later it was discovered that she had gone out secretly and spent the night in the barn, her behaviour was considered most indecent. Of course, at the time, we did not understand why; afterwards one's sense of the indecency got shifted to other shoulders.

On another occasion, word came that the mother of one of our maids was dying. I heard her, in great distress, asking leave to go home. It was granted; but I was told afterwards, "They make a great fuss, but they don't feel about these things as we do." Even in recent years, when I have quoted that opinion about the feelings of "the lower classes," I have heard it endorsed.

There was one instance, however, when leniency took the place of moral judgment. One of our gardeners and a domestic help mated before they married, and he was not dismissed for it. Not only did they mate but they set up house together; and we were actually allowed to call and inspect the domestic arrangements, while they were still "waiting to get married." The bride-that-was-to-be showed us the only bedroom; and one of my sisters, assuming it to be the husband's, said, "But where do you sleep?" There was a moment's hesitation. "Oh, I sleep anywhere," was the answer, which at the time satisfied us.

We attended the wedding; and the union having been thus made respectable, the whole of our domestic staff went that same evening to the wedding party; and there, though I did not know of it till years afterwards, the bridegroom gave a very Rabelaisian recitation, which would certainly have procured his dismissal, had our parents heard of it. About ten years later I heard it myself. The occasion was a birthday party (when Ben and his wife were no longer in our employ) which I attended surreptitiously; and there, elated by the occasion, Ben stood up and broke forth. I was a little scared, but no one else seemed to mind, or think it unsuitable for mixed company. And when it was over—"Ben has never said that," was his wife's comment, "since the night we was married." And I wonder is there an orgiastic tradition for such occasions among country folk about which the more sophisticated of us know nothing?

When my Rabelaisian old friend Ben was dying, he saw angels standing about his bed, and his wife told of it with great joy and consolation. "What superstition!" said my stepmother when she heard of it. But I think she would not have objected had the vision been vouchsafed to a relative, or to one of her own class. The apportioning of pews in a parish church according to social importance does colour—or did in the days of our youth—the whole religious outlook of quite kind and well-educated people. Lord Curzon's surprise, when he came upon "Tommies" bathing during the war, to find that the English "lower classes" had such white skins, was shared in things spiritual as well, and amounted not only to surprise but to incredulity.

Some years ago I met an old cottage-gardener who had recently lost his wife. For many years she had been stone deaf. The tears sprang to his eyes as he spoke of her. "Ah," he said, "she was a lovely soul!" The beauty of that phrase and of the feeling that went with it would have been, had I needed it then, a good corrective to that pronouncement of fifty years ago, "They make a great fuss, but they don't feel as we do."

The depth of feeling of simple villagers and farm hands used sometimes to surprise me. A fine farm horse, named Blackbird, was stabled on the premises; and sometimes, rather fearfully holding on to his mane, I would ride him down to pasture for the night. One morning the carter, John Tong, found him lying in his stable dead, and came to us weeping with the news. On another day I remember that same humble friend of our childhood, fiery with anger. We had been teasing his small son. Class-distinction was forgotten then, and he told us what he thought of us.

At the bottom of Fockbury field, in a small cottage under a wall of rock, lived the poaching family I have already mentioned, an old gypsy-like father, three unmarried sons, and one daughter. The old man's heart was in the pursuit of ground game at which he was an adept. "When I can do no more ratting and rabbitting," he said one day, "then I hope the Lord will take me." He got other things than rats and rabbits, but whatever it was, it went with his religion all right.

But for the lone daughter that was not a suitable or a safe home. In the pinched cottage accommodation she slept in the same room as her three brothers, divided from them only by a curtain; and one night she had to flee away in her nightclothes to the home of the man she was to marry. The matter did not seem to be very seriously regarded, and no blood was shed. I did not know of it at the time; but when I did, it told me something of social conditions which were then, I suppose, fairly prevalent. With those brothers some of us were on friendly terms; they were quite decent fellows in their way; and when my father went out for a day's shooting, he generally had one of them carry the bag for him, and look after the dogs.

Now and then things were told us by our village neighbours of which I have since made literary use. The gardener who followed Ben in my father's employ gave me this: He was going one day by a neighbour's house when he smelt a savoury smell. "What have you got there?" he asked. "My dinner," he was told: "Will you come in and have a bit?" He went in and had a bit, and unable to deny that it was good, had a bit more. Having finished, "Did you like it?" his neighbour asked him, and he owned that he did like it. Then came the question, "D'you know what you've been eating?" He confessed that he did not. "Hedgehog," said his neighbour. And then came the finish of his story. In a tone of deep moral satisfaction he said, "I brought it all back again!"

By this time my two eldest brothers, Alfred and Robert, had been at school for some years. The rest of us—my two sisters Clemence and Kate, Basil, myself, and the youngest, Herbert—were getting our education from a governess; and on the whole I think that learning interested us and gave us no pain worth talking about. The learning of things by heart, both poetry and prose, came easily to most of us; and every day of our lives we learned two or three verses of poetry, and a passage of Scripture. I can still remember the Psalms which I learned in my childhood—those, at least, which interested me; those which did not have gone from me; and that, generally speaking, is true of all the things I memorized in early youth. What fitted stuck; what did not fit lost its hold on my memory, having never secured my interest.

But what interested me and excited me far more in our learning of Scripture than my own memorisings were those passages from *Isaiah* learned and recited by my elder sister. In those early days they struck for me the high note of poetry—and have done so ever since. Why, then, was I not set to learn, or did I not ask to learn those or similar passages from the same writer? I suppose because, at that early age, desire was inarticulate in the face of an educational scheme which gave no choice to the pupil as to what he should learn. Often poems were chosen for me which I rather disliked; Cowper's *Rose;* Wordsworth's *We Are Seven;* Tennyson's horrid little *May Queen,* which I still think a detestable poem; a passage from *Paradise Lost* which so bored me that it has never recovered hold. I liked better such inferior things as *The Death of Gellert, Sir Ralph the Rover, The Battle of Ivry,* and still more such superior things (showing that taste had already begun to form) as *The Fall of Sennacherib, The Burial of Sir John Moore,* and *Hohenlinden*—which last I admired enormously.

Sitting together in the schoolroom, we all heard each other's poetry, and even then I could feel the difference in the poetry said by the elder sister, to whom it came as the breath of her nostrils, and that of the younger, to whom it meant little more than a jingle of words, easy to memorise. And so it was that the death of Constance from *Marmion* stood far higher in my estimation as poetry than the opening canto of *The Lay of the Last Minstrel,* which I think now is the better thing.

That gift of quiet expressive delivery has remained with my sister through life; and two memorable events in my initiation into poetry during my teens were her reading to me of Mrs. Browning's beautiful but very faulty poem, *The Song of the Morning Star,* and her recitation as we walked along Pont Street of the choruses from *Atalanta in Calydon*—the first Swinburne I had ever heard. In each case her rendering raised the poem to a higher rank than it probably had any right to. Had all Swinburne's verse made the same appeal to me as that first hearing, I should have become his devout worshipper—a fate which perhaps I escaped thereafter by reading him mainly to myself.

It is a curious fact, in view of the attitude of my two sisters towards poetry, that a few years later Kate wrote two poems better than any that Clemence ever produced either up to that time or later—the one was a welcome to a new-born baby, the other a lament over a General Election. The baby-poem has been lost, the other has been happily preserved, and shall appear in its right place.

At Fockbury family reading became an almost daily institution, especially during the winter months, and school holidays. It was, I think, our stepmother's happiest contribution to our early training. She was a good reader, and though not caring greatly for poetry herself, she did her duty nobly, and read to us much of what she believed to be best for us; the narrative poems of Scott and Thomas Moore, most of Shakespeare, *Esmond,* and a few of the *Waverley Novels.* One day Alfred came to call us in to reading. Some book had just been finished. "What is she going to read now?" we asked.

"One of the nicest stories that has ever been written," he answered. And that was our introduction to the delights of *Cranford.*

In the evenings our father was the reader. *Pickwick* was his first choice; and I have never liked Dickens better, or so well. But Sheridan's *Rivals* did not interest us, and certain other of his selections have passed out of my memory for the same reason. But on the whole those family readings formed so satisfying a bond of common interest between elder and younger, that I can hardly think of family life without it; and I marvel when I hear of families in whose upbringing it has had no place.

About this time we began to act plays—generally of our own composing, unwritten and impromptu. Alfred would come into the schoolroom while we were having tea. "We are going to do a play tonight," he would say. And there and then, he would tell us the plot and assign to us our parts; and when the elders had finished dinner—without any rehearsal, so far as I can remember— the play was performed, less to their entertainment, I imagine, than ours. I don't think we acted well; and I don't remember that we ever got praised for our performance. Once when a real ham was dropped on the floor by an escaping thief, my father loudly protested; but as a rule the elders accepted what was set before them without much criticism, and endured as wise elders should when their young are harmlessly experimenting in the things which interest them.

My main interest in these five years at Fockbury, now that I look back on them, is the way they date a period that has passed almost out of memory. Among the villagers illiteracy was common, and those who could read for the most part could only read out loud— not to themselves—following the lines with their fingers. At Catshill there was a struggling church-school, always in financial arrears; and in a neighbouring cottage a very primitive dame-school run by the wife of a farm labourer; her pupils twelve to fifteen small children, sitting round on low stools, each with a slate, and she busy all the while preparing her man's midday meal.

They were a strange couple; the wife had a refined face, once it must have been beautiful, and she did not look unhappy; but her husband was about the ugliest man I have ever seen. He was deformed as well; his legs were stunted and absurdly bowed, his face—a caricature by nature—was further damaged by an accident which had happened in early youth; from that same accident he carried on his body an unhealed wound. They had no children. What strange conjunction, one wonders, had brought about that union? Had a woman of such comely attraction given herself willingly to that poor scarecrow, or had tragic circumstances compelled her? Her queer little school proved her to be a woman of energy; perhaps it was that which gave her happiness. But before we left Fockbury her school came to an end. The Education Act of 1870 had come into force. One day, much to the family's amusement, an investigating official called at our house to find out if we were being properly educated. The fact that we had an unqualified but resident governess quite satisfied him; and our home education was left undisturbed. But the poor little dame-school up the lane had to go; and I wonder which of the two things was the wife's greater tragedy—her marriage, or the loss of her school?

But in the years that followed, while lessons under a governess of no special qualifications were considered a sufficiently finished education for girls, we boys went, as a matter of course, to Bromsgrove School; and when I entered in 1876, there were four of us—all Foundation Scholars—receiving a good education at less cost for the whole lot than that which went to the engagement of the governess.

The appropriation to one family of four scholarships (and eventually of five) out of the twelve available for all natives of Bromsgrove, naturally caused some local jealousy; but the terms of the Foundation required that those who got top marks in the entrance examination should get whatever scholarships were vacant, and that particular qualification each of us honestly fulfilled as it came to our turn. When it came to mine I was in terror lest I should disgrace the family record; and I was told that when with the other candidates I came before the Governors to hear the result, I presented a face of such acute apprehension—and, a moment later, of such ecstatic relief—that as we retired from the Presence, the Board broke into laughter.

There was also laughter between the headmaster and my parents over one of my answers to the history paper which had been set me. Called on to give an account of the chief events in the life of Nelson, I gave a list of his battles, in one of which I said he lost an eye, in another an arm, and then added, "He was also in love with Lady Hamilton."

I could not myself see why this was amusing. Having come upon one of Romney's portraits of the lovely lady, it was the incident in Nelson's career which, coupled with his physical losses, most interested me. I was already a romantic humanist, and such, I suppose, I have remained.

With school my childhood ended. At the end of my twelfth year we returned to Bromsgrove and the old home. Ten years later Fockbury was in the occupation of a most friendly family with whom I spent many happy days, and the place still had its old charm for me, though alterations and extensions had already been made. More recently I returned to find that it had become a mansion—almost unrecognizable so far as the house was concerned. But one old feature had been restored; at the end of a new wing a clock-tower has been built, with a clock to give time to the neighbourhood, and the "Clock-House" is once more its name.

Chapter VII

SCHOOL DAYS

I WENT to school in my eleventh year, and there the easy days of childhood ended, and the more difficult ones of youth began. During my first term I was placed in a class with boys bigger than myself, who used to stick knives and pins into me if I dared to go above them. It was the old bad system; "taking down" in class was the crude and lazy way which schoolmasters then employed for registering merit and progress. Quite naturally the older boys resented it, when in a manner humiliating to themselves a small junior was allowed to exhibit publicly so insignificant a thing in school life as mental superiority.

But it was equally natural that, when for the moment I could do so, I should feel a certain enjoyment in pulling down the mighty from their seats, and exalting the humble and meek; for, outside the class, those bigger boys led me a terrible life, and inside, so far as discipline and decorum allowed—in that sort of League of Nations atmosphere which school hours established—they wished still to do the same, and bully the small nations.

I use the political parallel because that was really my first training in politics; from it I had the sense to learn that physical force is not the basis of government as the materialists would have us believe. The basis of government is human nature. My human nature stuck it out, and the human nature of the bigger boys, being fundamentally decent, grew ashamed of itself, and they ceased to stick pins into me. In spite of my being the smaller and weaker, they allowed me at last to take them down. The small object-lesson of the limitations of physical force in a world where school-boy honor (or the taboo that stands for it) allows no appeal to the higher authorities, helped to make me an idealist.

I can still remember the last occasion when that particular form of intimidation was practised on me. Just before the end of class, a question was being passed down. I knew the answer to it; perhaps my face showed as much. As the question came nearer, warning looks and gestures were directed towards me of what I was to expect if I defied public opinion. I was up against the whole class. The question reached me; I answered it and went up top. And there I was safe in my pride of place, for the hour was already striking. We numbered down; the bell began ringing for evening chapel. The master went out, followed by the rest. I lingered collecting my books, papers, and inkpot, hoping that the call to chapel (which, as a day boy I had not to attend) would clear the way for me. But when I came out round the corner of the corridor, there was the whole class waiting for me. The buffeting that fell upon me was short (for chapel was calling them) but it was as sharp as they could make it. Books and papers were violently scattered, inkpot broken; dazed from the pummelling of a dozen fists, crouched on hands and knees I watched them rush off and reach the chapel door just in time. I collected my scattered belongings, with a queer sense of pride—a feeling that somehow I had won. And the next day, though I was not able to remain top of the class for long, I let it be seen that I did not willingly relinquish my position. After that they either let me alone, or made such slight attacks on my right of self-determination that I no longer remember them.

Defenders of the Public School System—as it existed in my days, and as they would like it to continue—maintain that the bullying of small boys is good for them, and has a healthy and hardening effect on their characters. It may be so; but what of its effect on those who do the bullying? It seems to me a cowardly and despicable thing for the strong to afflict the weak; and I am inclined to think that the divine right of imperialism to swagger through the world, exploiting subject races for their supposed benefit has very largely had its origin in the bullying and fagging which have been countenanced in our public schools.

I have come to the conclusion rather as an observer of, than as a sufferer from, the system; for after my first two terms the bullies did not much trouble me, and, as a day boy, fagging was not one of my duties. But throughout the school an atmosphere of upper and under dog was prevalent; and until they reached the fifth and sixth form all day boys were made to feel it in varying degrees. In this the headmaster aided and abetted. He disliked the trade element (to which, on the terms of its Foundation, the school had to give admission) and wanted to be rid of it. I remember on one occasion, when the day boys had beaten the lower school boarders at football, how the Head insisted on a return match at short notice, so that the disgrace should be wiped out. I also heard him, on more than one occasion, use in the playground the insulting nicknames given to certain day boys by their class-conscious school-mates. "Bacon" and "Carthorse" were two of the names in question, given respectively to the son of a grocer and the son of a farmer; the grocer, much to the Head's annoyance, no doubt, being also on the Board of Governors.

But in this one particular my school life was blessed to me that, though it meant belonging to a despised section, I had the great luck to be a day boy. For that I have never ceased to be thankful, for I am quite sure that my home life formed a more valuable element in my training than anything that the tender mercies of the best boarding-school could have provided. This may not apply to all kinds of boys, or to all kinds of homes, but I am in no doubt that it was true about my own home, and about myself. And though, looking back upon it, I now regard my school life as a miserable one—a life beset with repressions, snubs, ignominy, and a general sense of unfitness to my environment, and though it had in it horrid moments of pain, apprehension, and paralysing fear, I am quite sure that I was not continuously miserable or even depressed. The young have infinite powers of evasion; disposing Fate stands over and claims them—they are not the masters of it; but they often manage to dodge it, and belong again to themselves. Being a day boy, my half holidays and Sundays were free, or could be made so with a certain amount of dodging. Even on school days

I had two or three blessed hours to myself and my real interests. And give a prisoner that proportion of release from the treadmill of uncongenial drudgery, his lot is none too bad if he can remain consciously individual—even libertarian.

But I am sure that a life of so much furtive dodging was not good for me, and would have been much worse had not most of the dodging taken place in that old home setting to which we returned, after my second year's schooling. Until then our continuing to live at Fockbury involved a double journey of over two miles, in summer term a six o'clock breakfast, through all terms alike a scratch meal in the middle of the day, and a make-weight on getting back at six-thirty. As a consequence one was ready for bed before one's evening work was done, and preparation was often scamped. But the standard of scholarship in the lowest form where duffers congregated was an easy one. I had a form-master whom I loved, and for my first three terms did not do badly.

During my first term I was caned only once, and could set against that the prize which I took for poetry-recitation. But though I moderately deserved it, that caning had a curious effect upon me, which I find difficult to account for. I thought, after having received it, that I was in permanent disgrace with my headmaster; and though I had taken a prize at his hands at the end of term, when I went to a party at his house during the holidays, I feared to meet his eye, or to presume on friendly relations. He had beaten me, and the social bond was broken. It may have been the shock of a too-unaccustomed punishment—for I had never received it at home since early days in the nursery. But while from my beloved form-master whom I did not fear I took a caning without any mental trouble, I remained morbidly sensitive to similar punishment from my headmaster, whom I feared more than I have feared any other person before or since. I can only make a guess that his infuriated manner when he caned anyone—a sort of white rage, sometimes hot, sometimes cold—had a terrifying effect on me. There was in it something evil; and when he caned me unjustly, as he did twice, my resentment went deep and has lasted to this day.

Why is it that one finds it so much harder to forgive the wrongs and injustices of one's youth than those encountered in later years? Often the latter are materially the much more serious; but they are not so devastating to a mind which has become set to life's accidents. Is it because those earlier wrongs have done me an unending harm that I find them so difficult to forgive? That headmaster of mine—a strange mixture of artificial manners, shallow charm, and real enthusiasm, left on me not merely a mark but an unhealed wound. Until after my fortieth year I had terrifying dreams of him—a prolongation into the subconscious of the nervous damage he had done me. There must have been in his nature a streak of sadistic cruelty, which was, I suspect, not merely mental but physical. My earliest experience on the mental side was when, before the whole class, he told a small boy he must come to school better dressed, as though the boy were himself responsible for the clothes with which parental carelessness had provided him. As I happened to be that boy, I remember the distress it caused me. The shabbiness of my outfit was already a daily discomfort, for my schoolfellows had taken a derisive note of it. Now they had the backing of the headmaster in the class-snobbishness which was beginning to give the school its social tone. How the wish is still alive in me that I could have given him the right answer, returned him insult for insult, and got myself expelled! The stupid presumption—or was it not stupidity but cold malice?—that a boy of eleven had the ordering of his own clothes (I remember them still—coat, waistcoat, and breeches, of three different patterns) remains an amazement to me; and as I think of that moment of humiliation, again I grow hot.

My solution, I remember, was—*not* to pass on word of the public disgrace that had befallen me (of that I was too miserably ashamed), but to put on surreptitiously each day my Sunday coat and waistcoat—leaving for school in the morning before the elders were up—and changing again on my return, till, my Sunday best becoming noticeably shabby, I was provided with a fresh outfit, and the misappropriated suit was passed into school wear.

But though that was the most searing experience, being the earliest, there were others. On one occasion, our form-master being absent, the Head took us for Latin at short notice—indeed at no notice at all. We were the lowest form; and in order to inspect the work of term, he put us through the exercises we had done during the previous weeks. We stood round him a nervously in-capacitated class—for the terror of going to the Head was at that time general through the whole of the lower school—and each in turn translated the sentence which fell to him. Whether others were as nervously paralysed as I was, I cannot tell—probably not. The boy next to me translated his allotted sentence, inaccurately; the Head flew out at him, "Be accurate, sir, be accurate!" I drew a breath of relief. The sentence which lay before me admitted of *perfect* "accuracy." Word for word, in strict order as they stood, I translated, "The king wise citizens has." For that I was caned.

And I wonder now, did that intellectual ass think I was insulting him with a too-literal "accuracy," or was he simply out for my blood on the smallest excuse he could find? It remains a mystery; for at the end of that term, in the report sent home, with its various entries—Latin, French, Mathematics, English, all fairly good, I think—his own report was not unfavourable. "But, alas, so in-accurate!" was his only word of blame. How willingly at that time would I have given up all my imaginary cleverness for the comparative safety of that quality of accuracy which I never attained!

Many years later I asked Alfred, who was the shining light of his sixth form, what he thought of our late Head as a teacher. "Excellent!" he said, "for those of good ability to do the subjects he cared about." Over the rest there was silence.

It may have been for that reason that, in the midst of my terrors, there was one set of lessons with him which I almost enjoyed. For some freakish reason, in my first term at school, he took the lowest form in English grammar. And I suppose that, having for grammar a natural interest and aptitude, I was more alive to its charms than others, and showed a better standard. In this subject I found him stimulating and delightful, and through that hour each week a strange sense of security accompanied me; I was temporarily without fear of him.

Probably it was those hours of comparative bliss which went to my after undoing; for he must have then formed the opinion that I was a "clever" boy; and according to his code all clever boys had to be classics; and if, in the classics, their cleverness did not show, it was their own "won't obstinacy." In the classics I was certainly not clever. When I came to Homer and Virgil, I could see the beauty of both languages; the sound of them was lovely to me, and still is. But in their structure—moods, conjugations, declensions, and horridly involved misarrangement of words—they floored me as much as they floored the merest dolts whose recognised stupidity secured for them comparatively mild treatment. The Head never forgave me for being good at English, and bad at Latin and Greek; and when with pain and difficulty I reached the sixth form—driven to the constant use of cribs to make any headway at all—I got turned out of it again for saying that ἕκαστόν meant a hundred. Re-admitted the next term, I took the part of Odysseus in the *Cyclops* of Euripides, and delivered the verses which I had learned by heart with so much ease and zest for their beauty that the Head was more exasperated with me than ever, when, in my "unseens," I stumbled over strange words, and scattered false quantities in every paragraph. And it was, I suppose, as a sort of revenge that he snubbed all my attempts at English.

But it was the general rule throughout the school in those days for English literature to get only scant and careless attention. I remember the lacklustre lessons which we got in my third year on Milton, from a master who had not one ounce of poetry in his composition, and who clearly regarded the whole business as a foolish waste of time, as—under his tuition—it certainly was. And it stays a wonder to me that, even after such a deadening experience, the *Lycidas* should have remained, or rather should have become, almost my favourite poem in the English language.

I suppose that these conditions were largely Victorian, and could hardly be found now in a school of the same class. And even there there was an exception; for a year later I came under the tuition of a form-master, the Rev. F. W. Parsons (I record his name with

gratitude) who did actively encourage my love of English literature and poetry; and next to my own family there is nobody, I
think, to whom I owe so much for that "leading out" of my young
mind, which is the right literal meaning of education, as I do
to him.

He was the only one of our masters who consistently joined up
our work in Latin and Greek with English literature. He had a
beautiful voice, and his soft gentle delivery of poetry was very
attractive. I liked everything he read to us; and though he made
the mistake of thinking Lewis Morris a great poet, and gave
exaggerated praise to Kingsley's hexameters, he had also good
things to say about Browning, whom then it was somewhat heretical
to admire—among teachers of the young, at any rate.

Another of his virtues was the setting of impositions that required intelligence. This took a form that on one occasion landed
me in embarrassment. To try us out in our powers of English he
made defaulters translate their Ovid and Virgil into verse; and
when those incapable of the task got an imposition of this kind
set them, they came to me for the doing of it. This was all very
well when I did not get an imposition myself over the same ground.
But one day, having already done Ovid's *Song of Arion* into verse
for a schoolmate in difficulty, I got caught in it myself, and had to
turn out as my own a version which was bound to be inferior. The
task might have floored me—did, indeed, till I bethought me of the
expedient of doing a comic rendering, to which I was helped by
the fragment which my schoolfellow had been able to compose,
but which I had not used. This—the only bit of the two versions
which I now remember—ran thus:

> "What sea does not know of Arion?
>   What land does not honour his name?
> For he conquered the wolf and the lion,
>   And made them excessively tame."

This, with the rest to match, I took to my form-master; and he—
God rest his good easy soul!—accepted as an allowable joke what
with any other master I might have been caned for.

A little later I was given another translation to do, which brought me a greater satisfaction. It was another of Ovid's *Odes*, but which, I cannot now remember. Having finished it, I took it to read to my sister Clemence. In a corner of the room sat Alfred deep in study. I did not suppose he was listening. Presently I came to these lines:

"When fate hath snatched our choicest flowers away,
    Vex not my spirit with these idle tales!
Say not that holy men may hope for Heaven,
    When nothing holy, nothing good avails!"

Voice from corner: "Excellent!" And because of that single word of commendation, those lines, and those alone—as the result, I suppose, of my reciting them to myself so many hundreds of times—have remained in my memory—Alfred having said they were "excellent"!

My school experience taught me early the truth of that wise Greek saying, inscribed in the temple at Delphi: "Would you know a man, give him power." Wherever I have seen power in operation—the kind of power which its admirers are fond of describing as "benevolent despotism"—its effect has always been to show very plainly the true character of the man—the good and bad of him; and very seldom indeed have I found human nature capable of sustaining the burden without moral and intellectual deterioration both in the operator and those on whom he operated. The atavism of cruelty is far too deeply engrained in the human race for even saints to be entrusted with uncontrolled power over the lives of others; and it is not usual for headmasters, governors of prisons, or rulers of states to be chosen for their saintliness. But power seems to bring out not only the cruelty and injustice of the masterful ones, it brings out also their stupidity. A headmaster, who afterwards became an archbishop, flogged a boy into confessing to something he had not done; the old foolish mediæval belief that torture was the way to extract truth was still in him. History in that respect had taught him nothing. And I am quite sure that at my own school the rule that a boy who was caught telling a lie must be flogged for it bred far more lies than it extirpated.

There was also the inconsiderate stupidity which set impossible tasks, with the natural result that we resorted to cribs as the only means of performing them. The most flagrant instance of this was the Greek Testament lesson, for which a whole chapter was set regularly to a class whose usual measure of Greek construe was not more than thirty lines a lesson. Yet every Monday morning we were supposed to have mastered between one and two hundred lines of Greek Testament, without any aid from the English version which lay so conveniently to hand. This being quite impossible for a fourth-form standard of scholarship we did not attempt it; but woe betide us if we were caught falling into the phraseology of the authorized version, or the occasional traps which its mistranslation set for us—for then, not only had we been lazy in our preparation, we had been dishonourable.

This unintelligent treatment could not fail to produce bad results both in scholarship and morals; a large number of the class would sit with their Bibles surreptitiously open on their knees, and when set to construe would give a deceitfully stumbling paraphrase from the page of text concealed beneath the level of the table. Once, through a careless practitioner, the trick was discovered; and then, while wrath was falling on him alone, all round the table there was a stealthy closing up of knees, and the Word of God was restored to its proper position by a dozen guilty hands without further detection. But though afterwards more caution was exercised, the practice was never abandoned, and we continued to combine with our lessons in Holy Scripture our lowest standard of morals, the responsibility for which did not lie, I think, wholly with us. Nor was it very much to be wondered at that when we came to examination in that particular subject we always failed gloriously; for during examination we were too well watched for cribbing to be possible.

These six years of rather unsatisfactory schooling for mind and morals were finished off by a piece of unexpected and, if I guess right, of undeserved success. My lack of classical attainment had made it quite evident that I was not going to be able to make my living by my brains in any scholarly sense; and as I had always shown an interest in colour and pattern, and was fond of drawing, it was decided—with little enough to show for it—that I had in me the makings of an artist; and so, a year before I left school, the thing was settled—I was to go to London and study art. But before that was to be allowed there was a ditch that I must cross; and I did not believe that I had the capacity for crossing it.

My four brothers and I had all entered school on Foundation scholarships, and those ahead of me in years had on leaving passed an examination called the Higher Oxford and Cambridge Local which qualified for entry to the Universities. My father decided that, in order to round off the family record, I also must pass this perfectly unnecessary examination before leaving. It may only have been held over me as a threat, not seriously meant; but I took it to be real, and I entered for the examination with a sense of failure and the doom of another year's schooling lying ahead.

The examiner who came to us that year was the famous Doctor Spooner, in whose name so many "Spoonerisms" have been invented. I knew that I had done pretty badly in two at least of the papers that had been set, and when I entered his genial presence for my "Viva," I entered without hope. He put me on to a piece of Virgil over which I stumbled badly. Very soon he stopped me.

"What" he inquired amiably, "are you intending to do when you leave school?"

"I am going to study art," I said.

"Then you are not going to the University?"

"No, sir."

"Then why have you entered for this examination?"

A flash of inspiration descended upon me. I told him the truth. "Merely family pride, sir. My father says that if I don't pass it, I am to stay for another year."

He smiled a beautiful smile. "Oh, indeed!" was all he said.

A week later I had left school for good—very much for good. Doctor Spooner had passed me! And how I have loved him ever since!

CHAPTER VIII

THE FAMILY CIRCLE

OUR return from Fockbury to our original home at Bromsgrove
was shortly followed by a period of serious financial strain. We
were a large and fast-growing family, and for each of us in turn,
as we left school, education became more expensive. Alfred went
with a scholarship to St. John's, Oxford; two other brothers to
Mason's and Queen's, Birmingham, but in the case of one there
was waiting and delay before the money could be found for it. My
father was a practising solicitor, whose practice did not increase
with the years, and as his employment of an office staff diminished
certain members of the family had to take on the necessary clerical
work. To this two of us gave up some of our school leisure; but
the main brunt of it fell on my sister Clemence, who until she left
home to share my life in London, became virtually my father's
head clerk, and was, for two or three years, the expert who worked
out all the income tax calculations for the County of Worcestershire. When the main pressure of that work was on, it became the
regular thing for the family to go to bed leaving her still at it;
and how many hours past midnight she worked nobody knew.

One night, however, I was able to make a guess. A relative was
staying with us who had a large and very obstinately tangled
skein of fine tatting thread, which as she looped the loops, she
slowly and painfully disentangled yard by yard. As I enjoyed undoing knots, I boastfully said that, if she would give it to me, I
would have it all unravelled for her by next morning. She went
up to bed, leaving me the skein. I started on the job. It took hours.

I was quite interested, but it was a longer game than I had
bargained for. There was no question, however, but that having

83

so boasted, I must get it done. It must be on my Aunt's plate next morning. And while I worked at my tangled skein, there was Clemence working at her income tax papers. But while my job was only for a joke, hers was a regular thing, done for necessity.

It was, I think, between one and two in the morning, after I had repeatedly refused her advice to go to bed, that she came to my rescue, and in a short while, with two pairs of hands working, the job was done. And next morning to the amused and grateful surprise of my Aunt, there on her plate lay a large and beautifully wound ball. But I had this to remember that, when it was done, I had gone up to bed, while Clemence had remained working.

During those years of strain much was secretly done of which my father knew nothing—perhaps preferred not to know, for he had always the gift of taking things more easily than others could; and we would often see him going his own way, showing but little sign of inward disturbance, when the domestic situation was very disturbing indeed. Though sociable, and preferring to talk rather than be talked to, he enjoyed his own company, and would drift away, "lonely as a cloud," from the family circle, absorbed in his own thoughts, and talking quietly to himself—a habit which increased as he grew older.

One morning he came down to breakfast wearing a strange waistcoat—one half of it blue, the other half brown. There was a family cry. "Look at Father's waistcoat!" Investigation followed; and it was found that, while too thoughtfully dressing himself, he had put on two, and having joined the wrong halves had let their remainders slip comfortably out of sight under cover of his coat. The accident was characteristic; it was over some like piece of forgetfulness that the Mater once remarked genially, "Your Mother used to say that a fortnight after her death your Father would be seen ambling down High Street in lavender kid gloves and pepper-and-salt trousers. Did you?" she asked him.

My father considered for a while. "No, I don't think so," he said, but there was doubt in his answer.

That bit of reminiscence has always pleased me for the special reason that it gave me a sample of what I had been too young to remember before sickness fell on her, my mother's blithe humour and amusing choice of phrase. That word "ambling" was good caricature: my father did amble—if, as I take it, the word stands for a mode of progression wherein aim and object are rather lacking.

In their early days my mother and my stepmother had been great friends; and it was always the boast of the latter that she had brought about the match, telling my father not to choose a wife till he had seen her friend, Sarah Jane Williams. I remember one day her reading to us the letters which she had received from my mother during the courtship, and also during the honeymoon; in this latter series came the remark, "I don't mind telling you that he is a very decent fellow." From which, and also from the general tenor of her letters, I gather that my mother's vocabulary was not characteristically mid-Victorian. One specimen of her quality I do remember, too intimate and personal to be recorded here—a little Rabelaisian. Our mother was no Puritan.

But during our stepmother's régime streaks of Puritanism did afflict us, and it was only gradually that we escaped into larger airs of our own choosing. Even among ourselves we were a curiously mixed family; and the blend of so many and such opposite qualities made membership of it a liberal, if not an easy education. But though with individual growth our interests began to separate, we had still much in common, especially in certain inventive games, in which we found good mental exercise, and lively amusement.

Most of these were of a semi-literary character, if the writing of intentionally nonsensical verse can be called literary; and one which at that time became a favourite was the writing of short poems containing a collection of nouns, each member of the company supplying one.

This game produced two poems which have remained in my memory. The one was by Alfred, of whose poetic beginnings there still exists an assortment similar in character, but not for general publication. Here the nouns were: hat, novel, banker, cucumber, yacht, and abridgment. Obviously the last was the crux: this is what Alfred made of it:

"At the door of my own little hovel
  Reading a novel I sat;
And as I was reading the novel
  A gnat flew away with my hat.
As fast as a fraudulent banker,
  Away with my hat it fled,
And calmly came to an anchor
  In the midst of a cucumber bed.
I went and purchased a yacht
  And traversed the garden tank,
And I gave it that insect hot
  When I got to the other bank;
Of its life I made an abridgment,
  By squeezing it somewhat flat.
And I cannot think what that midge meant
  By flying away with my hat."

The other poem was by my sister Kate, who was usually reckoned among the prosaic members of the family. But on this occasion (a General Election was going on at the time: the one during which I attended my first Liberal meeting) inspiration seized her, with the following noble result; the six nouns which formed its foundation being: Election, mangle, chestnut, liquor, slipper, and artifice:

"Oh, for the Election! Oh, for the Election!
  Rejection! Rejection! My young man has gone—
Gone to the Election, Rejection! Rejection!
  Rejecting the right, and voting for the wrong!

"Perhaps he'll come back mangled, with his chestnut locks tangled—
  Tangled with mud, and matted with gore;
Perhaps they'll impound him, sit on him, or drownd him;
  And perhaps I shall see him again never more.

"They will ply him with liquor, in the hope that he may flicker,
  They will use every artifice to turn him again.
He will drink like a nipper; and his head in a slipper,
  And his feet in a hat, he will sleep in a lane."

These two poems, I think, represent the highwater mark of our
domestic achievement in rhymed games. But one Christmas we
attempted something more ambitious, which produced memorable
results. We were each to write a story; and on Christmas Eve, or
thereabouts, the stories were read out to the assembled family;
and once more it was Alfred, and another non-literary member of
the family, who beat all the rest. Alfred's contribution was a
domestic sketch in verse and prose entitled *A Morning with the
Royal Family,* the opening sentence of which ran, " 'Pigs on the
front lawn!' cried the King. 'Lend me a cannon somebody!' Nobody lent him a cannon; so, seizing a tea-spoon from the break-
fast-table, he rushed from the apartment." The whole story—the
only work of fiction, I think, which he ever produced, was published
a few years later without his permission, in a magazine of which my
brother Basil was editor, and has remained ever since a prized but
rather private family possession.

Later in the reading came a story by Herbert, the youngest,
called *Why They Eloped.* He did not read it himself; far too shy to
hear his own composition made public, he had disappeared, and
another read it for him. It was, I think, almost as good as *The
Young Visiters,* which it somewhat resembled; and how we
laughed! At the end there were loud calls for the author; and out
from under the sofa crawled the bashful "Babe," who thus, in his
eleventh year, woke like Byron to find himself famous, but never
followed up his early promise in the literary direction, except in
the rather imaginative letters which he wrote home of his military
experiences in India and Burmah, where he served first in the ranks,
and later as a noncommissioned officer, ending his short and adventurous career at Braakenlaagte in the South African War.

It was a mark of development that we had begun by that time to
write things separately; previously most of our compositions had
been corporate. Apart from the poems which Alfred used to father
upon us, unwilling to acknowledge them as his own, we had
started on several literary adventures as a stock company, with
Alfred as contributing editor and a good deal more as well. Our
first experiment of any length was a novel called *Veronica,* in

which each was to be responsible for a separate character. Alfred's was the villain, mine was the parish curate with a long beard beginning dark and ending light; and if I remember right, as soon as Alfred heard of that beard, the curate's fate was sealed: he was to die an early and violent death, strangled by the villain in the beautiful beard with which I had provided him. But the story never got so far; its place was taken by an imaginary history of Europe, in which we were all different countries, and all at war with one another either as enemies or allies. Alfred was Napoleon with France as a necessary accompaniment; Robert was England with Wellington and the ghost of Marlborough to help him; Clemence was Frederick the Great; Kate, I think, was Alva; Basil Peter the Great, and I was Maria Theresa. In the first chapter war had been declared all about nothing—the only point which was at all true to history—the first battle had been won by the French, and Napoleon was going to romp home against all the rest of us. But the history never got into its second stride; having satisfactorily drawn first blood, it died a quiet death, other interests taking its place.

And the next may possibly have been one started by myself; for one day Alfred came upon the beginnings of a play which I had started to write in blank verse—*The Tragedy of Lady Jane Grey*. At once he decided that we were each to write an act, which—if we had all written one would have made seven—or perhaps only six, for at that time Herbert did not count. The character which attracted Alfred, and which we were to leave to him, was "Bloody Queen Mary," but the play never got so far, and mine—the first act—was the only one which got finished. I remember enough of it to know that it was very bad indeed.

But even from that abortive venture something rather good emerged. To Clemence, who had an inborn appetite, which she had never lost, for heroes and heroines in suffering for the sins of others, was allotted the scene of Lady Jane in captivity, nobly awaiting death; and having a Shakespearean sense that for such a scene a song was the most suitable opening, she applied elsewhere for her material; and the following poem, of which the authorship may be guessed, was supplied her:

"Breathe, my lute, beneath my fingers
  One regretful breath,
One lament for life that lingers
  Round the doors of death.
For the frost has killed the rose,
And our summer dies in snows,
  And our morning once for all
  Gathers to the evenfall.

"Hush, my lute, return to sleeping,
  Sing no songs again!
For the reaper stays his reaping
  On the darkened plain;
And the day has drained its cup,
And the twilight cometh up;
  Song and sorrow all that are
  Slumber at the even-star."

But the project went no further, and I think that it was the last
that we undertook corporately. Nearly twenty-five years went by
before I again made any serious attempt at play-writing, and when
I did, the Censor forbade its public performance. After that shock
I waited another four years; and then, with Granville Barker,
wrote *Prunella*.

I have heard since, though I did not know of it at the time, that
a certain amount of secret censorship was, in those early days, being directed against my attraction toward the stage. My parents
feared that I might wish to become a play-actor, and from my fourteenth year onward small hindrances were put in the way of my
visits to the professional theatre. On one occasion I was prevented
from going up to Birmingham to see Kyrle Bellew in *The Corsican
Brothers* (I had previously seen him in *As You Like It*), the
invitation intended for me being passed on to another. A little
later, when those taking part in the school play at the end of the
term were sent up to see Irving as Shylock, I was not allowed to
go, although, as the school Odysseus, I was playing a leading part.
I was aggrieved, but I did not understand; and certainly at that
time I did not act well enough to have any idea of going upon the

stage. Yet had I gone it might have given me the technical knowledge of stagecraft which I never acquired, and enabled me to start earlier, and do better, in that form of writing which has now become my main interest.

In those days there were still travelling companies which went country rounds, and played under canvas; and it was thus that I first saw Shakespeare acted, and the part of Othello very decently done by an actor who dropped a few *h*'s, and Mrs. Jennings, in her own company, as Hamlet, looking like George IV, "fat and scant of breath," rather absurdly rigged out in a black-plumed head-dress, but doing the part better and more honestly than Beerbohm Tree, though she also dropped and put in *h*'s.

A hundred yards from the ground where these performances took place was a barn in which Mrs. Siddons had once acted, perhaps in a company no better, and no better equipped than those I am telling of, from one of which I got the material for the first article I ever wrote. It was a ridiculously crude play called *Faith, Hope, and Charity,* an impossible plot with acting to match; and out of the unholy delight it gave me, I constructed an article called "Strollers" which I sent to *Cornhill,* and James Payne, who was then editor, accepted it. I wrote it when I was eighteen; it did not appear till seven years later; and how, all that time, I languished, waiting for my literary career to begin!

Looking at things now, I think my heart was always more in literature than in what is called "Art." But I was far more secretive at that time over what I wrote, than over what I drew. Anyone might see my drawings, but it was generally only to my sister Clemence that I showed what I wrote, in prose and poetry. About my poetry she told me afterwards that she had been very much afraid I should never get away from my Byron stage; but she did not damp my ardour with her doubts; and indeed, took a hand collaboratively in something which was worse. It was a commission—the first piece of writing for which I received payment. One of my schoolfellows had offered me a shilling if I would translate the Ninth Book of the *Odyssey* into English; and as I was totally without pocket-money for most of the years I was at school, it seemed worth while. The translation involved no scholarship; I simply got hold of the two verse translations by Pope and Cowper, and with the laudable determination that my verse should be as good as Pope's, and as close to the original as Cowper's, set out upon my task. With my sister's help, I considered that I had achieved my aim; my employer was well satisfied, and paid me the shilling, for which—like old Daffern—"I was very thankful." And I wonder does the Rev. Archibald Cochrane remember that it was he who thus gave me my first footing as a paid writer? And has he treasured, as he ought to have done, that translation, which was supposed to improve upon the virtues of Cowper and Pope, of which I can now remember only a single couplet, descriptive of the drunken sleep of Polyphemus after Ulysses had plied him with liquor? It was hearty but ungrammatical, and for its heartiness I still admire it. Here it is:

"And drunken hiccoughs, sounding loud and deep,
Rankled his belly, and disturbed his sleep."

And if my collaborator claims to share the glory of that couplet, I deny it to her; it was entirely my own.

It was, I suppose, at about this time that the pairing of our interests in art and literature became evident. Both in drawing and writing Clemence was then well ahead of me, and had already shown so much mental ability that my headmaster—though not one who favoured the claims of women to higher education—had said that he wished he had her in his sixth form. Eventually, when it was decided that to study art, I must go to London, Clemence was released from the Victorian bonds of home, for the sole reason that it was considered too risky for me to go alone without some one of more stable character to look after me. So when I left school we began studying together, first at the local art school; then, having each come into a small legacy upon the death of our grandmother, and Clemence into a somewhat larger one on her coming of age, we went up to London together—she to learn wood-engraving, and I to find out in the course of further study what particular line of art I was made for.

I think now it was a very risky thing. It took me nearly seven years to find myself, to discover, that is to say, in what direction my individual interest and abilities were to find expression; and for some years the routine training of the art schools I attended did nothing to help me, leaving me with the depressed feeling that I should never do anything but pot-boiling. For though during that waiting period I had formed many enthusiasms, I was unable to give them an individual application; and though while at South Kensington I took a few prizes in the National Competition, I did not get near to having a style of my own.

But among the influences which were then biding their time was one to which, years before, I had wilfully turned a cold shoulder. And in view of the great hold it had on me in after years, the story of it, as one of "Life's Little Ironies," seems worth telling. In my fourteenth year I had gone up to London for the first time, to see as many of the sights as could be got into a fortnight. And at the National Gallery I had been curiously attracted by the picture of *The Spiritual Form of Pitt Guiding Behemoth*. It was by an artist I had never heard of; and then I saw to my sorrow that he had lived in the eighteenth century; and having at that time a fixed belief that, except in portraiture and landscape, the art of the eighteenth century was all wrong, I turned my back on it, and must even have forgotten his name. Two years later I went to stay with my godfather, who was a clergyman of terrific religious zeal, but with no interest in art except for church decoration; and in his study were bookshelves filled entirely with works of theology and the lives of heavy divines. But he had recently married, and one or two of his wife's books had found a place among the sterner stuff in which on previous visits I had tried and failed to find interest. And as I roamed the shelves I sighted two volumes which had golden angels on their backs, not badly designed. Going nearer, I looked at the title. *Life and Works of William Blake*. But in the library of my godfather *Life and Works* had only one meaning for me. It meant the life and works of a clergyman, and to the life of this particular clergyman had been given an attractive cover of angels with uplifted wings. So I did not probe further. There were the two books of the life of the man I was born to adore, and I did not take them down. The Gates of Paradise were before me waiting to be opened—and I did not open them! Two more years were to go by before I knew anything about William Blake.

Many years later, when his wife died, my godfather gave me the books as a remembrance. I have them now, and whenever I look at them they remind me of those two years of possible help and inspiration which I so blindly wasted.

Chapter IX

LIFE IN LONDON

WE ARRIVED in London without knowing what address we were going to. Alfred met us at Paddington, and directed us; otherwise we should have been stranded. After a week in temporary lodgings we found a landlady in South London, with whom we stayed for sixteen years; for when we decided to change from Kennington to Kensington, she moved house and came with us; and under her devoted care we lived for fourteen years in Marloes Road, facing the workhouse gates—a situation which offered us the combined attraction of a good open space for outlook, Sunday night incidents between inmates returning drunk from their homes and the police, and the stately funerals with which well-to-do families resumed possession of impossible relatives when death had rendered them innocuous.

We chose Kennington in the first place, so as to be near an arts and crafts school which included wood-engraving among its subjects. We also joined the Millers Lane School in South Lambeth, which had then a high reputation, John Sparkes, Principal at South Kensington, being its Head, and William Llewelyn, now P. R. A., assistant master. Among the students at both schools were Ricketts and Shannon, already inseparable, and one named Hill, who afterwards became the "Ravenhill" of *Punch*.

While my sister learned wood-engraving, Ricketts and Shannon were doing the same in an adjoining room; but though there were communicating doors, the men's and the women's classes were kept respectably separate. Also at Millers Lane were senior and junior classes which did not mix, and I did not know Ricketts and Shannon to speak to till years later. Indeed I only saw them on

94

the nights when the Senior Sketch Club came to Millers Lane to be criticised; a matter in which the Junior to which I belonged had a decided advantage; for while we were criticised by Sparkes, whose caustic knifings did us good, he would bring down to the Seniors men of distinguished names—artists and art critics whose woolly remarks were seldom worth listening to. Amongst others I remember Alma Tadema, Frank Dicksee, Marks and Yeames (R. A.'s prominent in their day) and Edmund Gosse. Most of them came and went leaving no impression; Gosse gave a peck or two, but did not seem to be enjoying himself; only Tadema took heartily to the job, and amused us with his vigorous declamation.

But Sparkes really knew his business, and his quiet biting remarks were greatly enjoyed by all except the recipient. I remember encountering one of these unfortunates when class was over, still trembling with indignation. He had done his own portrait, and had done it too well, for he was no beauty; and Sparkes regarding its stubborn realism with disfavour, had remarked "Yes, horribly like!"

"It's more than a man's stomach can stand!" exclaimed the poor victim. "He makes your flesh creep with his insults! He makes your blood boil!"

Perhaps with the thin-skinned ones he did; but most of us, I think, found that his adverse comments were worded in such a way as to stick in the memory and become useful; and though it was not he who helped me finally to my feet in the choice of method and material, and in deciding to become an illustrator, he did give me a grounding in figure-composition which helped me considerably upon the way. And while I remember many of his jeers, I remember also the unexpected encouragement he once gave me in early days, before I had begun to know how to draw. I had just lighted upon Blake, and without any approach to his unity of technique in line and composition, had begun imitating him. And one day I brought to the Sketch Club a drawing which set all my fellow students laughing. As Sparkes went around criticising the drawings, my heart went down into my boots, for if my attempt appeared so ridiculous to the rest, what would it seem to him? He left it to the very last (having first passed it by without comment) ; as he approached it a titter of happy anticipation went round the class. Then came his first words, "This drawing interests me enormously," and the titter stopped. He went on to say, quite truly, that I did not yet know how to draw, and that my figures were ludicrously wrong and ugly; but he said other things as well. I saw him asking the secretary whose sketch it was (for our exhibits went in unsigned), and when class was over he came and spoke to me about it, saying, "Blake, I suppose?" From that day he kept a friendly eye on me; and two years later, when I had gone on to South Kensington, he got me my first job, which though of a pot-boiling character was a heavenly godsend at a time when my share in our joint expenses was coming from the small and rapidly disappearing legacy which had been left me.

But before we left Kennington an alarming thing happened, which to our apprehensive minds seemed to threaten an untimely end to all our plans for a life of shared interests. We had been from home a year, when it was found that Clemence could not be spared during the extra pressure time of income tax work which came annually. My younger sister's health was breaking down under it, and as my father could not afford to pay a competent clerk's wage, my classmate had to go.

The right of daughters to earn independence, and be as free from the claims of home as their brothers, was not as well-recognised then as it is now. And it was quite on the cards that if the elders decided that I could be trusted in London alone, Clemence would be called on to sacrifice herself to domestic claims which would make no provision for her future.

With a pile of work awaiting her, which might have taken two or three months to get done, she went—and working night and day, was through with it in a few weeks. Before home had become too much re-accustomed to her services, she was able to claim a return to freedom; and twelve months later was on safer ground, having then begun to earn her wage as a wood-engraver.

Her employer had an office in Chancery Lane, doing work for the weekly *Graphic* and other illustrated papers; and for the next

eight or nine years my sister was one of a small band of workers
involved in a desperate struggle—not only for their own livelihood,
but for the survival in the commercial world of a noble craft,
which—with the coming of "process"—was being slowly strangled
to death. In the last effort to keep it alive, a rival weekly, called
Black and White, was started in the early '90's, but as that too
turned to "process," the struggle became hopeless; and when my
sister's employer shut down his office, he stood heavily in her
debt for work done but not paid for.

It was then, when wood-engraving was commercially dead, that
my own work got the benefit of her skill and devotion; and most
of my illustrations from that time were of her engraving. Subsequently she engraved drawings by Reginald Savage, and C. R.
Ashbee for the Essex House Press, by James Guthrie for his own
Peartree Press, Paul Woodroffe's illustrations to *Aucassin and
Nicolette,* and finally a set of drawings of the beautiful buildings
of Chipping Campden by F. L. Griggs. A few years ago a collection
of film-proofs of her best work went by request to the Print Room
of the British Museum, and one of her woodblocks to the Tate
Gallery, together with the original drawing which it facsimiled so
perfectly.

It was with the beginning of my sister's employment as an
engraver, and my own entry as a student at South Kensington, that
we moved to Marloes Road. I had at that time begun writing
things which I had no thought to publish—crude essays on social
and religious subjects, about which I had ideas, the outcome of
emotion rather than of sober reading and study. On fiction and
fairy tale I had hardly begun. There, Clemence was well ahead
of me. Before we left Kennington she had written, for the amusement of her fellow students in the engraving class, a story called
The Were Wolf. It was far too good to be kept only for private
circulation. So we submitted it to A. W. Pollard, who as a college
friend of Alfred had visited us at Bromsgrove, and become a
friend of the family. On his recommendation it went to the editor
of *Atalanta,* was accepted, and published as the Christmas Number.
It made a considerable success; the number sold out and in course

of time the proprietors sent to the author a check for five pounds. Alfred Pollard undertook the necessary remonstrance; and after some parleying a more adequate sum was extracted. But what made the whole thing doubly shabby was that the proprietors had themselves been struck by the quality of the story, and had asked my sister to call on them, with a view to further work, and having discovered that this was her first publication, and that authorship had not yet become her profession, they sent her the remuneration which—without naming the amount—they had assured her would be satisfactory.

Publishers are supposed to have a bad name with authors; so here I would say that though, in my long and varied experience, I have met instances both of stinginess and sharp practice, they have been the exception and not the rule. Publishers and editors have been kind to me and more than once I have had work taken that I was anxious to publish, in which, for the publisher, there was no likelihood of profit.

The personal kindness of my first publisher, Mr. Kegan Paul, came to me through the friendly interest of Alfred Pollard, to whom I owed most of my early introductions both to editors and publishers—and not introductions alone; he was a constant help to me in his criticism of my immature beginnings in verse and prose, and also in the loan of books for the bettering of my very haphazard knowledge of English literature, limited till then to the books which we had at home. Through him I received a commission from Kegan Paul to edit a selection of *The Writings of William Blake.* This was my first book; it was prentice-work, done at a time when Blake was far less known and appreciated than he is now; and Andrew Lang began his review of it with the words, "To admire Blake is the mark of a clique." It was true then; it is not true now. In the National Gallery of British Art, Blake has a room all to himself, and a floor paved with mosaics inspired by his designs for the *Book of Job.*

It was that *Book of Job* which, when I first encountered it, gave me a dim sense that Blake was one of the greatest of English artists: for *me,* at any rate. And when I came to read his poems, a similar discovery was waiting for me. One of my most vivid memories of that time is of going to meet my sister for an hour's wait at the pit door of the St. James Theatre, and as we stood there in the crowd, about to see Mrs. Kendal for the first time, I whispered to her the words of Blake's *Divine Image*, which I had just read, and which has always remained to me the most perfect expression of religious humanism in English poetry.

My failure, during the first five or six years of my art training, to get set in the right direction, and the disappointment which it caused me, drove me the more persistently into writing as an alternative. But though I wrote much and constantly, I had no confidence that I could become an author. And it was that lack of confidence, I suppose, which made me keep the first book I ever wrote lying idle for five years, before trying it on a publisher, and it took three more years to find one. This was *Gods and Their Makers* which I wrote in my twenty-third year. I was just then going through a healthy reaction from the orthodoxy of my youth; religion had become for me not so much a possession as an obsession, which I was trying to throw off, and this iconoclastic tale of an imaginary tribe was the result. A good many years later, George Tyrrell told me that he regarded it as the best of all my books; but that was the rather personal preference of one who was so much of an iconoclast himself. Nevertheless that book was the symptom of something that has persisted till now; I have never been able to lose my interest in man's false gods, and in his age-long quest for one which, though unprovable, may yet be true. Charles Ricketts, under whose influence I was presently to run a zigzag course of acceptance and escape, told me that I was "dotty about God." Though an unsympathetic criticism, it was, in a way, true; for I still think that if the human race, or even one nation, could only get right about its God the rest would follow.

After Blake, the firm of Kegan Paul published three books of my fairy stories, another of imaginary legends, called *All-Fellows*, which still has my heart, and a monograph on the work of Arthur Boyd Houghton. My illustrated tales they continued to publish, in spite of the protests of their head traveller, who, in his country rounds, not merely failed to find a market for them, but was met with derision when he offered them. My illustrations were not popular with the country booksellers; and to have his wares ridiculed hurt his sense of dignity, and also his standing with the trade. When I heard of it, I suggested that the right solution was for him to agree heartily with my detractors, but to say that just now they were "the thing," and that his firm had to publish them to meet a depraved taste. The idea was not my own; a friend had told me that she had heard two children discussing those same illustrations—one objecting to them, and the other saying that she must try to like them because now they were "the thing."

The newspaper critics were similarly divided: the "Thingummyites"—and the others. But these divided opinions did not much trouble me. Dr. Richard Garnett had given my fairy tales a welcome with higher praise than I should have given them myself, and though the illustrations were liked by few, the stories were generally commended, and have had sufficient life in them to recover from the "out-of-print" condition into which they lapsed a few years after publication.

In the year before the appearance of my first fairy tales, an introduction from Pollard had secured me work both in illustration and writing from Harry Quilter, editor and proprietor of the *Universal Review*. In this case relations were not quite so friendly; but the work which I did for that boreal blast of a character, honest at least in his opinions, and uncompromising in the expression of them, led to a meeting which had a decisive effect upon my work. A story of mine called "The Green Gaffer" with several illustrations, had appeared in the *Universal Review* and this, coupled with my attempt to obtain a copy of the first *Dial*, already out of print, brought me an invitation from Ricketts and Shannon to call at the "Vale." Within a month Ricketts had dragged me away from my timid preference for fuzzy chalk-drawing, as a means of concealing my bad draughtsmanship, and had set me to pen-work, with Rossetti and the other Pre-Raphaelites as my main guides both in composition and technique. From that time on,

I felt set—I acquired a new confidence; I had found out at last what I wanted to do.

Ricketts and I did not remain friends; and parting from Ricketts I had also to part from Shannon, whose gentle character with its quiet blend of modesty and confidence presented so curious a contrast to the strained and restless brilliance of Ricketts, ever laying down the law with an arbitrariness which the quick change of some of his admirations did nothing to modify. But though we finally clashed, and preferred no longer to meet, the few years during which I was frequently in his company, and very much under his influence, taught me far more of what I wanted to know than all the preceding years of dull schoolwork in which much of my interest got wasted. And that debt must ever remain.

It was at the "Vale" that I first met Oscar Wilde—the only time I did meet him in the days of his success. It was from him that Ricketts had heard of my story "The Green Gaffer."—"A strange tale," he had said, "with strange illustrations, and containing a beautiful sentence, (which some day he intended to use himself); 'the smoke of their wood-fires lay upon the boughs, soft as the bloom upon a grape.' " And not long after he did use it, giving it a setting in his own polished prose, where it seemed so much at home that the kidnapping became an adoption. And perhaps because thus microscopically in my debt, he turned to me courteously in the first pause of general conversation to say, "And when, pray, are we to have another work from your pen?" Like most of his remarks, the enquiry was phrased with a certain decorative solemnity, in excess of what the occasion required; but the kindness and courtesy of it were very real, coming from one who was then a great figure in the contemporary world of letters, to an author then unknown.

My connection with the *Universal Review* brought me also another commission of special value and interest. Quilter, claiming the right to republish in book form a poem by George Meredith, called *Jump-to-Glory Jane,* set me to illustrate it, and I learned later that although Meredith very much resented Quilter's interpretation of his "serial rights," my illustrations had the good fortune to please him. For myself not only was it a great joy to illustrate a poem by one who was at that time my favourite among living authors, but the poem itself had a peculiar call for me. I have already told of my early interest in Mrs. Girling and the Shakers, and this interest had been curiously rekindled a few years before by an incident, which though it might seem mystical, was in fact, I believe, nothing but a strange coincidence. I dreamed one night that I heard somebody say, "Mrs. Girling is dead." The next day her death was in the papers. For anyone out to get proofs for spiritualism, that was good enough. But shortly before, I had been staying with my godfather in his Birmingham parish, and while there, I had heard him speaking more than once of a poor woman of the district, also named Girling, who was dying. The name had caught my attention, and that, I believe, was the explanation of my dream.

And now again, in this poem which had been given me to illustrate, I found myself face to face with a replica of Mrs. Girling—not dead, but in a strange mixture of tragedy and comedy very much alive, and as I drew my pictures of "Jumping Jane," I had Mrs. Girling in mind.

Twenty years later, we had a holiday cottage near Hordle, between the New Forest and the sea. One day my sister came to me and said, "Who do you think used to live close here?" It was Mrs. Girling. The call had come; here once more was Mrs. Girling trying to attract my attention; and suddenly it struck me that she was a subject waiting for my pen. The next day, or thereabouts, I began writing *The Sheepfold*.

The Mother of the Shakers, though forgotten now and her community no longer in existence, must have been a remarkable character, and the faith she inspired in her followers was not only intense but beautiful. She taught them joy. Her powers must have been partly hypnotic, for on one occasion a footman from Beaulieu Abbey, having attended a Shaker meeting with its usual accompaniment, was seized that same evening, while serving at dinner, with a fit of the "shakes," and these proving uncontrollable, he had to be removed forcibly from the room.

Another poem which I illustrated about this time—Christina Rossetti's *Goblin Market* I did of my own choice, author and publisher consenting. But this time I did not satisfy the person who mattered most. I had hoped to get word that my drawings pleased her; but the only comment that reached me was her answer to a congratulating friend who liked them. She shook her head, saying, "I don't think my Goblins were quite so ugly."

From another quarter they brought me better encouragement. Sir Frederick Leighton, who, as official head of English academic art, kept a fatherly eye on new arrivals, sent me a letter of appreciation, and asked if I would do a drawing for him. Eventually he chose my title-page design to *Goblin Market* saying that what struck him most in my work was the combination of figures with decoration. After Leighton came Aubrey Beardsley, asking me to do a drawing for the *Yellow Book*.

From that time on, I did a good deal of work for John Lane, the publisher most closely identified with the movement of the '90's, on which he built up his business. He published the re-issue of my sister's *Were Wolf* which I illustrated, also my first poems, and after that *Gods and Their Makers*. It was over one of these two that he asked me to meet at dinner an American publisher, with whom he hoped to place the American rights. "If you interest him," said Lane, "he'll take it; so I want you to be brilliant."

"All right," I said, "give me champagne, and I will be." The meeting took place, and we had champagne. The next day I called on Lane at his office. "You were!" he said. He had placed the book to his satisfaction.

Lane was always friendly, but was not always businesslike. Probably he was running his output on a small amount of capital. Whatever the reason, cheques were sometimes long in coming from him, and when one pressed for them, there was in his response more promise than performance. As, at that time, I was living (to put it figuratively) with only a pound or two between me and the workhouse across the road, this often caused me considerable inconvenience. So, one day, after having already extracted from him two or three promises which had come to nothing, I wrote to

ask if he would, as a friend, lend me the five pounds which my
publisher had promised faithfully to send me a week ago. This
brought me a cheque by return; and Evelyn Sharp tells in her
Reminiscences that Lane was so pleased with the joke that he
went about repeating it. But in doing so, to give it more body, he
enlarged the amount from five to fifty—a sum which in those
days was far beyond my dreams. I never received a check for fifty
pounds till I was thirty-five; and then (being for a far less deserving piece of work) it was a good deal more.

My doubts of my ability to make a living, either by illustration
or writing, had had plenty of confirmation during the first ten
years of my life in London. My first scanty earnings had been for
the job which John Sparkes got me—the revision of Vere Foster's
and Poynter's drawing-books; and after that, the designing of small
devices for commercial firms connected with the printing trade.
Between the year 1887 when I finished my training at South
Kensington, and 1893, I earned £277. 15. 6d., an average of less
than £50. a year. During the two decades following (from my twenty-eighth to my forty-seventh year) I made incomes of the following
amounts: £146. 13. 6d.; £156. 9s. 0d.; £130. 7s. 6d.; £150. 3s. 0d.;
£105. 9s. 6d.; £192. 9s. 0d.; £291. 18s. 11d.; £252. 13s. 9d.;
£317. 1s. 3d.; £179. 16. 11d.; £224. 13s. 2d.; £223. 9s. 9d. These
are fairly, but not quite consecutive. In other years I did better;
in the year of *An Englishwoman's Love-letters* I made £2072.
14s. 1d., but even with that mighty windfall for the worst book I
ever wrote, my average for those twenty years was only £365. Yet
for the last fifteen of those years I was fairly well known both as
author and illustrator, with one book to my discredit which had
almost ranked as a "best seller," and part-authorship of a play
(Prunella) which has been a continual source of income ever since.
In the second year of the war I made £85. 1s. 10d.; in the third,
£165. 2s. 2d. Since the war I have had an income amply sufficient
for a bachelor, sharing house with a relation who is also self-supporting.

It is not usual, I suppose, for an author to give so detailed a return of his income for the information of the general public; but

I do so for two reasons—first because my indifference to a paying popularity has, I believe, in the long run helped and not hindered my output of the things which seemed to me most worth doing; and secondly because my small income has not prevented me from living a happy life. It is true, that such an income made it impossible for me to marry, had I wished it, in the class to which I was supposed to belong; I could not, until I was well over forty, have run the risk of a family. But as the "not impossible She" never came within the horizon of my waking dreams, that deprivation was more theoretical than real. Nevertheless there remains a large disproportion between the respectable reputation which I began to acquire in my early thirties, and the monetary return I got from it. And I wonder whether other authors—my superiors in quality and my equals in the favour of the critics—have had similar experiences; whether an author who does not aim at popularity must always have a hard time, unless his needs are as modest, and as unmatrimonial as were mine.

It was, I suppose, the pinched circumstances of my home life, and the accompanying anxiety, which made me in after years so painfully scrupulous—not so much over the spending and lending of money when I had it to spare, as over the earning and the borrowing of it. I have spent, and I have lent carelessly; but I have borrowed only rarely, and with such reluctance that I have never felt quite comfortable until repayment has been made; and though of what I spend I keep no record, I have kept record—if not of every penny that I have earned, at least of every pound, and probably of every shilling.

That form of the "anxiety complex" has stuck to me through life, and has sometimes perhaps made me a little hard in my judgment of those in whom it is so conspicuously lacking; for I have never been able to feel that a man is quite honest who goes on allowing himself the luxuries of life while owing money which he has borrowed from a friend. Indeed it is, I think, my experience of easy borrowers which has made me realise how narrow, morally, is the dividing line between the criminal and the non-criminal. For your easy borrower, though he promises faithfully, has no real intention of repaying, nor does he dock himself of any of the superfluities of life, because of his broken word to a friend who has trusted him. Yet probably he is a charming fellow, and very good-natured—so long as his good nature does not put him to inconvenience.

I had a very charming acquaintance, who—to put it mildly—had borrowed from me far more often than he had repaid. One day he came to me in great distress: his honour was involved; he had pawned something which did not belong to him—would I save him?—he would repay me in a week. I advanced the necessary amount, and heard no more from him when the week had gone by. Presently a mutual friend reported that J—— was again in pocket, and had been seen standing treat in champagne to a whole company at a Strand restaurant. When we next met I told him what I had heard, and I spoke my mind. "After this," I said, "if you came to me starving, I would give you food, but I would not give you a penny." He professed shame and penitence; but nothing came of it. Some years later, having forgotten, or not believing what I said, he applied to me again for what he described as the "needful." The needful in the form of food I was willing to give, but nothing more. After that I saw him only once again, meeting him in the street by accident. He was as charming as ever; but I was no longer on his visiting list.

Of all the people to whom I have lent money, the one who has always repaid me most fully and faithfully on the date named is one of the criminal class. Twice, on coming out of prison, he has asked me to help him to his feet again, and though it has been a struggle for him to get back into decent society—for the world does not make things easy for those whom it legally punishes when punishment is over—he, without any asking on my part, has paid back what he owed me long before I expected it—for indeed, in the first instance, I did not expect it at all. There, truly, was an honest man, which your professional borrower is not; but he happened to be, in matters other than monetary, a social misfit, a son of tribulation not of his own making; and for that he had to pay the penalty.

I often wonder with amusement over the existing proportion between detected and undetected criminals. Prisons, we are told, are necessary for the protection of society; but it is only a minority of offenders who get there. For even leaving out all the thefts by people in good society which when detected become "klepto-mania," the undiscovered murders, and the offences against mor-als, which the law—perhaps wisely—makes no real attempt to cope with, there must be, I imagine, far more people in this country, making false income tax returns, and smuggling goods through the customs than the whole of our prison population put together. And yet society, while hobnobbing with this large herd of undetected criminals, still manages to survive, while the scape-goats—one in ten, perhaps, or thereabouts, do penance for the rest.

I shall always remember it as a compliment, how, one day when I was clipping my garden hedge, and being interested in my job tried to turn away an unwelcome tramp, who came interrupting me—how with an instinct for the right word, he finally got round me. "No, no, no," I had kept saying; and had meant it, until with shrewd spiritual insight he said, "Don't be hard on me, sir; I've done time!" That bit of intuition pulled me down from my perch; the man who knew that he could get my sympathy by telling me that he "had done time" was the right man for me at any rate.

Would it not be a rather good thing if every judge, on his ap-pointment, had to undergo a month's imprisonment, so as to real-ise what kind of punishment he was empowered to inflict, and also—unless he were a conscientious objector to its infliction on anyone—three strokes of the "cat," well laid on? What a judicial symptom conscientious objection might then become!

But what has this to do with my early years in London? In a way, nothing at all; but as life is full of parentheses, so, if true to its original, must autobiography be also.

CHAPTER X

COMINGS AND GOINGS

In the Art Library at South Kensington where, as a student, I read once or twice a week, sat a Permanent Official—one of many. What distinguished him from the rest was that he merely sat. He had nothing to do. He came at eleven; on his desk his newspaper was waiting for him; he read it till twelve-thirty; he went out to lunch, and was away for over an hour; on returning from lunch, he slept in his chair, not always silently; he left at three. For this the country paid him six hundred pounds a year. The reason was that the post to which he had been originally appointed had been re-organised into nonexistence; there was nothing left for him to do. Had he been of the working class, he would quite rightly have been sent to look for another job; but because he had passed a civil service examination, he had a permanent claim on the gratitude of his country. At the age of forty he became useless; for another twenty years or so he was paid for his uselessness at the rate of six hundred pounds a year. Then negotiations were set on foot, and he was retired from office with a pension of four hundred or four hundred and fifty pounds for the rest of his life, an example of how, in spite of red-tape rules, Government can be exceedingly humane in its treatment of its out-of-works, when they belong to the higher classes of the civil service.

Other games had been played at South Kensington over staff stipends, which did not make for efficiency. Under the régime of Sir Henry Cole, the Art School staff had been persuaded to forego their pensions in exchange for an immediate increase of salary, with the result that, while I was a student, we had over us at least two masters too senile and out-of-date to be of any use, whom the

108

authorities had not the heart to retire to an old age of penury. They had accepted the proffered increase, but had not saved.

Many of us in order to escape from their inefficiency, would leave our easels, when they made their rounds. They were delightful old men; but they belonged to the time of the Great Exhibition, or thereabouts; and they preferred Herbert R. A. to Watts, and Goodall to Whistler. One of them told me pathetically of the greatest compliment that had ever been paid to his work. It was a small statuette, and in an auctioneer's catalogue it had been described as a "perfect gem." This, the voice of posterity, coming thirty years after its production, had made the old man proud and happy. He used to put his hand on my shoulder as he talked to me, and I liked him, but he was not a bit of use.

In the library I had begun reading Ruskin, and for a time was carried off my feet by the strange beauty of his winged eloquence. Later I came to value chiefly not his writings on art, but his political economy. But for a short while he shared with Blake (whom he did not sufficiently appreciate) my devout admiration. One day I was at work in the Antique Room, and was dimly aware that Sparkes had gone through into the Life class accompanied by a visitor. A while later, a fellow student said to me. "Did you see who went through with Sparkes just now?" It was Ruskin; but they had come and gone. I rushed out hoping to catch sight of that prophet of the Lord; but I was too late, and my lamentation went up to Heaven.—Why had fate let me be in the same room with Ruskin, but not set eyes on him?

I have not as a rule been anxious to meet famous men; even to Meredith, in the days of his deafness, I avoided introduction and my one meeting with Whistler was a nightmare. But for Ruskin I had a singularly personal affection; and when a year ago I stood for the first time by his grave, it all came back to me, and I felt that, in some strange way, Ruskin (though I had departed from much of his teaching) was my spiritual father.

I met Whistler, about whom Ruskin made one of his biggest mistakes, at Ricketts and Shannon's one evening. Walter Sickert had fortunately just gone—for at that time Whistler was full to flatulence of his quarrel with Sir William Eden over his wife's portrait, and Sickert, for many years Whistler's devout disciple, had not given his master all the backing that was expected of him. Whistler sprawled into the room with a slow defiant swagger, and almost without preliminary greetings started upon his grievance. "What? Have you heard the news? No? Oh, yes! Walter has been seen walking down Bond Street with the Baronet!"—This in a slow nasal drawl. "Walter's mistake," he went on, "is that he began life as an actor. On the stage there is always an exit. Now Walter is going to find that there's *no* exit. He's been seen walking down Bond Street with the Baronet." This evidently prepared phrase became the burden of a monologue which did not permit of interruption. In a momentary pause, when Shannon was inviting him to "say when" to a whiskey and soda, I asked Ricketts to show me a drawing which he was then doing for *The Pageant*. Whistler turned and pounced. "Hey? What's that? What's that? Oh, yes! Walter has been seen walking down Bond Street with the Baronet." When the tedium of it became too much for me, I left; and as I went down the passage to the door, I heard Whistler still at his refrain. "Oh, yes! Walter has been seen walking down Bond Street with the Baronet!"

No doubt it was all calculated; Whistler knew that Ricketts and Shannon had not cut Sickert for his disgraceful association with the Baronet as they should have done; perhaps he had seen Sickert leaving the house. And so they also were to be taught that there was "no exit" for those who did not take up his quarrels and share his antagonisms as he expected of them.

Great men are not always nice, or even interesting to meet; and it is not my intention to follow the example of those who, in writing their reminiscences, give a list of all the notable people with whom they have had contact or acquaintance, who tell you of dinner parties at which they met so-and-so, and so-and-so; and inform you that the conversation was very brilliant and interesting; but of the brilliance and interest convey nothing—leaving you intellectually on the doormat, since for them the main interest is to tell you that they were of the company. And what interest has that, except to themselves?

If I were to give a list of my most worth-while acquaintances and friendships, of those who have blessed my life, giving me warmth, comfort, encouragement and a better understanding, it would consist, with a few exceptions, of people whom the world does not know. Even men to whom in art and literature I owe much, have seldom had for me the same personal value, as those whose names to the general public would have no interest at all.

Some of my friends were people whose literary work I did not admire as much as they admired it themselves; and in consequence there had to be a certain amount of dodging, which was not quite comfortable. One of my kindest and most generous friends in those early days was E. Nesbit, who, when I began contributing to *Atalanta*, wrote asking that we might meet. She was an able and energetic writer of stories for children; but her prose was better than her poetry, and this she did not know. It was, indeed, rather an offence to hint it; and when, after some years of happy association, I said that some poem she had written was "good verse," she replied with a quiver of indignation mixed with triumph, "That is the *first* time you have ever praised my poetry!" I did not know that I had been so honest; it was difficult—she hungering for appreciation, and I liking her so much—to remain quite sincere without seeming to be unkind.

With another friend of those days, I had less difficulty. Mabel Dearmer, in her beginnings, was one of the most amusing people I have ever met. She wrote good nursery rhymes, with illustrations rather crudely drawn but of the right kind. These I admired and corrected for her, so far as correctness was desirable; and we had great fun together. She had social ambitions, and liked to be surrounded by an admiring crowd; probably even then she did not know that the charm of her work lay not in its cleverness, but in its exuberant spirits and simplicity; but we laughed at her so much that she did not trouble to take herself seriously.

In that circle of friends I had a nickname, which I still value for its happy associations. One day, after one of her "at homes," she came running to be told what I thought of it. She talked as she entered: "Odrik, did you like my dress, last night?"

"Your *dress* was very nice Mabel," I said.

"Well, wasn't *I* nice too?"

"Yes, you were very nice too."

"Then what was the matter? I know you've got something hidden in your nasty mind!"

"Well," I said (and I knew that I was going to catch it), "it may be a silly prejudice, but I never think that pince-nez and a very decolleté dress go well together."

She opened her eyes at me in joyous contempt. "Why, you idiot! I wear my pince-nez in my bath!"

At that we laughed heartily, and she went away very pleased with herself. The next day she came back, looking serious. "Why did you two laugh," she demanded, "when I said that I wore my pince-nez in my bath?"

"Because it was funny," we told her.

"Well, as you laughed so much, I thought it must be," she said. "So I went and said it to another man, and he didn't think it funny at all!"

Such lack of caution was characteristic of her at that time. And then came a change. How or why it came about, I don't know; but all at once she began to take herself seriously. Ceasing to write funny books for children, she turned to sombre novel-writing, and then to things of a mildly mystical character; and as her writing changed, she changed also; she became "good"; and it did not improve her, for it diminished her sense of humour, and still more the unconscious comedy of her behaviour. We remained good friends, but we saw less of each other as time went on, and when she began producing her plays by the aid of committees including archbishop and bishop, I was not of the company.

I wonder sometimes if I have been unfaithful in my friendships; so many have come and gone, not through any active breach or loss of kind feeling, but from the fact that we have each become different people; and as we became different our points of intimate contact have diminished. It was Emerson, I think, who maintained that for sincerity in friendship, change must be recognised—and accepted; and the real test of the genuineness of a friendship, when

circumstances have brought about separation, is whether one does
or does not regret that the friendship was ever formed. In very few
of my friendships has that sense of regret followed; over all the rest,
when the period of intimacy has ended, I have retained a lively
feeling of gratitude for benefits received, and to some, whom I
never now meet or even hear from, my thoughts go constantly,
still registering the old affection of the days when meeting was an
exciting pleasure and parting always a regret.

Sometimes I have very much wished to become intimate with
people who had not the corresponding desire, and sometimes I
have avoided meeting those whom I afterwards discovered to be
more than most, the very people I was in search of—not knowing
that they existed. The benefit that has come from those foolishly
delayed meetings has, I would like to hope, been mutual; but in
one instance at least the heavier debt has remained so much mine,
that I would like to tell its story—beginning with an avoidance
on my part which remained effective for five or six years, a similar
case to my encounter with those two closed volumes of William
Blake, which I might have opened to my exceeding great delight,
but did not.

It happened during my early years in London. I went to a
musical "at home," and heard that, in an interval of the music,
there was to be recitation. One of the reciters was pointed out to
me—a comely and rather stout lady dressed in blue velvet; and she
was to be followed by a "boy-genius," her own son, whom she
herself had trained in voice production.

It was a hot afternoon; and to hear a lady who had character-
ised herself in blue velvet, and after her a "boy-genius" of home
production, was, I thought, something to be avoided. And I
had at least this excuse, that there was at that time a fashion for
drawing-room recitations so crude and incompetent that they made
one's flesh creep. And so, just before the blue velvet took up its
position, I made the unfortunate mistake of creeping unobtrusively
away, and so missed hearing a quite good reciter, and after her
the man (then only a boy) whose knowledge and manipulative
skill in the rendering of English for dramatic purposes I came

afterwards to put in a class all by themselves—Granville Barker. Some years later, I saw him for the first time on the stage taking the part of Eugene in *Candida,* and thereafter I hunted among my friends till I found one who could bring us together; a service which I owe to the kindness of Alfred Sutro. At the time nothing more came of it; I had no plans then of collaboration, or even of writing for the stage; it was simply a case of intellectual satisfaction at meeting an actor who had brains as well as temperament, and was apparently without vanity. We did not meet again for a year or two; and then during the discussion over a Shakespearean lecture of his at which I was present, he gave me one of the surprises of my life—saying that I was one of the people whom he wanted to persuade to write for the English stage.

I asked him afterwards if he really meant it. He assured me that he did, and the proof of his sincerity was that a year afterwards he came and asked me if I would write a play—"a grown-up fairy-tale play" he called it, for the Barker-Vedrenne Management then about to start at the Court Theatre. And when he did so, God gave me the grace to say that I could not do it alone; but only if he would do it with me. And that was the how and the why of our joint production of *Prunella.* And when people, unnecessarily curious, ask how much of it was his, and how much of it was mine, I can only truthfully tell them that in that happy collaboration the yard measure had no place, and the only fact which mattered was that his joint authorship made the play twice as good as it would otherwise have been.

There was also the added satisfaction, rare in the history of collaborative play-writing—we never quarrelled, and have remained friends to this day.

CHAPTER XI

CHANGING VIEWS

WHEN home for the holidays, we began to find that life in London
was having a bad effect on us; or, if we ourselves did not find it out,
it was found out for us. In books, politics, and religion we were
beginning to have views of our own; and though we were still
willing churchgoers, and still reckoned ourselves Conservatives,
we were so with a difference. Happily for family concord, we still
detested Gladstone, and Home Rule for Ireland; but we had begun
to read books and admire authors of whom our elders disapproved;
and on one occasion the disapproval descended upon us, very much
to our surprise, with almost excommunicative weight.

It came about through our having been left by ourselves at home
while all the rest were away on holiday. From the local circulating
library came a form for the recommendation of books for the
coming year. Innocent of offence, we put down two books which
were just then being much talked about—*John Ward, Preacher,*
and *Robert Elsmere,* and a better one which was then less known,
The Story of an African Farm. Whether the Bromsgrove Library
Committee saw danger in the first two, and so did not fall into the
pit we had digged for them, I do not know, but never having
heard of *The Story of an African Farm,* and supposing from its
title that it was merely an account of colonial life in which anyone
might find interest, they got it, and a few weeks later it went
into circulation.

Then followed explosion. We had gone back to London, but
word of the scandal we had caused soon reached us. A father of
a large family found his eldest daughter, aged eighteen, reading
it. Having read a few pages of it himself, he rushed off to the vicar

115

and the headmaster to demand why they had permitted such poisonous stuff to enter the library; and they in turn, finding that my father's recommendation list was responsible for it, came to him to know what he meant by it. Thus charged with responsibility for a thing about which he knew nothing, he asked for the book and read it, and was horrified to find himself tarred with the brush of so odious a production.

His letter denouncing it, and us, might almost have been written had we let loose on the community a book as free of speech as *Lady Chatterly's Lover,* or James Joyce's *Ulysses.* And though I was able truthfully to say that it had been recommended to us in a sermon, that did not excuse us from the guilt of having passed the recommendation on. It was not only for its bad morals that it deserved reprobation; it toyed also with unbelief, and thereby endangered that "simple faith" of our Victorian sisters which Tennyson so mistakenly supposed to be a frail plant of delicate condition, instead of the thorny thicket which it actually was, in which even rams could be caught and bound against their will. But when he quoted to me Tennyson's lines as a guide to wisdom, I accepted them at their false value, only remarking that I had not imagined my native town to contain so many "sisters" and so few brothers. It was not a conciliatory remark, nor was it meant to be; and I think that it was after that encounter that we began to be suspiciously watched for the development of heretical notions, and suspected of far worse opinions than we had at that time actually acquired. But conciliatoriness has never been the characteristic of religious controversy; pious opinion has always brought out the worst side of human nature; and in both camps—Christian and anti-Christian—the desire for disagreement has been far more fervent than for agreement or mutual understanding.

It was somewhere about this time that I heard a venerable old Canon of Winchester thank God that, "in this Christian land of ours," unbelievers had on their consciences not only the sin of unbelief, but hypocrisy as well; since, for worldly reasons, they were obliged to conform, and pretend to faith though they had it not. And it was true, at that date, in country parishes at all events, that a doctor who did not come regularly to church would have suffered in his practice; and with all the other trades and professions, religion had a commercial value which it was well to recognise.

In that matter, at any rate, things have greatly improved; and bowing in the House of Rimmon has become a much more voluntary performance than it was fifty years ago. It is no longer necessary to go to church in order to prosper professionally.

But, as I look back on it, the parish church of my youth was still a fortress for class distinction and "the appearances." In the middle aisle sat the gentry, here and there among them a few of the more prosperous tradespeople; the south aisle accommodated the smaller shopkeepers, and the more respectable of the working class; in the north aisle sat the Sunday-school children and the riffraff. But as a symbol of Christian equality (which, however, went no further) one front pew under the reading-desk was given to the old men and women from the almshouses. Also, in the choir, the gift of a singing voice levelled out class distinction.

Another social rule, which concerned only the gentry, was that a newly-arrived bride did not go to church till she was ready to receive visitors. After she had joined in congregational worship, calls began.

I suppose that even now, in small country parishes, the Church of England is pre-eminently the church of the gentry and their retainers. But it would seldom now be made a condition for a maid entering domestic service in a gentleman's family, that she must forsake her own connection and become a churchgoer. That, however, was the rule in our own family; and, elsewhere throughout the neighbourhood, the class barrier between church and chapel was rigidly maintained. It was some while after we left home that we heard of the sensation caused at Catshill, when the leading lady, having quarrelled with the vicar, betook herself to chapel as a protest. Before long, however, the adulation and attention which she received from her fellow worshippers drove her back again; for a lady to become a chapel-goer was too much out of the order of nature to be simply accepted even by those to whom it gave most spiritual satisfaction.

One hears a good deal of talk nowadays about the decay of

religion, and the Victorian age is spoken of as though it had been an age of faith. My own impression of it is that it combined much foolish superstition with a smug adaptation of Christianity to social convention and worldly ends; and that the main aim of the Established Church was—with as little mutual disturbance as possible—to make Christianity support Conservatism, and Conservatism support Christianity.

Yet already, beneath the surface, change was beginning; and even in some who still held conventionally pious views, beliefs were getting curiously mixed. Our stepmother, having an ardent passion for antiquity, had decided that it was compatible with faith to believe that the world was more than six thousand years old, and had taken longer than six days to create; but when one day—having read an article in the *Contemporary Review* which propounded the theory that the builders of Babel were astrologers, and their Tower reaching for the Heavens merely an observatory for the study of the stars—when, with pleased interest, I quoted that proposition as making for sense instead of architectural nonsense, she turned upon me, and said in a voice of stern rebuke, "My dear, don't lose your faith!" and I was smitten dumb. What she meant by "faith" only a Victorian mind could explain, yet, without in the least intending it, she did perhaps help me more than anyone else to lose my faith in a good many things social and religious to which she tried most conscientiously to bind my mind.

I remember her shocked denunciation of Mrs. Josephine Butler's impious crusade against the C. D. Acts, which was then agitating public opinion; and about the cause of which, till then, I had known nothing. I remember also her defence, against my horrified protest when I discovered it, of the Victorian practice of allowing prospective brides to marry without in the least knowing what marriage meant. "We can't afford to give it up," she said. "It's too attractive." A remark which shocked me far more than that made to me quite lately by a young member of the Society of Friends, who hoped that his wife, before they married, would have been initiated (in the full sense of the word) by someone else. He owned that it was rather a selfish wish, but that was how he felt about it.

The Story of an African Farm has become now a little old-fashioned, and troubles nobody; but I can still hear the tone of vengeful relish with which a lady of respectable intelligence told me how, having read it, she "took it up in the tongs, and put it upon the fire." She had not held it in the tongs while reading it; but, when reading was over, the tongs became the symbolic instrument of her virtuous disgust. Similarly, Sir Edwin Arnold informed his public in the *Daily Telegraph* how, after reading Zola's *La Terre* with absorbed interest to the very end, while crossing the Atlantic, he had leapt from his seat, and running to the ship's side had hurled the book as far as he could make it go to safe death. It is curious how much satisfaction a little ritual gives to the human mind, and with what pleasure we tell of it.

The savage imposition of ignorance under the Victorian code on virgin minds has become almost unbelievable to the present generation. Sometimes its results were only comic, but sometimes tragic.

One of our friends, a girl well up in her teens, had a rapacious interest in babies; and as soon as any of her friends married, she would begin, without proper waiting, to enquire for results. When this became embarrassing, her mother said to her one day, "My dear Emily, you ought to know by this time that people don't have babies till they have been married at least nine months." This information of nature's slow way of doing things greatly surprised her; but she accepted her mother's word for it, till shortly after (it happened on their "at-home" day) someone announced over the teacups the safe arrival of a baby to a recently married couple. Then, from the insufficiently instructed Emily, came astonished protest: "Oh! I'm sure *they've* not been married nine months!" Having said it, she saw that she had dropped a brick, but she did not in the least know why.

Much more serious was the effect of ignorance on the wife of a doctor friend of mine, in her young days. He told me that she had been allowed to grow up with the fantastic notion that if she looked upon a man "to lust after him" (to have, that is to say, any feeling of attraction towards him) she would land herself with a baby, and become a disgraced character. The frantic "holy custody of the eyes" which this imposed upon her, ruined her health; she became a semi-invalid—a state from which marriage only partially rescued her.

Taught by these monstrous perversions of modesty, I had become a feminist and a suffragist long before the day of battle actually arrived; and when I first heard of the device used by the Abyssinians for the preservation of pre-marital virginity it seemed to me hardly more cruel than that stitching up of minds which one encountered everywhere as regards the "facts of life," until some forty years ago.

Nor did the damage fall only on the weaker sex. In my own social class, boys and girls alike were given at least some book-knowledge in languages, living or dead, other than their own; but as they approached the most critical age, the language of life in their own bodies was strange to them. Boys at school did, indeed, pick up knowledge of a kind, but nothing that could be called either help or instruction. Girls were not supposed to pick up anything—for them knowledge of that sort was a contamination. It made them "less attractive."

It was this sanction of obscurantism (of which *The Story of an African Farm* incident was symptomatic) which started the breach between myself and the narrow conservatism of my upbringing. I could not feel that any religious or social system, which so sedulously refused to tell and to face the truth, deserved respect; and though for a while I still conformed it was without heart or conviction. Quite recently a relative, for whom intellectually I have a great respect, said that he considered the Church of England "the best religion ever invented;" it was so undisturbing. That, I think, is what separated me from it; its undisturbingness disturbed me. Today, over the most burning of all moral problems—the relation of Christianity to war—it takes a back seat, and still signing itself with the Cross, does nothing. Too often, at Peace Meetings, it is the representative of the Established Church who gets up and defends war without shame or embarrassment.

Photo. by Vandamm Studio

Helen Hayes in the New York production of *Victoria Regina*.
(Victoria has just learned that she has become queen.)

For the same reason, though I once had a hope that I could find rest for my conscience in the Roman Catholic Church, I can do so no longer. The moral obstacles have increased as time has gone on; the Church's tolerance of war has become the final barrier between myself and any form of institutional Christianity.

Roman Catholicism, as a medium for devotion, has always attracted me; but I have been generally repelled by the hard arrogance of its apologists, though the repulsion has sometimes been mingled with amusement. Once, in a discussion with an ardent young Catholic, I happened to say that since Rome admitted the validity of Orders in the Greek Church, she must also admit the validity of its sacraments. "So it comes to this," I said, "the Real Presence being upon their altars just as much as upon yours, what you find is not good enough for you, Christ yet finds to be good enough for Him." To which argument I got this amazing reply, "Ah, yes! but He's there under protest! He's there under protest!"

That proposition of Christ led daily to unwilling sacrifice in the Blessed Sacrament, though it scandalized my sense of spiritual values, did rather delight me as an example of the grotesque lengths to which the *odium theologicum* can lead its victims.

Until my fourteenth year, since I had no friends or acquaintances in its communion, Roman Catholicism had no interest for me. If I thought about it at all, it was as a superstitious form of religion lying outside the pale of genuine Christianity. But in that year, circumstances drew me into a closer relation through the beginning of a very great friendship with two members—mother and son—of a Roman Catholic family. She was a distant cousin, quite unknown to us until, with an invalid husband and two small children, she came to live at Bromsgrove. She was young, charming, and beautiful, and her two children were adorable little creatures. Very quickly we became intimate. Her husband's health failed rapidly, and for some weeks before he became finally bedridden I went daily to carry him up to bed—a task which was easier than it sounds, for illness had made him a living skeleton.

In this household I found religion to be a real thing, though in its long-winded forms rather cruelly oppressive to such young children—to the boy, at any rate, whose resistance to evening prayers full of vain repetitions, and the invocation of a dozen saints for whom he had no use, resulted in whippings which rather shocked me, and did him no good.

But from that closer acquaintance I began to view Roman Catholicism differently. I saw that it had a real meaning to one whom I loved. It was not a matter of more conviction that I had met before in others; my elders were quite convinced of the religion they professed, but it had no marked effect on their life and actions; our home religion was mainly an act of conformity, an affair of family prayers every morning, grace before the meal which included potatoes and pudding, but not before breakfast or tea, and Sunday observance. Family prayers we disliked because of their monotonous unreality. Sunday observance we rather liked so far as church-going was concerned, because of the music and the hymns, and also the human interest of watching a large congregation of the various classes in their Sunday best, decorously behaving themselves, or not, as the case might be. Its other restrictions, the prohibition of games or the reading of fiction, we dodged fairly successfully.

But now as I grew older, having been confirmed, I found that so much unreality had brought uncertainty. I was no longer sure what I believed, or whether I believed anything. As a communicant, I had a great wish to believe in the Real Presence; but I required certainty; and the Church of England, with its doctrinal variations of High and Low, could not give it me. That certainty, I saw, existed at any rate in the minds of the Roman Catholics I knew; and for the next fourteen years my problem was whether to accept uncertainty as a natural and inevitable condition of human knowledge concerning the unseen, or to batter myself into a fictitious certainty which habit might presently make real, for—man having a peculiarly human faculty for making himself believe anything that he sets his mind on—any fixed ritual or observance, carried through, day in day out, with a certain solemnity of mind, gets into the blood till something which cannot rightly be called knowledge becomes conviction; and it is far more out of conviction than out of genuine knowledge that the world has grown its religious beliefs—beliefs about things which, in their very nature, are impossible of proof.

Can one believe, it may be asked, what one is uncertain about? Yes, surely! One can say quite truly, "I believe he went yesterday," in a case where to say, "I *know* he went yesterday," would not be true. Belief is a state of mind short of absolute knowledge, and must therefore admit of uncertainty of a kind. And yet, though it does not amount to absolute knowledge, belief may amount to absolute conviction; and that is the danger when we start imposing our convictions on others. You may say of a man charged with murder, "I am convinced he did it," yet your conviction may be wrong, and his conviction on the strength of yours might be a miscarriage of justice.

In those early days, I had far more hope than I have now that belief might become a certainty; and from about my twenty-eighth to my thirtieth year I did what I believed to be my best to accept intellectually the faith of the Roman Church, which emotionally made so deep an appeal to me.

But emotion was not enough; I knew it to be a danger. Emotionally I enjoyed, and almost accepted, all that it seemed to offer; and at that time I was writing stories and poems which to the unobservant might have marked me down as already a Roman Catholic. I had just written two such books, *Spikenard* and *All-Fellows,* when I made the acquaintance which grew into friendship of George Tyrrell, S. J., not then at loggerheads with the powers at Rome. From him I tried hopefully to extract the certainty I was in search of. He told me frankly that he did not think the kind of absolute certainty that I craved was obtainable—only a reasonable certainty on the basis of every other alternative to the Catholic faith being less reasonable; then—when reason had made its choice—religious experience would confirm it, and give it an engrained quality which would meet my need. That I take to be quite orthodox teaching, having in it no taint of modernism. Coming to me from a man whom I liked and whose intellectual powers I admired, I wished to give it every chance of getting hold of me; and as Tyrrell was due to conduct a Retreat at Stonyhurst during Holy Week I went there with a Catholic friend.

Fortunately or unfortunately, Tyrrell was at the last moment snatched away to be operated upon for appendicitis, and a very dear old Jesuit Father took his place. I found his ministrations pleasant and soothing; he said nothing that disturbed or shocked me; I was interested, attracted—I was even happy, believing that conversion was about to come. But in the end I remained unconvinced; and on Holy Thursday, when relics were produced for the veneration of the faithful, I found that I had too much respect for my fellowship to take a sham part in the observance.

My experience of that Retreat ended in a sharp sense of isolation, which I hoped would be only temporary. On Easter Day I attended an early Mass, and saw the Communion taken by my friends and companions in the Retreat, while I, of course, had to remain a non-communicant. I was then on a threshold which I longed to cross, but could not.

A week later I went to Paris on journalistic work for the *Manchester Guardian,* and when I saw, in some of the lovely French churches, the tawdry statues, emblems, and ornaments with which modern Catholicism allows its altars to be desecrated, I began to be glad of my escape; unreasonably glad, perhaps, but I cannot dissociate false art from false worship. If there be a personal God, the beauty they produce and cherish is for me the surest sign that His worshippers have the truth in them; if beauty is betrayed, God is betrayed also. And so the foolish vulgarity of modern Roman Catholic art was a decisive aid to my escape from St. Peter's net—an escape for which I became more and more thankful as the years went on.

What finally shocked and saved me from acceptance of Roman Catholicism was not its theology—in the mystical side of which there was much that attracted me—but the damning historical record of Rome's claims, under divine guidance, to impose on her followers policies of an anti-Christian character; her blessing of the Crusades, her excommunication of rulers who refused to take part in them, her countenance to religious persecution, her official sanction to judicial torture as being "without sin," and the arrogance with which—in the face of such contrary departure from the teaching of Christ—she yet claimed to be His sole commissioner upon earth. It seemed clear to me that if the Keys of Peter—the power to excommunicate and to absolve (with consequences not temporal but eternal)—had been employed to make acts and policies of a non-Christian character compulsory, they had been so grossly misused as in effect to render the claim a usurpation and an imposture.

Baron von Hugel's strange dictum that man is God's greatest rival, has behind it the underlying truth—that it is the failure of authoritarian religion to be humanist in its practice which has roused against it so widespread a revolt among those who believe that by man's treatment of man must the truth of his conception about God be judged, and that if he gives religious sanction to devilish devices, then there must be something devilish in his God also.

Of my leanings towards Roman Catholicism during this period my elders knew nothing. I was only suspected of High-church tendencies—by one of them with secret satisfaction, by the other with stern disapproval. But one day, in discussing some religious matter with the Mater (I cannot now remember what it was), I must have expressed a certain degree of sympathy with something that had a Romish flavour. For that I was brought sharply to book, and when I ventured to argue the matter—"My dear, I am older than you; which of us then is the more likely——?" The completion of that sentence (so typical of the Victorian age) is unnecessary.

"Well, as for that," I replied, "the Pope is older than you are!" But as a countering argument it was quite useless.

"Yes," came the reply, "the poor old Pope, with all his superstitions, is older than I am."

Religious discussion is not in itself amusing, but it does sometimes produce amusing answers from its disputants. The most amusing answer I ever received was from my Roman Catholic friend who, till the day of her death, gave me more varied and unexpected entertainment than anyone else I knew. She was a devout believer, and over most matters lenient and charitable in her judgments (over the troubles of a young relative living in India, for instance, she was quite sure that "our Lady would make allowances for the climate"); but she could not stand the Jews. One day some rather extreme expression of her pet dislike caused me to say, "My dear C——, I do wish you would sometimes remember that Christ Himself was a Jew."

She drew herself up; she was not going to be deflected by *that!* "Only on His Mother's side," she said.

It was a devastating answer; and, coming from a devout Roman Catholic, had in it a touch of genius. I passed it on to a French friend. He said to me when we met again, "That is the most successful English joke that has ever crossed the Channel." Yet the best of the joke was that she had not intended it as a joke.

Nevertheless one of the debts which I owe to that dear and most entertaining friend was the glimpse she gave me of the ability of good Catholics to connect their religion intimately and happily with the affairs of life. I remember her saying one day—apropos of the cleanliness which is next to godliness, "I would as soon think of not cleaning my teeth every day as of not saying my prayers." As at that time I was in the habit of neglecting both duties, the remark struck me. Here was someone doing voluntarily and *con amore* what as a child I had been made to do, and had left off doing; and I saw, even then, how much better it might be for me if I resumed those two duties, which compulsion had made distasteful, in a spirit of free will.

One day—she and her two children fresh back from a stay in Brittany—her small daughter propounded to us a French riddle of which the English would be—What is it that a common man sees every day, but that God never sees? Such a riddle was all right in the *bonne famille* atmosphere of genuine Catholicism, but it was horribly all wrong when propounded in the hearing of a family respectably brought up in Protestantism. There was a frozen silence among our elders over the flagrant irreverence of a riddle dealing with the Deity. The true answer—"His equal"—was of unimpeachable orthodoxy; but when some spirit of mischief prompted my sister Clemence to say, "A joke," the riddle was no longer an impropriety; it became an obscenity.

And yet her answer was perfectly true. The God of Protestantism, in whose worship we had been trained, could not see a joke; and it was, I think, for me one of its main recommendations that the God of Catholicism could.

I can seldom think of that friend of early days, even in her misfortunes, without some accompanying amusement, due to her way of taking them. Years later, after a drastic ordeal with her dentist, she went with her daughter to Italy. A complete set of teeth were to follow her. Presently she wrote from Ancona that the teeth had arrived. I wrote back, "Take care not to wear your new teeth when you go bathing." By return came a woeful postcard: "Why didn't you *telegraph?*" It was tragic, for she could ill afford the loss, yet her postcard made it amusing—and it was so like her!

She was partly of Irish blood, which helps explain her; and how we became connected with that Irish blood is a story not without interest. Somewhere at the beginning of the nineteenth century we had a great-great-uncle named Higgins, and he, on a visit to Ireland, stayed at the house of an impecunious family named Bellew. The family consisted of a number of sons, and one daughter—plain, no longer in her first youth, and apparently unmarriageable. So one evening the Bellew brothers made their English guest drunk, locked him and their sister in a room together for the night, and the next day demanded marriage to save "the honour of the family." Faced with the alternative of half a dozen duels, Higgins accepted the proposal forced on him. They married, she proved an excellent wife, and became the mother of a son John, who, adopting the name of Bellew, made a considerable reputation for himself, first as a popular preacher and then as a public reader. He had four children, my dear cousin friend and Kyrle Bellew, the actor, being two of them. The actress who in later years assumed his name was no relation.

In his youth Kyrle Bellew was reckoned to be the handsomest man on the English stage, and might easily have become one of our leading actors; but the higher monetary rewards of America attracted him, and there, in partnership for some years with Mrs. Brown Potter, the handsomest of American actresses, he spent the rest of his life. When occasionally he returned to England he no longer seemed quite English. He had great acting capacity, but America had somewhat spoiled him.

CHAPTER XII

EDITORS, CRITICS, AND PUBLISHERS

I WAS still rather badly off, when, in my thirtieth year, the chance writing of a single article provided me with the basis of an income for several years to follow. The article itself only brought me five pounds; but it also resulted in a fixed stipend, so from that day I was sure of making a living. The circumstances were these. My friend, Alfred Pollard, had become the editor of a book-lovers' quarterly called *Bibliographica;* wishing for variety, and something less erudite than the exploration of mediæval texts, and examples of early printing, he asked me for an article on any modern illustrator I chose to select. I chose Arthur Boyd Houghton, and my article was re-issued a year later in monograph form, with numerous illustrations, drawn mainly from Dalziel's *Arabian Nights* and the early numbers of the *Graphic*. Just then I chanced to meet R. A. M. Stevenson, who, wishing to give up his post as art critic to the *Manchester Guardian,* was looking round for a suitable successor to recommend.

As I was both an illustrator and a writer, he thought that I might do; and having asked if I was willing, he sent in my name. But naturally, before appointing me, the editor wished to see a specimen of my work, and the only thing I had then written, in the way of art criticism, was my article on Houghton. I sent it along, and it secured me the job.

To my connection with the *Manchester Guardian* and its wonderful editor, C. P. Scott (a connection which lasted for sixteen years), I owe more than I can say. Not only did it relieve me during the first five years, from the fear of starvation, but it gave me confidence and a power of ready writing which till then I had lacked. Hitherto I had waited too much upon mood, and when dissatisfied with results would often put away a piece of writing and not look at it again for months—sometimes, indeed, never; for I still have by me a large pile of fragmentary stories and articles begun in the '90's, which I am now never likely to finish.

But most of the press notices which I wrote for the *Manchester Guardian* had to be wired from the London office early the same evening; and though that is all in the ABC of journalism, it was for me a strange, and at first an unnerving, experience. But even before I got the nerve, I found it was good for me; and my "pot-boiling"— if so it must be regarded—has, I believe, enabled me to write better, and certainly to write more of the things I wished to write than would otherwise have been possible. In the course of a year or two, I got so inured to the habit of writing against time, that once I actually took on the job of doing a double set of Academy notices (the hardest bit of work in the year)—when Bowyer Nicholls, the art critic of the *Westminster Gazette,* was on the sick list. It was rather mental gymnastics to write twice over in twenty-four hours, a notice of all the principal pictures of the year, and to say the same thing about them but to say it differently, and with the added consciousness that I and the critic, whose place I was temporarily filling, did not usually see eye to eye in matters of art. Incidentally the double job enabled me to perform a lordly gesture, the memory of which amuses me. As I was writing for two papers, I had received two press tickets which gave admission also to the private view—a very acceptable convenience for preparing one's second notice, and also a social privilege, which perhaps at that time I valued foolishly. Hitherto the ticket had remained mine without question for both days, but it so happened that Massingham, having broken with the *Daily Chronicle,* was temporarily acting as London editor for the *Manchester Guardian,* and wanting to go to the private view himself, he wrote and asked for the ticket to be returned. Stiffly and without comment, I sent it back to him *before* press day; this gave him a considerable shock, as I intended that it should; and the ticket was expressed back to me in haste, with permission to keep it for private-view day if I required it. Once more I sent it back to him, saying that, as I had another, I was able (but only for that reason) to spare it. He did not ask me for any of my private-view tickets again.

The most flagrant piece of pot-boiling I ever did for the *Manchester Guardian* was also the most desperate race against time. A few days before the end of the nineteenth century, I received a wire asking for three columns on the history of art in Europe during the last hundred years. It was required in twenty-four hours! I suppose I am proud of having done it or I should not now be making the confession, but I hope that nobody will think it worth while to search through the back files of the *Manchester Guardian* for that particular history of nineteenth-century art. As a piece of sprinting it fulfilled its purpose; but its information can be better found elsewhere.

At the larger press views which I attended humanity became an amusing study. Certain critics were regarded as authorities, especially where Old Masters were concerned; they moved round, each with his own cluster—a note-taking crew; and one could occasionally trace the influence of their pronouncements on what was genuine and what was spurious, in the unanimity of certain press notices that followed. Among these figures, a little aloof from the rest, moved two brothers-in-arms, whose minds were as one; they were pleasant to watch by reason of their extreme physical contrast and their inseparableness. D. S. MacCall was lank and long, especially in neck and leg; Bowyer Nicholls was correspondingly short. One never saw them apart, and when MacCall strode down the gallery with Nicholls bustling urgently after, three steps to his one, it was for all the world like the partnership (equally inseparable) of a stork and a duck in a certain French hotel garden, of which a friend once told me, or like that more famous partnership of the duck and the kangaroo in Lear's *Book of Nonsense*.

Some of the authorities (one especially) I sedulously avoided; others were kindly patronising, without too much insistence upon submissive agreement; but the only critic with whom I became at all friendly and communicative over the job in hand was Clutton Brock, whose mischievous depreciation and even dislike of Sargent, then at the height of his reputation, used to amuse and please me though I did not quite agree. But it was pleasant, at a time when the praise lavished on Sargent was almost fulsome in its extravagance, to meet one critic who boldly declared that his dexterous performances were often cheap and vulgar in quality. Clutton Brock's weakness lay in his reluctance to disturb the harmony of his hatred when Sargent did a really fine thing; and when we met at the Academy on press day, his opening remark, made with a sideway cock of his head and a wicked smile, "Isn't Sargent awful this year?" became a stock phrase for which I had to be prepared with reservations.

From the material point of view, my appointment on the *Manchester Guardian,* coming when it did, was as I have said a godsend; but from the beginning I had scruples whether my acceptance of it was quite honest. Was I right to take a position which at least gave me a certain amount of influence over the reputations and market value of men who knew so much more about painting than I did? My qualifications were of the slenderest kind; my own practice was entirely in black and white, and only line work at that. I did not know how to paint; I did not want to paint; about the technique of painting I knew almost nothing; I still do not. But I loved pictures, and good composition attracted me. I had a fair gift of expression, and by descriptive analysis could dish up a readable article on pictures, which would enable the general public to know a little—but not much—more than it did before about the aims of individual artists, and their characteristics; and I had strong likes and dislikes with which I was probably able to infect a proportion of my readers. On this equipment my notices won so much approval from my editor that when, on the first opportunity (an undeserved windfall from the success of a certain book having come to me) I asked to be let go, he continued to hold me on very generous terms, asking me only to undertake at a raised fee the bigger shows of the year; while for the smaller ones he provided an understudy from his London staff.

As a result of this arrangement I found before long that I was being specially retained to write reviews of an inferior quality to those which my substitute—a brainy Scotsman—was very soon able to produce; and after a prolonged tussle between the too-kind reluctance of my editor to let me go, and a hesitating conscience disinclined to part with an easy job, I secured my release, and the better man (whose reviews I continue to read with the respect they deserve) took my place.

Now I am not pretending that my notices were any worse (sometimes they were rather better) than the majority of those which were appearing in the big London dailies, but on that showing, the question does arise how much real use—except for enabling pictures to become a market commodity and attract purchasers—has the generality of art criticism which appears in our daily press? It does, I suppose, help people at social gatherings to talk semi-intelligently about the pictures of the year and fancy themselves art lovers; but I doubt if it does much more.

The most useful and conscientious thing I ever did in my position as art critic involved me in my only big row—not with my editor but with members of the outside public. It was put upon me by James Bone, of the London staff, who wrote to say that an attempt was being made to raise a public fund and purchase at an extravagant price a very second-rate example of Holman Hunt's work for presentation to the National Gallery. While welcoming the proposal that he should be so honoured, we both objected to the bad selection, merely made because the picture was waiting for a purchaser; the price—if I remember rightly—six thousand pounds; we felt strongly that only if the work was representative of the artist at his best, should it be so purchased and presented.

I wrote my letter of protest; then came rage, and for a week or two in the correspondence columns of the *Manchester Guardian* the fight was waged. Some of my personal friends were angry with me because they knew that the old man wanted the money; and it was both cruel and in bad taste that I should seek to deprive him of it. But though I thought that Holman Hunt deserved a national pension or its equivalent, I did not think it should be provided in that way. When challenged to say what example of his work would content me, I was fortunate enough to name (amongst others) the one which was eventually chosen, while some years later—after Hunt's death, I think—the bone of contention found its way to the National Collection as a private gift. When it was all over, Bone wrote to apologise for having let me in for such a kettle of fish; but apart from the annoyance I had caused to certain friends—whose loyalty to the veteran painter exceeded their loyalty to the National Gallery—I had rather enjoyed the fight, and naturally was pleased over its successful outcome. Anyone who knows anything about art will agree that *The Ship* is a very much better picture than *The Lady of Shallot* (second version).

While on the *Manchester Guardian,* I had a show of my own at the Fine Arts Society, Bond Street, a selection of my book illustrations up to date, to which, as far as I remember, my fellow critics were fairly kind, and the patrons of art more receptive than I had expected.

In the event the show was rather a farewell to illustration, for after it I did little more, partly because my eyesight no longer served me for the very detailed style of drawing which was what most interested me, partly because I had found that I was more naturally cut out to be an author than an illustrator. At that show there were four or five drawings which had a curious history; and as it can no longer hurt the feelings of the man who commissioned them, I may now tell it. He was a publisher with whom I had not previously had any dealings; one day he wrote asking me to call on him. He told me he was about to issue a series of famous poems, suitably illustrated. Would I undertake—and he named a poem which for years I had wanted to illustrate. I told him I should be delighted; he asked me to name my price. I did so; he shook his head sadly; he assured me that he was not expecting to make a penny out of the venture, he was doing it entirely for love of art, could I not make a lower quotation? It did not then occur to me to suggest that he should buy only the copyright, and let me keep the originals, nor had I then any notion how much work I was going to put into them. Instead I accepted what he offered, but suggested that when he had covered his expenses, he should give me a royalty on further sales. To that he agreed, and I started work. When I had finished the set, I was aware that here was something technically in advance of anything I had previously done. He was rapturous in his appreciation. In course of time the book came out followed by others of the series. A year later he had an exhibition at his place of business of all the originals; they were for sale at moderate prices—in the case of mine the same price he had paid for them. When I visited the exhibition some of them had already been sold; I plunged and bought the rest of them back, and when I had my exhibition in Bond Street I sold them again for double the price.

Presently I got from my publisher a letter of lamentation, "I find I have sold *all* your beautiful drawings, I had intended to keep one as a souvenir; will you kindly do one for me?" I told him I would do so at a price. I did not get the commission. Time passed—a year or two, I think, but I received no royalties. I wrote and enquired whether, having sold all my drawings at the price he gave for them, he had not yet covered expenses. In reply he explained to me that his sale of the drawings was quite a separate matter, and could not be set against the cost of the publication. Probably our agreement was so informal in its wording that he was legally right; but I need hardly say that I never did any more work for him.

I found later that, in commissioning other artists for the series—men younger than myself—he had reduced some of them to his terms by quoting me as having accepted them, without however mentioning my stipulation for an additional royalty in the event of the book paying its way.

It was a lesson to me, coming late, not to undertake work on blackleg terms, also not to put any trust in the professions of those who offered them, with "art for art's sake" as an eye-washing accompaniment.

With other publishers I have had far pleasanter relations—even a degree of friendship; and their consideration over difficulties has often been generous as well as kind. I remember especially Mr. John Murray's noble acceptance of a correction of proofs, which amounted almost to the rewriting of whole chapters which did not satisfy me. It was a novel which I had been writing against time and so had lacked opportunity for second thoughts; indeed I was still writing the concluding chapters when proofs began to come in. My corrections were voluminous; John Murray wrote very reasonably to protest; I replied that they must be made, but that I would pay for them. Eventually the bill for corrections amounted to over a hundred pounds; but instead of taking me at my word and charging them to me, Mr. Murray wrote to say that he found the book so much improved in its revised form he would himself pay the damage. I'm afraid the book did not have the success which such generosity deserved. It had been rushed into print to follow up the success of my one and only "best seller," and was a very much better piece of work; but while *An Englishwoman's Love-letters* is remembered against me, *A Modern Antaeus* is forgotten.

That book had in it a good deal of autobiography; and though for actual publication it was written in haste, I had been nursing it for years, before I could afford to sit down and write it. While it was still only a mental mirage, I had a chance encounter which resulted, years later, in a strange coincidence. I was waiting for a train at High Street, Kensington, when down on to the platform came a very alert dark youth, on whom as I set eyes, I said to myself, "There goes Tristram,"—Tristram being the hero of my projected story. As our eyes met, he smiled and said, "Does the next train go to Westminster?" All trains from that platform, I told him, did go to Westminster. He explained that he was a stranger in London, having come up from Oxford only for the week end, and this being term time, and he an undergraduate, he was up unbeknownst to the authorities. We got into the train together, and talked all the way to Westminster; he told me his name—Harold Lascelles. I never saw or heard from him again, but in my memory I had him firmly registered—he was "Tristram." Years later, about a month before the publication of my book, I saw in a paper the account of an inquest on one named Harold Lascelles, and with it an account of a broken and troubled life. Sent down from Oxford, an outcast from his own people, he had disappeared from civilized society and in August of 1901 was found dying in a gypsy encampment on the Cotswolds. It was the same end I had written for Tristram after a failure not wholly of his own making.

Whenever a striking coincidence brings great good fortune, or salvation from danger, it is regarded by certain people as an act of God—they call it "divine intervention," but the most striking instance of "divine intervention" that I ever encountered was in so trivial a connection that I have remained sceptical ever since when miraculous coincidences have been hurled at my head by those who put their trust in a materialistic and interfering Deity. It happened that while illustrating a certain book for Messrs. Macmillan, I had to draw some dandelion heads popularly known as "what o'clocks," and I was worried about them. I could not remember just how the light and shade fell on them. It was at a time of the year when "what o'clocks" were not available; it seemed necessary therefore that I should go to the art library, and look up some book of botany with illustrations. Just then there was a knock and a ring; and my landlady came up to say, "Mrs. Stratton to see you, sir." And when Mrs. Stratton entered, there, in her bonnet, was a bunch of "what o'clocks." Without in the least believing it, "God has sent you!" I exclaimed, and forthwith I sat her down, and made her bonnet-decoration my model for a drawing which the curious may find, illustration number four, in Jane Barlow's *End of Elfintown.*

CHAPTER XIII

BUBBLE REPUTATION

DURING the 'nineties many books of verse were published; and out of them many mushroom reputations were made. John Lane had what he called his "nest of singing-birds," of whom, I imagine, only Francis Thompson would now count as important. In 1895 I became one of the ruck, and he published my first book of poems, *Green Arras,* with illustrations. Before submitting them I sent them to my brother Alfred for criticism; and his long critical notes which I still cherish were both kind and caustic. Thanks to him I left out several poems which I am now glad to have left out; had I accepted his advice without question, I should have left out a few more. I was just then designing book covers for John Lane; so naturally I did what I thought an extra-good one for myself. It was, at all events, very rich and elaborate. Alfred had not at that time published his own poems, but without having told us, was then writing them. Some years later I received from him a letter telling me how at a dinner his next-door neighbour "thought to interest me by talking about you and your poems. He said that he liked *Green Arras:* he added that *A Shropshire Lad* had a pretty cover. I am your affectionate brother. A. E. Housman. P. S. He did not say that the *Green Arras* had a pretty cover—nor *has* it.

"P. P. S. I was just licking the envelope when the following envenomed remark occurred to me: I had far far rather have my poems mistaken as yours, than your poems mistaken as mine."

As by that time we were constantly being taken for each other I had other letters from him of a like kind. Without malice he much enjoyed putting me in my place, though I was already sufficiently aware of it.

137

It was in the year following the publication of *Green Arras* that the bright blow descended upon me. I had begun in a small way to make a reputation for myself; there were just about a thousand people who liked my books sufficiently to buy them—my prose books that is to say; my poems were only wanted by about half that number. But this meant that publishers were willing to take what I brought them, though royalties usually did not begin with first sales. But I was happy, and hopeful, and prolific; and having the *Manchester Guardian* as a standby was able to indulge in the luxury of writing poems and stories which did not bring me much profit.

And then like a bolt from the blue out came *A Shropshire Lad,* and straightway, as an author with any individuality worth mentioning, I was wiped out. I became the brother of the *Shropshire Lad,* and for the next five years I laboured under the shadow of that bright cloud; then once more I got my own streak of the sunshine of popular favour: this time on a larger scale.

I came by it very easily, and very unexpectedly. I have always been a writer of letters, and of long ones; so, when I first thought of writing a book in the form of letters, I knew that I could do it quickly and easily. I had indeed already written a good number, to a domestic address but undomestic in character, which I could draw upon. A visit to Italy in 1899 provided me with a nucleus of material round which I had only to weave a story, or insert into it a plot. I happened to hit on one which mystified my readers (a concealed discovery of relationship within the prohibited degrees, preventing marriage) ; also (since a woman's love-letters followed by a man's name would have looked absurd) I had to choose anonymity, which made quite a lot of people think that the letters were genuine. With those two simple aids I wrote in a few weeks a book which, for a brief period, became the talk of the town. My agent, Pinker, hit on the ingenious device of planting the rather obvious fake on that most respectable and staid of publishers, Mr. John Murray, whose reputation seemed to guarantee authenticity. Thereupon, as soon as the book appeared, a feverish search for the author started and ran for nearly a year. Among

the numerous authors suggested in the press three of almost dia-
metrically opposed character were suggested: Mrs. Meynell, Marie
Corelli, and Oscar Wilde.

The hunt was up before I knew. When the book had been
published about a week—expecting nothing, but wishing to see
if it was being properly announced—I turned one day to the
advertisement columns of *The Times,* and there read Mr. John
Murray's apologies to his readers for the book having sold out;
a new issue was in the press, and would be ready immediately.

I went home feeling that my fortune was made, and bought
myself an overcoat, such as I had never been able to afford before,
and two beautiful Persian rugs.

A hectic time followed. The continued success of the book with
its deluded public now depended upon secrecy; had my authorship
been discovered, its main interest would have gone; and as I had
not supposed it would have any success at all, I had told about
thirty people. But they were friends and staunch; the quest grew
rampant but they did not betray me. The secret was finally given
away by a certain editor who had been told in strict confidence. At
first it was not believed, for I had not written anything of the
kind before; I was even accused of making fraudulent profit by
deceptively sitting tight and saying nothing; but now with a fear
that it had perhaps been "spoofed," the chatter-press, which had
tumbled headlong into extravagant praise, began to hedge; memories were short, it must save itself from its own folly.

The herd instinct is strong in the world of journalism—on this
occasion the herd was a jumping one; it wasted no time in practice; in less than two weeks its jumping feats were amazing, and
gave me a new form of enjoyment in addition to all that I had
before. I sorted out my press cuttings, and compiled a very pleasing list of quotations which I sent to Pinker, hoping that he might
get it published. No editor would touch it. As a curiosity from
the field of journalism, I give here a few extracts:

"They [the letters] were written by a girl who died at the
age of twenty-two, and they reveal an exquisite nature. . . .

She was a woman of parts; hers was a rare mind and a beautiful soul. . . . The love-letters written by this unhappy girl have a quality, a literary finish, and a delicate abandonment that give distinction to the volume." *Academy*

" 'An Englishwoman's Love-letters' is without the living wind that blows through true literature: it is essentially vaporous and not quite wholesome." *Academy*

"Guesses at the authorship of 'An Englishwoman's Love-letters' continues to amuse the town. We believe the author to be Mr. Laurence Housman." *Academy*

"We beg to inform several correspondents that guesses as to the identity of the author of 'An Englishwoman's Love-letters' have ceased to be amusing." *Academy*

" 'Who?' " (a two columns article). *Academy*

"I could not define why the letters fascinated me. Yet this I know; if every adjective of commendation that has been lavished on this little volume were set out before me I would subscribe them with a light heart. . . . Whether it is a great book or not, the test of time alone can prove. . . . For my own part I have no doubts." P. H. O. W. in *The Onlooker*

"The anonymous outpourings of an ingenious if somewhat mawkish sentimentality." P. H. O. W. *The Onlooker*

"How good the love-letters really are the following excerpts will serve to show. . . . The volume is full of delicate felicities, tender humour, and the ecstasy that comes only to those whose love is perfect." *The Outlook*

"The thing fails to interest because it is overweighted with pages that have nothing to do with the case, and that provoke the yawn." *The Outlook*

"Only at very rare intervals does a book so delicate in quality come into our hands. . . . We have heard it suggested that this little book, which cannot fail to touch a tender heart, may possibly be a literary *tour de force,* that is to say, a volume of letters that passed in the brain of the writer between imaginary lovers. We can hardly think this to be probable, though we admit the possibility of such a feat. To us, however, the letters seem real cries of joy and grief." *Literary World*

"Mr. Barry Pain has availed himself of a splendid opportunity. Ridicule is said to kill, and Mr. Barry Pain ought to put the quietus to this new movement. . . . Here is a specimen of the burlesque. . . . Put in this form the childishness of the whole thing strikes one, and wonder is created that the sane British public has gone wild over a young girl's extravagances." *Literary World*

"She has swift penetration and a vivid touch. . . . In its artistic reticence, in its directness, its simplicity, by the admirable way in which it realises the emotional value of the incident, that passage has the flavour of literature. . . . It is by just such flashes of insight as that, flashes that gleam all through the pages, that this little volume is made interesting and even noteworthy." "Hubert" (Hubert Bland) *Sunday Chronicle*

"From a literary or psychological point of view they are in no way remarkable." "Hubert" (Hubert Bland) *Sunday Chronicle*

"We can only be grateful that some discriminating mind has decided to publish these remarkable documents without excision or suppression. . . . Never was there written a confession so tender, so exquisite, so tragic." *Pall Mall Gazette*

"For our own part we are philistine enough to think that nobody need have written 'An Englishwoman's Love-letters'." *Pall Mall Gazette*

" 'But Dumas, through a dozen absurdities, knows apparently how to stalk his quarry: so large a genius may play the fool and remain wise. You see I have given your author a warm welcome at last.' *An Englishwoman's Love-letters,* page 82.

"He tries to make her read 'Le Vicomte de Bragellone,' but she obviously does not care for the great Dumas." Mr. Andrew Lang in *The Daily News*

Among the whole lot of commenting journalists the only man who showed honesty and discernment was Mr. Clement Shorter, and though his comment tells against me, I quote it, out of respect to his memory:

"The amusing thing is that from the moment that everyone knows the author everyone will scorn him, or her, for having written a poor book, whereas now everyone finds the said book to be charming." Mr. Clement Shorter in *The Sphere*

I suppose it was cruel of me to put this list of weathercock opinions into the hands of one of the writers thereof, who happened also to be a personal acquaintance, but we had never much liked each other. After that the gulf widened, and we met but seldom.

Certain members of my own family had not been let into the secret: I cannot remember why. When it leaked out there was excitement, and a little resentment that they had not been told sooner.

To one member of the family I knew the book would not appeal; but Herbert, then about to start with his regiment for the field of action in the Transvaal from which he was not to return, expressed a great desire to read it. "After which," commented Alfred, "the Boers will have no terrors for him."

But the Mater, whose literary taste was influenced, if not entirely guided, by popular favour, was at last pleased with me. Only a short time before she had commented on my lack of success as a writer, and with a firm belief in my ability had told me where the fault lay. "The reason why your books don't succeed," she said, "is because you don't choose good titles. If you wrote one called 'Who stole the diamonds?' it would be popular." She was probably right; unfortunately I could not see myself the writer of a book so named.

My titles were also charged against me by another member of the family; and it was not until I published *The Royal Runaway* that she admitted I had at last hit on an attractive one. Yet if there is one thing on which I pride myself it is my titles: *Gods and Their Makers, A Farm in Fairyland, The House of Joy, The Field of Clover, John of Jingalo, The Sheepfold, Trimblerigg, Cornered Poets, The Love Concealed, Palace Plays,* are all titles which, for the contents, could not I think be bettered.

CHAPTER XIV

HAPPY DAYS

My visit to Italy had come about through a new friendship, formed at Buildwas, in Shropshire, in the same year as the publication of my brother's poems with a title which has made so many people suppose that we are a Shropshire family. Percy and Mabel Dearmer—he in holiday charge of the living—asked me to go and stay with them; and there I first met three people with whom I became friends: Evelyn Sharp, Herbert Alexander, and his sister Marion. It was there and then that I got my name "Odrik," and got it in an amusing way. The whole party were known to each other by familiar names: I was the only one who remained "Mr." One day, as we sat at luncheon, I demanded that this should cease, and called upon each in turn to supply a letter for a more suitable name. "O" came as a natural exclamation from the first to whom I pointed; the rest followed: D, R, and I. Mabel Dearmer had to supply the last. She made a long pause, as though the suitable finish were hard to find. "Don't be silly," we said. "You know it has to be C." "K," she said; so "K" it had to be. When we parted I was made to promise that my new name should be used only by those who had given it me, or as passed on to their own relatives and friends; and so it is only by Alexanders, Dearmers and Evelyn Sharp that I am still so named; and for their kind sakes and for happy memories, I value it much more than a title.

In the following year I went to stay with the Alexanders at Cranbrook; and there, in the sheltered privacy of a large garden and grounds, I was introduced to tent-sleeping and sunbathing. It was the first time, since I had left home fifteen years ago, that

144

I found myself in the jolly company of friends all younger than myself, in carefree surroundings and a lap of luxury to which I was unaccustomed; and I enjoyed it enormously. Hitherto we had been unable to afford any holidays except just home-going, or occasional visits to elderly relatives; here was something entirely new to me, and though at first I found the tent and the sounds of night so disturbingly exciting that for two or three nights I hardly slept a wink, and was in consequence so dazed with sleepiness as I came in for tea one hot afternoon that I was suspected of being drunk—nevertheless I was in healthy and happy condition, with a touch of the pagan thrown in, when we varied our diversions by dressing or undressing for dinner (the elders of the family being away) in rather scanty Greek costume.

We did that also, on a later occasion, when Clemence had come and joined us. It happened that just then she was lame from an accident, and having got into my Greek dinner jacket I went to her room to help her downstairs. As I presented myself I asked did I not look beautiful? Rather reluctantly she admitted that I did. "But you are not *dressed!*" she objected. "Wait till you see Sandro," I said; and just then Sandro appeared, a scantily clad Cupid. This forced her to take an amended view of me. "Yes; *you are!*" she said.

It was all really quite decent, but it was not Victorian, though Victoria herself was still an influence, and even in that household, as I shall presently tell, had her representative in one who found some of the things we did a little disturbing.

People are sometimes asked if they can name or remember the happiest day of their lives. Probably they cannot, for strange though it may seem, they have in all likelihood forgotten it. But one can often recall certain days which, in the sense of well-being which pervaded them, were among those to be classed "happiest." One of my own I remember well. It was on that first visit to Cranbrook. Sandro and I had walked over to Goudhurst to see friends; it was a very hot day, we were in light summer attire, both, I remember, wearing white linen hats with wide brims. As we descended a field-path on our way to bathe, we came upon a group of hop-pickers, and heard suddenly a voice of Irish brogue cry, "Christ and the Virgin Mary!" The reference was to *us;* and it was, I suppose, the combination of hats set back like haloes, Alexander's virginal countenance, and my beard, which gave a distant resemblance.

Three other incidents of that day I also remember; while bathing I became entangled among the stems of water-lilies, but managed not to drown; then, a little later, I saw with delight a very beautiful girl (who a few years after died tragically in childbed) walk with perfect balance in high-heeled shoes along an iron field fence. Finally, as we raced home against time in the warm dusk of evening, we came upon a village postman held up from collecting his mail by a swarm of bees which had taken possession of the letterbox.

That visit provided me with another incident of which, shortly afterwards, I made literary use. I had come to Cranbrook in my poverty with a jacket exteriorly decent but with a ragged lining. Of this, when confronted with a manservant whose duty it would be to brush my clothes, I was weakly ashamed; and each evening when I dressed for dinner I hid it carefully away. But though I was ashamed of the servant finding it, I did not mind telling my friends; and one of those who heard the story was the beautiful lady who balanced on the iron rail.

Quite forgetting that I had told it, I put it next year into that surreptitious fake, the *Love-letters,* and while the hue-and-cry was on, my beautiful lady wrote to say that she had spotted me, but would not give me away.

It was on my second visit, I think, that an incident happened, which, starting in ominous gloom, ended in laughter. Colonel Alexander, the father, was then at home; also his eldest son, Boyd, the explorer, just back from bird-hunting in West Africa. Our tents and our sunbathing were in a corner of the grounds skirting the garden, shut off from the house by trees, and safely hidden from the road. Among the trees were some fine cedars; and early one morning, all in a state of nature, five of us climbed into their lower branches and were there photographed in monkeylike atti-

tudes as arboreal men. But when we went in to breakfast there
was dark gloom; our host returned our greetings with a nod and
a grunt, but would not speak. When he had finished he got up
and called Boyd into the library. We exchanged guilty glances;
we knew something must be up. Presently Boyd came back and
told us that his father, taking an early stroll in the garden, had
caught sight of our shameless performance, and had fled horrified
back to the house. "The place won't hold us, Boyd!" he had
expostulated. "We shall have to go!" His old-fashioned sense of
decency was badly hurt. What were we to do? We felt sorry for
him, and sorry for ourselves. It was all so innocent! A thought
struck me: there were those photographs. I asked for them to be
developed and prints to be taken as soon as possible. They came
out very successfully; I still have copies of them in my possession.
Merely from a decorative point of view, not for decency, we had
(by the favour of Heaven) girdled ourselves with vine leaves, and
we all looked very nice and almost proper.

Armed with these, I went into the library. "Colonel," I said,
"I've something to show you." I placed the photographs before
him. He could not resist their charm, their innocence, their *tout
ensemble*. He fell to laughing. I do not now remember whether
he kept them to send on to Mrs. Alexander, who was then away;
but we knew that we were forgiven.

Another happy folly of one of those visits was my learning to
ride a bicycle. Deceived by Sandro, who pretended to be holding it when he was not, I mastered the beast in a few minutes.
Hearing him shout from a distance, I immediately fell off; but
mounting again accompanied him for my first ride. He had put
me onto a bicycle that had no brake; we came to a hill, and the
bicycle began to run away with me. He shouted to me to "back-
pedal"; I did not even know what back-pedalling meant. I saved
my life by riding into the hedge without much hurt, but with some
damage to the bicycle. That same afternoon (strong tea must
have gone to my head) I did trick-riding on the lawn, Sandro
leading the way through a labyrinth of flower beds. Rounding a
too-sharp corner I felt myself falling; I threw my arms round a

large stone flower urn, and with the impetus of my speed lifted it from its pedestal and came crashing to ground. On that occasion neither I, nor the bicycle, nor the flower urn was hurt. It was one of those things that people call "a God's miracle": if it was a miracle at all it belonged much more to the devil. I am not usually an adventurous person; but looking back on that day, I feel that I was then not once but often nearer to death, or disfigurement, or broken bones than I ever was before or have been since—except only once. And that once also had a certain touch of comedy about it; though it was not then mad high spirits that led me into danger.

I was turning one day from High Street, Kensington, into Warwick Gardens, when there met me, bowling along at a sharp pace, a cart, on which piled up tier above tier and held together by crossings of rope were perhaps a hundred (they looked like two hundred) wooden chairs. As the cart rattled by, swinging sharply round the corner, the rope broke. I heard it swish past my head, then with terrific clatter a rain of chairs descended all about me— to right and to left, but amazingly not one of them struck me. I did not wait to see the cart loaded again; maybe I ought to have stayed and helped with my life so spared to me. But the man saw only the tragedy of the thing and was angry; I saw only the comedy, so it was better that we parted.

I have had no experience of the missiles of war, except distantly when air raids came over London; but a friend has told me how he enjoyed shells but could not stand bullets. The larger and more spectacular danger stimulated him; the smaller made him an arrant coward. Similarly with things of a slighter scale, I find myself of like mind. Spiders and mosquitoes I cannot abide; but a rain of chairs is not so bad as it sounds, for when heavy things miss hitting you it gives them a clumsy look—as of malign effort wasted—which is pleasing to the survivor.

But to go back to the point at which I began—my visit to Italy; a thing which in those days I should never have ventured alone, for to be abroad without friend or companion makes me discontented and homesick; speaking French badly, and other languages not at all, unable to mix with my fellow men I become solitary.

But when Herbert Alexander and another friend invited me to go and stay at their vineyard near Florence, and then on to Venice, I jumped at the offer; and in the late summer of 1899, we sailed from Southampton for Genoa, as second-class passengers on a German boat.

Romance awaited us. On the first-class deck above us we sighted a very beautiful lady—the centre of attraction to all the males who were her fellow passengers; she was young, slim, tall, and in all her movements as theatrically effective as Sarah Bernhardt. In twenty-four hours, without any sense of rivalry—our devotion being hopeless—we had all three fallen in love with her. A steward told us she was the wife of an elderly officer in the Danish Navy, and was going out to join her husband in China. As second-class passengers our position, even for making her acquaintance, seemed pretty hopeless, but what we could we did. Alexander had a mandolin and played well on it; and every evening when dinner was over we three sat with upturned faces and sang love songs to the upper deck, and presently she came and leaned upon the rail and listened to us, pretending not to pay much attention or to know that our song was addressed to her personally.

On the third day (while Alexander to pass the time was painting my portrait and I reading aloud to him *The Shaving of Shagpat*) she descended into our midst, and having purposely knocked over his easel in brushing past, apologised, and then sat down and talked with us. After that she joined us every day; and her first-class admirers hung over the rail and glared hatred at us. She gave them reason, having decided for the duration of the voyage to be romantically attracted towards one of us (it was not I), and though it all came to an end when we landed at Genoa, "Bharravar the Beautiful" (which was our name for her, as we were reading *Shagpat*) left her mark upon all three of us—and upon one especially. Two years later we heard of her end. Unsuitably mated to the elderly husband, she had continued to let her fancy stray elsewhere; and one day, coming upon her in a

Chinese teashop in forbidden company, her injured lord shot her and her fancy man, and then himself—dead.

Over that affair she may have been serious; but with us she was, I believe, only play-acting; and though in the last hours before our landing at Genoa she had pretended to play an elopement (not with me), I do not think my agonised counsels of prudence and morality were really necessary. "Horrid man!" she said to me when we last met, "we have decided to be good. I hate you!" And she said it so charmingly, and with such a tragic look of renunciation on her face, that I think in her the stage lost a great actress. To us she remained a fascinating memory.

During that ten days' voyage to Genoa an historic event happened of which we did not hear till we landed. The Empress of Austria was assassinated. In consequence, with a state visit from the Kaiser to King Humbert close ahead, Italian officials were on a scared lookout for arriving anarchists. And so, in the customs at Genoa, our luggage was rigorously searched; and my companions, swearing that my beard was the cause, made me take it off for the duration of our stay. After that we were no longer troubled. Two weeks later we arrived in Venice just in time to see the terrifically dramatic spectacle of a royal entry down the Grand Canal; the two monarchs sitting tight with strained nerves, the Kaiser jerkily saluting; to right and left and behind, vociferous police-boats warning everybody away; and all around them, wholly regardless of order, safety, or decorum—a jostling and fiercely combative crowd of two-oared gondolas streaming among the streams of old state barges with their long velvet skirts trailing behind them in the water: all Venice exuberantly enjoying itself in that explosive Italian fashion which looks and sounds so like fury, and is nothing but the ordinary conversational exchange of a warm-blooded race unusually gifted with the power of self-expression.

A memorable day, jolly to remember; yet I do not rank it specially amongst those which I call happy. But there had been one in the vineyard at Cercina, during our Florentine fortnight, when by great good luck we came in for the vintage, and were allowed to take part in an event of which the traditional accompaniments have probably changed hardly at all in the course of centuries. It was very beautiful to behold, peasants with bare brown limbs singing as they toiled—white oxen in a harness of red tassels, drawing a cart of antiquated design with wheels of solid wood, laden with *beguncias* (also of wood) into which we piled bunches of grapes, beating them down with heavy-headed truncheons; then, when full, crowning them with unbroken clusters to prevent the juice from spilling. And in it, I remember, were many drowned wasps and hornets, which we did not trouble to pick out, for the whole process was on too large a scale for such small incidents to matter. Then the cart carried its load of *beguncias* up to the great wine vat (how many hundreds of gallons it held I do not remember) ; and there for many days after lay wine in the making, of which presently signs grew audible: for, on about the third day, the vat began to hum like a hive of bees; and when, one morning early, men came to break the must, I rose from my sleeping-tent, and having begged for the privilege, washed my feet, bared my legs, climbed up the side of the vat, and taking hold of an overhead rope to save myself from drowning, stepped into that sea of bubbling pulp. It had unexpected qualities: it was warm like blood, and it drew like quicksand; and if one trod deeply it was only by strong muscular exertion that one got free again. In a few minutes I was exhausted, and glad to get out. I came down red almost to my middle, feeling like the prophet from Bozrah, as one who had trodden hot from slaughter in the blood of a whole army of enemies; and I was happy in the sensation.

Those peasants, I remember, did their vine harvesting communally, carrying exchange of labour from vineyard to vineyard, sufficiently paid for at the day's end, by a feast and dancing which each padrone provided in turn. Late at night among the hills we heard them with unquenched spirits singing on their homeward way, but their voices were not beautiful.

The accompaniments of that happy day in the vineyards went on for more than a week, and are hardly separable; but the most happy time of all was while my friends and I shared labour in the vineyard where we lodged—and with it the few exciting moments three days later when I was a treader in the wine vat.

In that Cercina vineyard, outside the vat house, was a large elder tree, then in full berry. How far it was an unusual feature I do not know; there, the explanation was that the wine of that particular vineyard had an English *clientèle,* that the English, to be sure they were getting good value for their money, liked their wine to be full-coloured; and so, to oblige, the juice of the homely elderberry was added. It affected the colour, but did not affect the flavour; so the Englishman got his money's worth without any spoiling of the wine.

This being a chapter of happy days, I will here give account of one, supremely happy, which came some years later. It happened among a people with whom I got on less well than with Italians, but on that day racial incompatibility did not come to trouble us. We had been lent a holiday cottage ten miles southwest of Cader on the Welsh coast. It was late spring, and there, living very much by ourselves (since the natives treated us as suspected foreigners) we invented summertime, and went our own way in happy idleness.

One afternoon Clemence asked if I would not come for a walk. Only a very short one, I said, for I was feeling lazy. We started at a crawl, going first towards the Falls of Arthog; then, something in the air caused lassitude to depart; the foothills of Cader attracted us; on reaching one of those low summits we found that the distance was amazingly clear, with all its brightness accentuated by the fresh colours of spring. There was no help for it, we had to go higher to get a wider view of so wonderful a day; and so, without having in the least intended it, we got to the top of Cader, and there, adopting the Japanese recipe for looking at a landscape with new eyes, we stood like capital A's, and with deflected bodies and heads almost touching earth, gazed on a world turned upside down. The recipe is worth knowing, for with the eye lenses thus inverted, tints become extraordinarily vivid, and the mild colour range of an English landscape assumes an Eastern intensity. I have often done it since, and always with the same result, but never on a day of clearness which gave so great a reward.

As we descended from that mount of transfiguration (getting slightly rockbound on the way), told by our legs that we had done enough, we turned in the direction of Dolgelly, reckoning on a train, the time of which we knew, to take us home. We had got halfway when we met upon the road a fine young farmer leading a great stallion by the halter, and on the stallion sat a most fair maiden, or bride, carrying a peacock's feather.

Truly for us that day had been dipped in romance. The beautiful three seemed stepping towards us out of fairy tale. Would beings so perfect know anything about trains? We doubted, but we asked the question. Oh, yes, they knew all about Dolgelly trains and lucky for us they did. It was a Saturday and on that day the train we had reckoned for did not run.

So there we were twelve miles from home with night coming on, and rather weary of foot, but happy, so happy. We wandered back through the foothills, on a track which had become almost invisible; but kind fate guided us. From lonely hill farms watchdogs barked at our approach full half a mile away, and the spring cry of the curlew sprang up from the hollows all round us. It was only half-past ten when we dropped into our beds; but by summertime it was an hour later. Having set out for a very short walk we had done twenty-four miles, with the top of Cader thrown in. It was a day in which free will had gone hand in hand with "divine intervention," a combination which comes but rarely in the lives of men.

Another rather happy day (two consecutive days making one) was also a day of distances. It stands out the more, perhaps, because it came in the middle-war period, when happiness of any kind was difficult. During the winter 1916-17, the Elliott Seabrookes had lent us their house in Great Langdale, in exchange for ours in Kensington, and one day we went up the Stake Pass and over bright frozen snow towards Borrowdale. There down in the valley we parted, Clemence going out beyond towards Keswick, to stay the night with cousins, I taking a track marked by stones that presently became buried in snow which led up over high ground under Stickle Pikes towards Easdale. I was feeling rather concerned when I found the stones no longer guiding me, and pockets of snow swallowing me well up to my waist, and was just beginning to wonder whether I had not been foolishly rash to adventure so rough a track with no experience of hill-climbing and very little sense of direction, when all at once I went in up to my neck. But I was close to what seemed the top, and I struggled on, and sure enough in a few more yards I struck the edge of the plateau, and there at once had under my feet hard wind-swept snow of little depth—a delight to walk on. From there the long Easdale descent into Grasmere gave me a sense of happiness in body and mind that have seldom come to me elsewhere, for walking in the Lake district has the same remove from ordinary walking as poetry from prose, and remains ever more memorable.

The next day I went out to meet my sister returning by the road which runs from Keswick to Grasmere under the side of Helvellyn. She met me stepping freshly, not apparently tired. She had walked farther than I. When we got home she had done almost fifty miles in the two days. It was, I think, the longest walk she had ever taken in her life, and her enjoyment of it was characteristic of a taste for trials of endurance of which time has not cured her.

Not so happy as memorable, was a day spent in Paris on my return from Italy, when, for the second time only, I met Oscar Wilde, then in forlorn exile, and from the conversation which took place as we lunched with a party of friends I obtained the material for the dramatic dialogue called *Echo de Paris* which I wrote and published twenty-four years later, and from the preface to which I may here give the impression made on me.

"My memory of him on that occasion inclines me to believe that those are right who maintain that as a personality he was more considerable than as a writer. The brilliance of conversation is doubtfully reproduced in the medium of cold print, and I may have wholly failed to convey the peculiar and arresting quality of what, by word of mouth, sounded so well. But the impression left upon me from that occasion is that Oscar Wilde was incomparably the most accomplished talker I have ever met. The smooth-flowing utterance, sedate and self-possessed, oracular in tone, whimsical in substance, carried on without halt or hesitation, or change of word, with the quiet zest of a man perfect at the game, and conscious that, for the moment at least, he was back at his old form again: this, combined with the pleasure, infectious to his listeners, of finding himself once more in a group of friends whose view of his downfall was not the world's view, made memorable to others besides myself a reunion more happily prolonged than this selected portion of it would indicate.

"But what I admired most was the quiet uncomplaining courage with which he accepted an ostracism against which, in his lifetime, there could be no appeal. To a man of his habits and temperament—conscious that the incentive to produce was gone with the popular applause which had been its recurrent stimulus—the outlook was utterly dark: life had already become a tomb. And it is as a 'Monologue d'outre tombe' that I recall his conversation on that day: and whether it had any intrinsic value or no, it was at least a wonderful expression of that gift which he had for charming himself by charming others.

"Among the many things he touched on that day (of which only a few disjointed sentences now remain to me) one note of enthusiasm I have always remembered, coming as it did strangely from him, with his elaborate and artificial code of values, based mainly not on beauty of human character, but on beauty of form—where, with a sudden warmth of word and tone, he praised Mrs. Gladstone for her greatness and gentleness of heart: 'her beautiful and perfect charity' I think was the phrase he used: 'But then, she was always like that.'

"None of us knew her: but from that day on, the warmth and humility of his praise left an impression upon my mind which a reading of her life only two years ago came to confirm. Perhaps—I like to think that it was possible—an expression of her 'beautiful and perfect charity' had come to him personally, so making her stand differently in his eyes from the rest of the world."

Chapter XV

BETHLEHEM

An Englishwoman's Love-letters gave me what I had never had before—financial elbow room, and apparent security for the future. The foolish fuss that was made about it seemed to suggest that its author might thereafter look forward to an assured income. Accustomed as I had been to live on less than two hundred pounds a year, and with no wish to spend on a much larger scale, I found myself in possession of a bank balance of over two thousand pounds. So I could now do many small things which I wanted to do, and a few bigger things which then, for the first time, occurred to me as both desirable and possible.

Among the small things the overcoat and the Persian rugs have already been mentioned; the overcoat has gone now but the rugs are still with me. More important, among the bigger things, I determined to risk, and if necessary to lose, a few hundred pounds in getting something done which was really beautiful and worth while. In the two previous years I had seen and fallen in love with Gordon Craig's first stage productions—*Dido and Æneas, The Masque of Love* and *Acis and Galatea;* it was over the last that I met Craig for the first time. Paul Woodroffe took me behind the scenes (it was a Saturday night) and introduced me. Craig's first words to me were characteristic. He threw up his hands in a dramatic gesture of despair. "Do you know," he cried, "*anyone* who will lend me a hundred pounds?" It was theatrically done, but the need was real; stagehands and sceneshifters were waiting to be paid; and the money was not forthcoming. The critics had done their best to damn with faint praise and civil leer something which was too new and original to escape their dislike. Had

156

the cry come two years later, I should have answered yes; but not having then made my pile, I was obliged to say no. Around me I heard, deep and low, the complaints of the stagehands to whom art meant little and wages everything. And it remained on my memory—an angry prick of conscience over the foolishness of critics—that here was a production of strange beauty which offered new hope for the art of the theatre, struggling for existence because its official guides had carefully deflected the public from giving it the attention it deserved; and would, of course, go on doing so until it achieved commercial success.

So now, two years later, had come my chance. I had written, with little thought of the possibility of getting it produced, my Nativity play, *Bethlehem,* and Moorat had, on the very off-chance, written some accompanying music which I thought beautiful. With this in hand, I went to Craig and told him that, if he would like to produce it, I was willing to put up the money on the terms of share and share alike, if any profit came out of it. Craig accepted with great willingness, only making the condition that I would allow him to produce it in his own way. The author was not to interfere during rehearsal, neither was the composer. We had no business agreement, we merely exchanged letters. Craig was to present us with the play in his dressing. Quite sure that the result would be beautiful, I left it at that.

What followed was a grotesque nightmare of uncomfortable comedy—not so comic at the time as the enchanting distance of years has made it. Craig did, as I knew he would, turn out a very beautiful production: but it was not the play or the music which had been given him to produce—of the play only a part; and of the music only mutilated fragments. It is true that he treated my play with more consideration and respect than he treated Moorat's music. He cut only chunks of it, without substituting patches from other authors; but three-quarters of Moorat's music went by the board; and, in its place, Bach, Beethoven, and Palestrina (improvements, no doubt, but not what Craig had been asked to produce) were substituted. And, of what was happening, not one word till the day of production drew near. Then it became necessary that Moorat should be allowed a look-in to hear the rendering of his own music—or what was left of it; and suddenly the situation was revealed to me. Something like breach of faith to Moorat, who had confided his music to my keeping, had suddenly been thrust on me. I told Craig at once that I could not countenance the substitutions without Moorat's consent; and I refused point-blank to try to wring consent out of him. The situation was of Craig's making, not mine.

Craig, therefore, had to do the thing himself. He went down to Campden, where Moorat lived, and told him enough of the situation (but not more than enough) to wring from him an agonised consent to allow Bach, Beethoven, and Palestrina to have an ousting share in the show. As I say, I don't know how he did it. I got a letter from Moorat which had in it more of weeping and wailing than of completed sentences—and small wonder; but to my amazement he did say yes. But when, a few days later, he came up to hear a rehearsal of his music, he found things much worse—from his point of view—than he had been led to suppose. He came to me, and told me that he must withdraw his music from the production. Regretfully I told him that he spoke too late; that I had insisted on his being given the chance of saying no, and should have had no quarrel with him had he then done so—being, indeed, sufficiently sore about it myself. But as he had not taken that decisive step, I claimed (it was then only a few days before the date of the production) that he must allow what was left of his music to remain.

We did not quarrel; he submitted to what was then inevitable, and *Bethlehem* (with the whole of the Virgin's spoken part, and most of Moorat's music left out) was produced very beautifully in the Great Hall of the University of London, and went on for some ten or twelve performances—I forget now how many.

In cutting the Virgin's lines, Craig curiously anticipated the scruples of Mr. Redford, the Censor, who, when in later years he granted the performing license which for the original production was refused, allowed it on the condition that the Virgin was not to speak nor the Holy Child to appear. On both those points Mr.

Craig, the apostle of art, was of the same mind as Mr. Redford; and as he made the play quite beautiful without those details, I did not too greatly complain.

But naturally these accompaniments to the production had not made things very smooth between us. My admiration for Craig's artistic gifts remained unabated, my appreciation for his qualities both as a man of business and as a collaborator had somewhat diminished. But as I look back on it all, how funny, how very funny, some of the incidents, which at the time rasped and annoyed me, now appear! Some of them have even my sympathy.

After the financial failure of Craig's previous productions, there were certain people who wanted his address, and had not got it. When the *Bethlehem* project was announced, an address for the production became necessary; and there were knocks at Craig's door. Bills were presented, importunate voices were heard; Craig's impromptu reply was—*not* "Go to hell!" but "Go to Housman!" And presently I was asked by an interested party whether I had taken over Craig's financial liabilities. I replied emphatically that I had not.

But the door knocks continued to be an element in the situation; so when Craig took a retired studio in a Kensington mews, in order to start producing, he caused a small wicket to be cut in the studio door—whereat, when knocks came, his face would appear; and after inspection, either the wicket was closed again, or the door was opened.

I, meanwhile, had plenty to do on the general business-management side of things, forming the "Bethlehem Society" so as to escape the Censor's jurisdiction, setting up a species of box office for the enrolment of members, running a publicity campaign, full of sound sense and fury against the traditional censoring of religious plays, and—most difficult of all—trying to discover a hall within my means suited to Craig's stage requirements. We went together to look at several, but as Craig nearly always wanted half the hall for the accommodation of his stage, there was not much space left for audience. At last, when things were getting desperate, I lighted by sheer fluke on the Great Hall of the Imperial

Institute, that pretentious failure of which the foundation-stone had been laid by Queen Victoria in the year of her first Jubilee, and which—finding itself useless—had become a seat of learning, and was now the University of London.

By great good luck the University had a chairman, or a president (I forget his exact standing: he afterward became Bishop of Exeter) who was willing to help me to flout the Censor; and I secured at a moderate rental, but under strict conditions as to fire insurance, the use of the Great Hall.

There was no lack of space and accommodation there. It was vast, but terribly resounding; and Craig saw at once that by some device it must be cut down in size, and made less resonant. As a canvas tent was his proposed solution, I do not know why he did not haul in, for trial and approval, the tent which eventually I had to hire. Instead he sent out his stage manager to buy six or seven hundred yards of a blue cotton fabric softly glazed, for which I paid a good many pounds, and this, cut into lengths, he caused to be festooned over the crossbeams and iron girders of the too-spacious auditorium, and having thus constructed a dissipated sort of tent, he brought some of his actors to speak their lines in it, and so satisfied himself that reasonable acoustics could be secured. The later history of that glazed cotton fabric, which thereafter became my possession, was curious and interesting: its career of usefulness is not yet over. Most luckily for me Craig's artistic eye (or his manager's) had chosen a blue of charming quality; and in the many years since then, all my changes of residence have had in their furnishing an ingredient of Craig's happily chosen colour: curtains, cushions, bedspreads, quilts, box covers, splashbacks, dust sheets—they are still with me; and doubtless some of it will remain over to make my shroud and to line my coffin. And not only has it supplied me with such furnishings, but many of my friends also, to whom I have made large gifts of it when occasion called; and I am not sure that a good many suffrage banners were not lined with it—dipped and dyed to another colour when my sister was chief banner-maker to the Suffrage between the years 1908 and 1914. So I may say that Craig's fantastic lavishness in discovering the acoustics of London University's Great Hall is one of his items of expenditure which I least regret—it brought me a very serviceable supply, and I have never tired of its colour or of happy meditation on its queer origin.

Other expenditure was less happy, and less fruitful of results. Craig was still at his experimental beginnings in stage production, and sometimes found it necessary to experiment with his material before getting his results. He did this for the opening scene of *Bethlehem,* which failing of its effect had to be scrapped on the very eve of production, and then, in a few hours, Craig's magnificent imagination devised a setting of perfect beauty and extreme simplicity combined—just a backcloth of a deep and intense blue, pierced by a few stars, a ruck of hurdles and a pile of stuffed sacks which gave somehow a suggestion of folded sheep. But those sacks, so lovely to look upon, were almost the ruin of us. They were, it seemed, inflammably stuffed, with shavings or straw. The fireman reported this to the authorities, the authorities required immediate fireproofing as a condition for further performances being allowed (the first having already taken place). Urgently I passed on word to Craig; nothing was done. A few hours before performance I received word that, unless alteration was made, the gates would be closed against us. I did desperately what had to be done to meet the situation. A few hours later Craig arrived for the performance (which I had managed to make possible) quite unperturbed. "Housman, don't be childish!" was his answer to my protest, at having been left unaided to solve a predicament which was of his making.

But in spite of upsets and hairbreadth escapes (including the turning away of an agent provocateur, sent presumably by the Censor, to offer gate money, and so bring us within reach of the law) the performances took place and ran a longer course than we originally intended; and though by then my nerves were badly on edge, the beauty of the thing satisfied me. There were roughnesses, of course, the company being mainly amateurs; but they had laboured devotedly, sometimes rehearsing into the small hours; and one of the actors (a fine professional singer, who took the part of "First King") was kept at it on the night of his marriage till about twelve o'clock. At last his beseeching looks secured his release. "You may go," said Craig. "God bless you!" he cried, and bolted off.

In the actual performances I remember only one contretemps, too comic to be called serious. In the arrangement of the lighting, there was one concealed lamp, which provided an important central effect for the Manger scene. It was set in the floor, and with its upward rays lighted the interior of the cradle in which, invisibly present, lay the Holy Child. On the departure of the Shepherds and Kings came a sleep scene, for which all lights had to be lowered—except that one. But just once a mistake was made; in the sleep that fell on mortals, Divinity also became extinguished, and a fierce whisper shocked the silence. "Here! you've switched off Jesus!"

That mistake was perhaps a little symbolic of what had spiritually happened in the course of the production. We had, between us, "switched off Jesus."

The comedy of our misunderstandings did not end with Craig's production—or non-production—of the material which had been given him to produce. I had thought that in offering to pay the whole cost of production, and go shares in the profits—if any—I was not indeed doing Craig a favour, but giving him an opportunity for which he had been waiting some while in vain. But after production, when an additional series of performances—still at my expense—were mooted, it was sprung upon me that I was the highly favoured one; and for that favour must accept new conditions of Craig's making. He required that he should have control of all future performances of *Bethlehem* and that I would undertake not to produce it again except under his direction. That I refused, but I offered him the rights for five years from date, and with that he had to be content. It came to nothing; nor was I very anxious myself to promote a revival under those conditions, but had we been able to secure one, I have no doubt that I should have been as much charmed by its beauty as I was by the first— more so, perhaps, since I should then have made it a condition that Moorat's music was to be given intact, and my words spoken.

My troubles over *Bethlehem* did not end with the lapse of Craig's rights when the five years were over. Moorat was a devout Catholic; he came to the conclusion that he could not, as a faithful son of the Church, allow his music to be performed by other religious communities, or for other than Catholic charities; and further it must be performed (under those pious limitations) without any payment of fees; it would be, he said, "selling our Lady" to allow such a thing to be done. I asked him whether in his Church Masses for the repose of souls were not bought at a price, and whether he regarded that also as an act of impiety? But it was not to be a matter for argument.

That trouble has now passed; but it did for a time oblige me to allow performances of *Bethlehem* without being also able to offer the use of the music originally composed for it. Now, however, it can be had for the asking—but also for a fee.

As regards the censorship, after a long tussle, *Bethlehem* has now won its right to public performance. The story of that concession I shall tell presently. I have no doubt that when I can no longer have the benefit of them, the rest of my long list of censored plays will follow and find grace with a department which has the unique power in this country of destroying property at the fiat of a single official, whose opinion in matters of taste has the weight of law.

CHAPTER XVI

FRIENDS, NEIGHBOURS, AND ACQUAINTANCES

IN THE three years following my visit to Italy we twice moved house, first going from an old lodgings in Kensington to a high flat overlooking Battersea Park with a view reaching to Hampstead, and then returning to Kensington, where we took over from Will Rothenstein a cottage in Edwardes Square which had become too small for his periodically arriving family. It was there, at the bottom of the stair leading to the attic, that he painted one of his best pictures, *The Doll's House,* with Mrs. Rothenstein and Augustus John as models.

At the far end of the garden was a still smaller cottage which, having been converted into a studio, gave good extra accommodation. Here, for the first time, we had a home in London really to our liking, with which we could feel intimate. The house dated from the beginning of the nineteenth century. In one of the windows were two panes of glass signed by the glazier, with date added; the rooms were small but comely; and the main room on the ground floor, extending through double doors from front to back, gave, as one entered it, an unexpected air of spaciousness in a house which, from outside, looked not much bigger than a bandbox.

During our sixteen years as lodgers, we had had an angel of a landlady; and it had been an anxious problem, when we began planning to set up in a place of our own, how to break to that faithful soul our intention to part from her. The problem solved itself very comfortably: one day she came to us looking rather shamefaced and miserable. "I don't know what you'll say to me," she said, "but I've decided that it is time for me to give up work

164

and rest: so now I shall have to give you notice." Gratefully we expressed our regrets, and the parting took place without any wounded feelings. Having recently come into a small legacy, and her two children being now self-supporting as schoolteachers, she bought herself a small house in the suburbs, and there, I hope, found the rest and refreshment she so fully deserved. She had a great devotion to my sister, and our debt to her was very real, but I think that possession was nine points of her love, for after we had parted, her manner, when occasionally she visited us, was formal and correctly polite. The intimacy of faithful service having ended, she adopted a new social standard to which we had to conform.

After our long sojourn with a landlady who had also been a friend, we now came into colder relations with a landlord (who was also our near neighbour) of less attractive character. But a character he was! He had a touch of colour—West Indian blood, I believe—wore diamond earrings, and high-heeled shoes like a lady's, and in the evenings, we were told, put on a sort of court dress with shortened sleeves showing ruffles, and gloves with the fingers cut off to display his rings. As he was a bachelor, with only an old housekeeper to look after him, he must have done this entirely to please himself, yet he did not strike me as having anything of the artistic temperament. When I applied for permission to turn a dressing room into a bathroom at my own expense, he agreed grudgingly, saying that "artists were a dirty lot, always having to wash themselves." But though he was cranky and crusty, we were equable in our relations; and to him of all unlikely people I owe a curious debt, since one day he provided me with material for a dissertation on the ways of ants, of which I twice made literary use, once as casual commentary by a minor character in one of my novels and once again in my *Little Plays,* as a speech for St. Francis himself—the manner of expression then being different, but the substance much the same. It happened thus. In his workmen's yard, which lay at the back of my garden, he was seen standing over a run of ants, and, talking half to himself half to another, this, or something like it, is what he was heard to say.

"Ants. Look at 'em! There they are, funny little creatures, all of 'em doing something, and you don't know what it is; but there they are—so busy, so full of themselves, and all about something that doesn't really matter. If they stopped working the world would still go on. I wonder what they think they mean by it all."

That (which I quote from *The Royal Runaway*) was my first and more literal version of what the old man was heard saying; and as an example of how one can make use of good material by changing it to suit a different character, here is the second version, as spoken by Francis to the Soldan in *Brother Sun*. "Soldan, as I came hither, there met me in the way a great army of ants—many thousands of them, all hither and thither running without rest. What was their toil, whose word they obeyed, I could not tell; but they were all very full of it—in a world of their own. So I stood and looked at them; but though very plainly I saw them, they saw not me. I was nothing to them. Yet had I so wished, I could have killed every one of them. . . . And they may have had Kings among them—yet I could not tell which *was* their King— they being all so much alike, even as we are."

It pleases me to remember how that passage, which comes so helpfully into one of my plays about the man whom I love best in the world, was supplied to me by a rather unattractive old man whom I did not like at all. It is a good commentary on life, and it has a moral.

While we were in lodgings, and afterwards in a flat, the problem of knowing our next-door neighbours had not troubled us. Our next-door neighbours had not wanted to know us, nor we them; and social usage did not require it of us. But when we came to have a house and a garden with others alongside to right and left, south and north, it became a question what should we do about it. We were perhaps rather morbidly anxious to keep our freedom and our privacy unimpaired, yet how is it possible to be "not at home" to your next-door neighbours? They know whether you are at home or not, and they come in accordingly. And you may not like them enough to wish it. And so, quite irrespective of their social standing or their attraction, we determined, in the most unneighbourly way, that our next-door neighbours should remain unknown to us, and we unknown to them. This led to consequences; to the cottage next ours came a young married couple—and we liked them. We watched them from our back window as they strolled in their garden, and we heard later that they similarly watched us. And in course of time, when their first-born was about to arrive, we saw the young husband walking with his arm encouragingly round his young wife's waist; and we liked him for it, as we also liked her; and with very genuine anxiety we shared their hope that everything should go well, and were very glad when everything did go well; and we watched the baby—who is now herself a beautiful mother of children—first toddle, then walk, then run. In a year or two she was joined by a sister, a year later by a brother, and they were all beautiful—beautiful in form and beautiful in motion, and still we did not know them. Their marmalade cat came over the wall (I put him into one of my stories) and after weeks of chilly treatment broke down our defences and made great friends with us— became in fact rather more our cat than theirs. And those dear people whom we had so cold-shouldered did not resent it. They wanted to know us, they saw that we did not want to know them (though they could not think why) yet they forgave us and bore us no grudge. But meanwhile, over the other garden wall, where lived people we did not in the least care about, there was indignation and resentment—of which, roundabout, we got word; and still, for the sake of our blessed privacy—with no compunction in one direction, but with a good deal in the other, we kept to ourselves; yet all the while with an increasing conviction that we liked those to the north well enough to know them even as next-door neighbours. And at last we did begin to exchange shy salutations when we passed each other in the street. The cat also became a sort of a link: for when they went away, leaving a shut-up house, we looked after him. And so, though it did not come to an exchange of calls, the barrier grew gradually less rigid, and would perhaps have broken down altogether, even with things as they were, had not something else precipitated us into better acquaintance. This was brought about by their need for a larger house in which the fast-growing family could better spread itself; so one day they moved further up Edwardes Square, about six doors away, and at once the reason for our stiff refusal of their acquaintance was gone. We did not tumble to it all at once; but when the war came other circumstances helped, and we were able at last to explain to them how much we liked them, and how much we had wished to know them, but had been unable to do so because they were next-door neighbours. They were angelic about it before, they were angelic about it still, and they have been angelic about it ever since. A few years ago, the eldest of those three children came down into Somerset to stay with us for a week, bringing with her a man whom she had only met the day before, and during the week she was with us (he dancing daily attendance from the inn near by) they became engaged, and are now married, and her name is Mrs. Lance Sieveking.

How that family eventually came to be occupants of the very house that had been ours, when we gave up London for a life of country freedom, I shall tell later. If our friendship had an unpromising beginning, all that has come of it afterwards has been lovely and pleasant. I can even fancy that the ten years of cold shoulder were good preparation—we got to like each other so well from a distance; but it is not an experiment which I would wish to repeat. Time has made us wiser; indeed, the house in which we now live was built mainly to enable us to become next-door neighbours to a family we already knew, and of whose proximity we had no fear whatever.

Except for that one streak of unneighbourliness, our possession of a house that so exactly suited us did make us a good deal more sociable than we had ever been before. We had many interesting friends, a few of them known artists and writers; occasionally also I got letters from strangers, with or without introduction, asking if they might come and see me; sometimes we found that we suited each other, sometimes not. One case of self-introduction had a horrifyingly amusing sequel, which took many years to mature; but if I begin the story now I must also finish it. One day there came to me by post a very slim booklet of poems printed on brown paper, with a letter in rather scrabbled writing:

"Dear Mr. Housman. I pray to God you like my poems! Please immediately inform.   Yone Noguchi

I read them: in atmosphere and expression, though rather lacking in form, I found them charming. I wrote in reply:

"Dear Mr. Noguchi. Your prayer is answered. There is a great deal in your poems that I like very much."

I suppose that I added a few criticisms. In a few days I received a second letter:

"Dear Mr. Housman. Doubtless you are a lovely person. I like to see you."

Very willingly I complied with his wish. He came—like all Easterns very polite and gentle in manner, but with a pronunciation of English so far removed from anything ever heard, that I had the greatest difficulty in understanding him. I did not see him again till we met in 1920 at a literary gathering in New York, where he was one of the three guests of honour. His English was then quite understandable, and had, I hope, made a quick improvement after our first meeting; for only about two years later he had been appointed professor of English at the Tokio University, and hearing of it, I had wondered how English learned of such a teacher could ever be spoken so as to be understood.

After his return to his own country, he sent me two subsequent volumes of his English poems. They had the same charm as the first; they were full of atmosphere and graceful fancies; but they were in free verse, for which I have never felt much attraction. And as I read those poems, I thought to myself how easily they could be brought into good form and metre; and so, selecting one or two, I myself tried the experiment. One in result quite pleased me. I did not destroy it. I laid it aside, and forgot all about it, since I could not possibly send it to Mr. Noguchi, with the suggestion that he might find it an improvement upon the original. So there it lay for some fifteen years among pigeonholed poems of my own. Until one day, having been asked by a publisher to let him have another book of my poems, I turned to old manuscripts and as I sorted them over came upon a very charming *Cradle Song* which I had quite forgotten, and wondered why I had not published it before. And so with others in a book called *The Heart of Peace* I published it; and for some years thereafter my conscience in no way troubled me, until one day I read in the *Sunday Times* a review of the collected poems of Yone Noguchi, and the reviewer picked out for special praise a *Cradle Song* which he quoted. It was in free verse—the words, as I read them, seemed strangely familiar. I sat up with a snort of indignation—here, surely, I began saying to myself, was barefaced plagiarism! And then, memory smote me, and I suddenly realized what I had done! The book is now out of print; the poem cannot be recalled; nor can I expect those who possess copies to black it out; I can but promise that never again will that poem appear under my name, and here express my humble thanks to Mr. Yone Noguchi that he has not prosecuted me for the theft. I can only plead in excuse that had God not answered his prayer and made me like the poem so well, I should not have done it. But it is not a commendable thing for one man to start re-writing another man's poems. The results are seldom good, though he who experiments may think so. Pope tried it on Donne, Dryden on Chaucer, and both had much better have left it alone. But I must own that free verse, which (if it is at all good) seems capable of being so easily made better, does tempt me to do the injudicious thing, a temptation, however, to which I shall never yield again.

I was now full of work, publishers were beginning to want me, but not always to keep me; and so under the skilled manipulation of Pinker, my agent, I passed from firm to firm—never a good sign; it probably means that one is either quarrelsome or unremunerative, uncomfortable to keep, or not worth keeping. But there are also publishers and publishers; and when, as sometimes happens, they go bankrupt, even if one shares the responsibility, one tends to part company. In England I have assisted in two such cases, in America in three.

My one experiment in editing was not a success, though I think it deserved to be. I was asked to edit, and collect contributors for a new annual called *The Venture*. It was to be on the profit-sharing system. No contributor was to be paid anything except on results. It came out, a little late, in the autumn of 1903. Among its literary contributors were Thomas Hardy, John Masefield, G. K. Chesterton, Mrs. Meynell, Francis Thompson, Laurence Binyon, Violet Hunt, Stephen Phillips, Havelock Ellis, Somerset Maugham, E. F. Benson, Stephen Gwynn, Richard Garnett and A. E. Housman. Among its illustrators were Ricketts, Shannon, Gordon Craig, Sturge Moore, Paul Woodroffe, Bernard Sleigh, and Lucien Pissarro. It was a collection to be proud of, but it did not pay for itself. Not one of those distinguished contributors received a penny. And not one of them complained. G. K. C. when accepting my invitation to contribute, and my statement of terms, wrote that he had as much respect for the proposed sharing system as for the editor; if he did not mean it ironically, his respect was ill-rewarded. My brother contributed on condition that I did not include two writers whom he disliked—Galsworthy and Maurice Hewlett; he also hoped that I would do without Meredith, giving as his reason an adapted scriptural quotation concerning the dead body of Lazarus, a delicate indication that, in his view, Meredith had, for about ten years, passed his day.

The whole thing was, of course, too highbrow to be popular. Perhaps had it been published at a guinea instead of at five shillings, it would have done better.

It was not till after the miss-fire of *The Venture* that we met G. K. C. for the first time, though we had been near neighbours at Battersea. Then one evening he and his wife came to dine with us at Kensington. My best memory of that occasion is amusing but entirely unintellectual. The paradox I have to record was not a spoken one, but it was characteristic. Returning to the drawing room after dinner we began, with one exception, sensibly to dispose ourselves. In a remote corner of the room, well tucked away, was a very small cane-bottomed chair, which had already seen its best day, and was meant only for children. G. K. C., paradoxical in action as in writing—rejecting the more solid supports nearer to hand—went over and sat down on it. He survived, the chair did not. He treated the incident as quite usual. Chairs, it would seem, had a habit of breaking down under him.

That same night between ten and eleven, there came a knock at the door; I answered it. A stranger demanded abruptly whether Mr. Chesterton was on the premises, and being told that he was, requested that he might see him. "I have to remind him," he said, "that at ten o'clock tomorrow he is to stand godfather to one of my children." It was Hilaire Belloc. The reminder having been administered he departed as abruptly as he had come; and Chesterton, finding that we were not as familiar with his friend's poems as we ought to be, began reciting them. I have a memory that they were nimble in rhythm and military in character, and that Chesterton, with generous enjoyment, evidently thought them as greatly superior to his own poems as my brother's are to mine; but even after so first-hand a recommendation I continue to prefer Chesterton's.

Unless one has the trained memory of a Boswell, it is seldom that one can remember the conversational brilliance of the clever people one has met. I know that I have listened with delight to the after- and before-dinner volubility of Bernard Shaw, but can hardly remember a word of what he said; once and once only I heard the usually reserved J. M. Barrie let himself go, yet what he talked about I have entirely forgotten; and the best talk, perhaps, that I ever listened to, was from G. Lowes Dickenson when for nearly one hour, the last time that we met, he talked to my sister and myself alone, yet though the memory of it stays beautiful, I have no definite recollection of what he said, or even of his subject.

I remember one evening Rothenstein coming to dine with us, and holding forth in brilliant monologue—saying, I rather suspect, a lot of those clever nonsensical things which require a good brain to produce them, and are such a pleasure to listen to. A young cousin who was staying with us sat and giggled delightedly; it was a style and standard of talk that he had never encountered before. A few days later Mrs. Rothenstein, who had been unable to come with her husband, reported to us his account of how things had gone. "I ate a lot, I drank a lot, and I talked a lot, and I enjoyed myself enormously." Could any host wish to have from an honoured guest a better testimonial to the success of an evening?

I remember once driving back with Stephen Gwynn from a *Cornhill* dinner, given by the head of the firm of Smith and Elder (the magazine's publishers) to certain contributors of the past year. "Now that," said Gwynn, "is what I call a good dinner; one was able to drink too much without having to eat too much." I cannot be sure whether I myself had qualified on those lines for testifying to its excellence, but I do remember that it was a very pleasant dinner, and that I found myself in very good company, especially with a young man sitting next to me, Frank Sidgwick, who, when a few years later he turned publisher, took my *Selected Poems* as his first publication. Since then he has published more of my books than any other publisher—except one; and it is my standing complaint that, for the easing of my conscience, they will not combine themselves into one firm. If only they would, my wanderings from publisher to publisher would come to a peaceful end. As it is, divided, they force me year by year to a seesaw attitude towards their respective claims which pleases none of us.

At dinner tables I have not found friendly relations with my next-door neighbours anything of a difficulty. In some instances they have even been intimate. On one occasion, quite casually in the course of conversation over the rights and wrongs of euthanasia, a man told me how he had killed his own father. There had, it seems, been an understanding between them about it beforehand, which made it all right. Self-inflicted euthanasia has, I believe, secured the moral support (under certain conditions) of so distinguished an ecclesiastic as Doctor Inge, though he hopes not to practise it himself, and once a well-known Roman Catholic, of modernist views, told me that she considered it one of the most striking remnants of barbarism that her Church sanctioned the infliction of death as a punishment, but not as an act of mercy, and had in the past countenanced even death by torture, as not contrary to the Divine will, while holding release from hopeless torture to be anathema. It is, I suppose, one of the products of the Church's close alliance with Cæsar that war and punishment have thus been allowed to obliterate the teaching of its Founder, whose recommendation of indiscriminate charity as the way of perfection (Matthew V, 44-48) has never caught on either in politics or religion.

Some people very much dislike being reminded of death at all, especially of their own, which I once forgot when I met at dinner an artist whose importance required that his obituary notice should be got ready for use beforehand. In my work for the *Manchester Guardian* it had been my duty to write the obituaries of various prominent artists; and he being one of them, it seemed to me an amusing way of opening conversation to say, "I had the pleasure of writing your obituary last week." But he did not think it amusing at all, though I assured him that it was a laudatory one, and explained that it was his degree of celebrity which made such previousness necessary.

About two years ago I found myself the recipient of a similar compliment. A certain newspaper wrote to me asking for biographical details about myself. When I indicated *Who's Who,* I was told it was not enough. I then realized why more was wanted; and I did not see why I should supply it gratis, so I made a charge which I thought suitable, and have now the pleasure of feeling that I have been paid for writing my own obituary. I passed the idea on to the *Manchester Guardian,* and that paper has, I believe, made use of it. Their own obituaries by G. K. C. and G. B. S. should be well worth reading.

My queerest experience of dinner-table conversation was in America, where, among certain circles, culture is pursued with an effrontery which is almost indecent. Our host was a man of wealth, who, having made his pile, was anxious to catch up in things literary and intellectual. And as we sat down to table he announced that the subject of our conversation was to be, "Did Shakespeare write his own plays?" We were none of us competent to deal with the matter—that soon became evident; but he had rightly gauged the amount of interest his proposition would arouse. The discussion was breathless and—if not exciting—excited; and the only thing to do, to be in the swim, was to make extravagant assertions, which had very little authority behind them, but which, as they were swallowed or rejected, helped to keep the controversy going. At the end of it all our host judicially observed, "Well, ladies and gentlemen, I do not think we have succeeded in deciding whether Shakespeare *did* write those plays."

We had not. Nevertheless it had been a very successful dinner— of its kind. It was the sort of thing they do better in America than here.

Chapter XVII

CONTACTS AND ASSOCIATIONS

MAN's sense of beauty lives largely on association. If a thing is good, use and familiarity make it seem better. It was on our return from abroad, in the train from Folkestone, that Sandro and I, looking out on an October dawn, turned to each other to say simultaneously, "England is the most beautiful country in the world!"

We had neither of us seen the world, except for small bits of it here and there; we had not even seen England at all thoroughly; yet it was a statement—extravagant, but genuine—which further experience was not going to alter. The beauty of England was in our blood, and only whole-hearted blood-transference could make us think or see differently. But though we said it to each other, and though—for me at any rate—it was and remains indisputably true, it is not the sort of thing one could decently say to Swiss, French, German, or Italian; for if their sense of beauty has been similarly formed, they will have their own native opinions about it; and why wish it to be otherwise?

And as with beauty, so with all other things where people of different race and breed are concerned. The patriotism which thrusts itself down the throats of other nations is a crude remnant of savagery, and it is only the ill-educated who make a boast and a virtue of it. I am sometimes inclined to think it is the same with religion. I am not at all sure that Christianity is the best for all races—certainly not that half-and-half version of it which precedes or follows the flag of commercial imperialism, and always assumes the blessing of Heaven to be on the side of its own nationals in war.

176

But though large-scale patriotism is always an ugly thing when it starts imposing itself on others, small local patriotism is often pleasant and amusing, even when it displays a very limited intelligence. One cannot help liking and admiring the old yokel, who, when talk of a German invasion was going the round during the war, turned it down with the remark:

"They won't come 'ere; Squire wouldn't allow it." It was a nice sizable point of view, and made life so much more comfortable for those who could hold it.

Squire's authority is no longer what it was; but I have come on traces of it, where in spite of its restrictiveness, it gave charm to the locality. In a very lovely Dorset village, presided over by a Jacobean castle, the inn (which bore the castle arms, and was castle property) closed its bar half an hour before legal time, because it was "Squire's orders."

In that village (where lodging was hard to find—Squire's orders again) and hardly a new house to be seen, beauty was everywhere. And there I met, for the last time, the pretty old-fashioned curtsy which the village children dropped to "the gentry" and to all strangers. Of course it meant that there was not a single man in that village who dared vote anything but Conservative; but as Conservatism ought to be represented as long as it exists (especially that type of Conservatism which, eschewing slate and corrugated zinc for the repairing of old roofs, remains faithful to thatch) a thoroughly rural constituency is its right setting. Within those limits it is picturesque, and does no harm worth troubling about.

I might say differently of a place that turned us out; for a few years after we had discovered it, and when Sandro, for three summers running, had made its small lonely bay his camping-ground by arrangement with a local farmer, from whom he also hired a ruined cottage for cooking purposes, he was told that he could have it no more. It was Squire's orders. If he let it again, the farmer's lease would not be renewed. Some while after, a friend of mine was staying at the castle, and there heard tales of us— how we had bathed too often, and sunbathed too continuously;

and how we had "a model" down from London, who occupied a closely adjoining tent to the scandal of the neighbourhood. The "model" was really Sandro's friend, Kathleen Bruce (who afterwards married Scott of Antarctic fame), a terrible person to have as bathing companion; for she was a slow swimmer of great endurance, with a temperature which sea water seemed not to affect; and she had a way of swimming out great distances, so that for an hour or two she became invisible, quite heedless of the growing anxiety caused by her long absence. And after we had searched the horizon in vain many times for a sign of returning life, and had begun to consider in what terms to convey the impending news to her family, she would become once more an insignificant speck in the mid-distance between Arishmel and Weymouth, and arrive at late leisure, in rather irritating composure, more ready for the next meal than we were after our agony of waiting.

The first night she camped with us a cow came and lay down against the side of her tent, causing it to collapse. After that, she put barbed wire round it; and though that surely should have been a symbol of respectability, the villagers gave it an interpretation which had nothing to do with the cows, and was not to our credit.

Today, I suppose, such social arrangements and diversions would be regarded as normal, and would cause no comment, but forty years ago they were not usual, and as a result we were ejected from a delectable spot which I have never had the heart to visit again. It provided the main setting for my second novel, *Sabrina Warham*, and several of the incidents there recorded actually happened. The scene of Sabrina and the trapped rabbits on the twilight downs was an experience of my own.

In the garden of the ruined cottage, where we did our cooking, we found a hedgehog, and petted him with saucers of milk, which he would come seeking through the open door. One day, inadvertently, we left a large tin of sardines on the floor. The hedgehog emptied it, and if anyone asks incredulously, "But didn't that make him ill?" the answer is, "It did—very, very ill." And some one had to go round and clean the illness up. Then, for two whole days, our hedgehog disappeared; and we thought he must have died of oily indigestion. But one night, as we supped, we heard on the steep cottage stairway a soft thud, and then another, and another. It was our hedgehog coming down the stairs, each (and there were about eight of them) ten inches high! Why, or how, he had ever got up there, we could not imagine; he was evidently a determined character.

I have never again been on intimate terms with a hedgehog, except once at the Carlton Hotel, where I was the eater and he the eaten. I had made Grant Richards a bet that he could not produce hedgehog at a London restaurant within twenty-four hours. But aided by a chef who phoned to Scotland of all places, and secured a specimen nicely fattened for its winter sleep, he won the wager; and I found it quite good eating, though it was not cooked, as it should have been, in true gypsy fashion. Alfred, who shared the feast, thought less well of it than I did, and preferred the snails that followed.

In spite of those two pleasant encounters, hedgehogs have not had an important place in my life; neither have dogs. Cats have. Indeed my affection for cats has become a sorrow, for now we live in a garden with birds which we encourage to become tame, and to keep a cat is not fair to them.

I am not going to indulge in cat stories, the interest of which depends on a personal acquaintance which my readers have not shared. But there was one curious incident which took place on the day when "Chim," our first London cat, died of rat poison, which seems worth telling. We were aware that Chim had a small cat friend whom we never saw, or only saw vanishing out of a barred window in the basement, when we came down in the morning. They shared a bed inside the trap window; but the friend never sought our acquaintance, nor even came upon the premises in daytime. But on the night of Chim's death, as we sat heavy in our bereavement, we heard in the passage a loud appealing cry, and into the room came the small strange cat whom we had never met before, asking for him. He sprang up on my knee and asked repeatedly what had become of his friend. We told him as best we could; he accepted our sad caresses as though he knew us, but never left off asking. After a while we carried him down and put him in Chim's bed, and there left him for the night. In the morning he was gone, and we never saw him again.

I think it is Chesterton who says that one's love of animals is entirely different from and essentially lower than one's love of humans. Only, I think, in degree. In both cases love is a mystery, and part of the mystery of the love we have for animals is in its power to make us feel humble.

Is it not, indeed, one of the charms of life to submit oneself to the dictation or pleasure of some creature completely within one's power, but so unconscious of its powerlessness, or so confident of man's friendliness, that it claims to do with one just as it likes? The thrilling embrace of a kitten, fixing upon you a murderous eye, as if to say, "Now I am going to tear you to pieces!" and then proceeding to the best of its ability to do it—yet doing it for fun; the confident perch of a robin upon your hand, or the dictatorial pecks of a pigeon as it feeds, demanding more, or telling tickling fingers to keep still; the belief of a very small child that you and the whole world belong to it and to it alone; the sleep upon your lap of any small confiding animal which—in spite of cramps and the calls of time—you have not the heart to disturb—or, if you must, the tender shame and regret with which you do it; these are flavours of life which appeal to some of us far more than the exercise of power—of what, in a theological connection, would be called "divine intervention." This holding of one's power benevolently in restraint, accompanied by the certain knowledge—I could do this, that, or the other, dispersive of the arrogant assumption of very small things that they may have their own will and their own way with me—is anything in life more delicately flattering to one's self-respect? I know of nothing as restfully satisfying to the recreative mind when one is in the mood of wanting to *be* rather than to *do;* just to see the reflection, or the reaction to one's own existence in other and smaller natures—to fancy we are seeing ourselves through their eyes.

We would like, were it possible, to get away from ourselves for a while, to see and to be like them. And in imagination we do so—but really we don't—not in the least. We watch these little lives, so alert, so individual, so characteristic; and as we watch their every movement and expression, we ascribe to it a meaning by self-comparison. It is natural, it is probably inevitable that we should do so, unless we have specially trained ourselves to an attitude of scientific detachment, not imposing even upon their most delightfully expressive habits or actions an anthropomorphic interpretation.

Unless, therefore, we are able to be rigidly scientific in our approach to animal life, we are almost certainly colouring the relationship with a whole set of attributes which are not really true, but which nevertheless add very greatly to the charm of the association. We like to say that a robin is "cheeky"; we like him to be cheeky, yet he is not really cheeky at all; he is not really daring us, defying us, "putting us in our place" as part of a game; but we love to think or pretend that he is so doing. The delicious impertinence of it appeals to us; and in our imaginations we fill him to the brim with small vices, which we correct in ourselves and in our children, but to which in him we extend delighted indulgence. We could stop it in a moment—strike fear into him with the flick of a finger; but we don't do it, and don't want to. We love to see him "being himself" as he sits in the hollow of our hand, in our power, which it delights us *not* to use.

What is it that makes this control of one's power in relation to small weak forms of life so charming, so attractive? What exactly is one then doing? In a small way, I think, one is experimenting in love—not on the spiritual but on the sensuous plane. And yet out of the sensuous pleasure arrives something which, in embryo, is spiritual; and while what I have instanced is but a playtime expression of the social contract between ourselves and the lower and weaker forms of life, it nevertheless sets up a relationship which may lead on to acts and thoughts which we class as "unselfish"— spiritual even; so that, for those small confiding lives, one would readily undergo (rather than betray the trust or lessen the bond) a very considerable amount of discomfort, hardship, or even danger.

Most of us would wish to save a kitten from a burning house,

and if it happened that from the kitten in distress came the appeal
of personal recognition—the reminder, "I have sat on your knee;
I have trusted you," (for that is how we should interpret the cry)
then, likely enough, one might make quite desperate efforts to do
something—something which next day, under the heading, "Man
gives his life to save a kitten," would be classed as "heroic." But
though heroic or quixotic to outsiders, to ourselves it would not be
heroic at all; we should only have done what we wished to do,
what we couldn't help doing—what was quite "natural" under
the circumstances.

And if that is the outcome of our friendly relations with certain
of the sub-human species, are we to believe that Heaven is less
kindly and considerate towards us, when we too follow our own
unreasonable ways? How indeed can we approach Heaven, or
enter into the mind of Heaven, except through our own experiences, finding in them at their best a likeness to what we hope
Heaven feels about us—if it have any feeling for us at all?

I remember hearing, thirty years ago, the cries of a little cat,
caught in the privet hedge of my front garden. I rescued it, very
dirty, for the hedge was a London hedge. It scratched me a little
in the process, but finding itself rescued, it kissed me with effusion
—transferring while doing so a good deal of its dirt to me. And
then, having expressed its brief gratitude, it fled away, and I saw
it no more. It might have pleased me better had we, as a result
of that brief encounter, remained friends and intimates; but was
there in my mind the slightest sense of reproach, because it went
off and continued to live its own life apart from me? Of course
not. It would have been very unreasonable of me to have such a
thought. And is Heaven more unreasonable than I am?

And now to finish with cats, which are my obsession. There is
one story which I will not tell in detail—for it would not be believed; how, on the night when he was given euthanasia, a certain
cat of my affections put his paws on the shoulders of the "vet"
(whom he had never met before), and how I received that gesture
of farewell in a dream—not knowing what it meant till a month

after. No, I admit that is incredible; and yet, in a queer corner of my religious convictions, I believe it.

One day I was going along Portman Square; and on the opposite side of the road a black cat crouched, waiting for a gap in the traffic. Making a miscalculation, she started, and running a neck-and-neck race with an unobservant motor, narrowly escaped death. Leaping for life, she landed herself on the pavement at my feet, and I, sweating with horror over her narrow escape, cried, "Oh, my dear cat, why *do* you do such things?" Two workmen were passing at the time.

"Was that *your* cat, sir?" inquired one of them.

"My cat?" I replied. "She's all the world's cat!" For some reason or another my answer amused them. They went into peals of laughter.

I have one other black cat story to tell; but that waits for another chapter. This one began on villages and their local associations, to which I will now return.

Chipping Campden is a very beautiful and still unspoiled village; William Morris placed it second to Burford among the glories of the Cotswolds. I first encountered its charm when I began writing songs and plays for Joseph Moorat to set to music. There, later, came C. R. Ashbee with his Essex House Press, and a group of London craftsmen to experiment in Guild co-operation on the lines laid down by Morris; and it was there, after a lecture by Granville Barker on the Shakespearean theatre, that I received my call to write seriously for the stage, and not merely for settings to music. Out of Campden, by Granville Barker, came *Prunella,* and after *Prunella* all the rest—now well over a hundred.

From Campden, too, comes a story of simple impropriety, which deserves preservation among the historic records of Victorianism. In the year of the old Queen's second Jubilee a parish meeting was called, with the Rector in the chair and all Campden attending, to decide what most suitable memorial of the event should be added to its beauties. The Rector, after making a few pious suggestions, invited general discussion. Then up rose a local farmer, and spoke these words, "Well, Mr. Chairman, we all know as how Her Gracious Majesty has been very useful to this country for many years; so what we should want to be putting up to her memory is something that will go on being useful to us here. Now what we in Campden most wants, *I* say, is a public urinal——"

There his speech ended, drowned in shouts of laughter; and when order was restored, the Rector tactfully remarked, "I think we will pass on to the *next* suggestion." And so eventually, some other less useful, and far less original memorial was proposed and adopted. And though that first proposition, put forward nearly forty years ago, then got such good publicity and was in itself so honestly self-serving and sensible, the need, I am told, still remains; and the proposal not having been revived in the recent year of Jubilee, Campden still lacks its memorial in that particular form to the usefulness of Constitutional Monarchy.

Of the three Jubilees that I remember, the first—that of 1887— remains the most vivid to my recollection. It was less ceremonious- ly staged than the one that came after; and I saw the Queen really enjoying herself, laughing and crying with happiness, and holding over her head a very long-handled parasol—so designed that it should not hide her face from the raised spectators in the stands and windows lining the route. And it was then, at Hyde Park Corner, that I saw the incident take place, which by dramatic license in *Victoria Regina* I transferred to the latter occasion: a mob of rough working men running alongside the carriage, on its return from Westminster, and shouting with the full strength of their lungs, "Go it, Old Girl! You done it well! You done it well!"

It was a happy scene to remember, coming at a happy moment in that memorable day, for the long ordeal, to which the Queen had looked forward with considerable anxiety, was then almost over. Everything had gone superlatively well; the crowd waiting for the return journey was more lively and demonstrative than the earlier one; and the Queen, letting herself go, was responding to the "Old Girl" greeting with jolly nods and laughter that had in them nothing of ceremony or stateliness, and yet for nice fitness to the occasion could not possibly be bettered. And when my memory warms to that funny scene of fifty years ago, I know that I am still "a Victorian," and do not wish to be other.

The last time I saw her was during the Boer War, driving past the Albert Memorial, bowing very perfunctorily, with a rather dull cross look upon her face. Even the Memorial as she passed it did not seem to interest her. If, as the papers said, she had come out "to show herself to her people" in a time of adversity, she seemed rather to have come to impersonate the prevailing depression than to give encouragement. A year later I saw a much more eloquent expression of the hold she had upon the hearts of her people, when in the February of 1901 on my way northward to see the funeral procession I passed a silent crowd lining the railings of Battersea Park watching for a train to come; and as it came along the raised track, making for Victoria, hats were raised and a sigh went through that crowd of poor working people, a real expression of reverence and of bereavement, which I found much more moving than the more voluble and excited attention of the vast crowds lining the way to Paddington. There stands and seats were being bartered for, and boys shouting from the boughs of trees, "Here she comes!" And she came to the sound of Chopin's *Funeral March* played far too quickly, in order to allow the ground to be covered in a given time; and old Lord Roberts, a popular figure in the procession, kept raising his hand to check the unseemly bubble of cheers which now and then greeted him from those who had come merely as sightseers.

Nine years later I encountered a more curious and individual expression of respect for the death of kings. On the night of May 6, 1910, I was supping late at a London restaurant with some friends, whom I had taken to see the revival of *Prunella* at the Duke of York's Theatre, when a waiter came and informed us in hushed tones that King Edward was dead. Immediately after, the lights of the restaurant were turned down to a glim, and a bill was presented to us for our curtailed meal. We were still hungry, but it was evidently considered unseemly that after hearing the news we should have any appetites left.

That same night the London theatres died also; hardly a play survived to make a profit for the producer and provide wages for the actors. *Prunella* had been running merrily and well, but even when the two weeks of ceremonial mourning were over, life had gone from the theatre, and it was not till autumn that prosperity returned to it. The blow to the profession and its commercial accompaniments was so serious that on all subsequent occasions of a similar character a request has come from high quarters that ruth for kings and their relations shall not entail ruin to the theatrical profession or to other forms of public entertainment.

That particular excess of ceremonial observance was, indeed, only an exceptional survival. Mourning in general and the mourning of widows in particular, was no longer then what it used to be—not outwardly at any rate. The "Widow at Windsor" had set a fashion which was sedulously followed by all women (all "ladies" at least) of respectable character; during her reign it was quite usual for widows' weeds to continue to the day of their death; and in my own family one widow remarked, when she was well over seventy years of age, that she found it "such a protection"; from what I did not venture to inquire.

The incognito of kings sometimes takes curious forms. Of this I had an amusing example one Sunday afternoon, when calling on Alice Meynell. The maid came and announced that "Mr. Smith" was waiting at the door. "Oh, yes, ask him to come in," said Mrs. Meynell; and there entered presently a tall comely gentleman of distinguished manner and appearance. Not until he left did I know that "Mr. Smith" claimed to be anything more than he seemed; then the matter was explained. Mr. Smith was by legitimate descent King of Great Britain and Ireland. "I don't think he is quite sane," said Mrs. Meynell; "not because of his claim, which as regards descent, may very possibly be true; but because he expects everybody to know it, and believe it, and behave accordingly. When he sent word that he was at the door, it was to give me the opportunity of doing the proper thing, and going out to receive him; and had we all waited for his permission to sit down he would graciously have given it." But why, in that case, I asked, did he call himself "Mr. Smith"? Because he preferred, while waiting for his full rank and title to be recognised, to go about under the most self-effacing and impersonal incognito that he could devise. Until restored to the throne of his Stuart ancestors he would make no halfway claim. I only met him that one time; but he cultivated the royal memory; and at Christmas I received from him the large historical card which Royalty is accustomed to send out at that season to those whom it wishes to honour. On the envelope was a subtle indication of his claim: the stamp, with the rival king's head on it, was not put on upside down—that would have been rude and uncourteous, but it was put on sideways, recumbent that is to say, *not* regnant.

I think this must have been the same gentleman, who annually, upon the feast of "King Charles, the Martyr" laid a wreath at the foot of the statue in Whitehall; but on that very ceremonial occasion he did not call himself "Mr. Smith," but something much more decorative and dignified.

I do not know what happened to the "White Rose League," when the Great War made the favoured claimant of our English Legitimists—Prince Ruprecht of Bavaria—an enemy of their own country. To continue supporting his claim to the throne under those circumstances, would, I imagine, have been treasonable— anyway it would have been foolish. But some forty years ago the White Rose League was in high feather, and very full of itself; and when, in the last decade of the nineteenth century, the Stuart Exhibition was being held in London, and the then Prince of Wales, with his son Prince Albert Victor, went to visit it, the secretary of the League found great joy and satisfaction in exhibiting to those two descendants from the female line the pedigree of the House of Hanover, side by side with the much more simple and direct pedigree of the House of Bavaria; and in hearing Prince Albert Victor exclaim in astonishment, "Oh, Father, I see *we* are not direct!" Whereat his father replied, "Yes, we are direct; but not so direct. Come on!"

That word "direct" is, of course, only a technical expression of the claim for succession through the male to rank higher than succession through the female. I had the pleasure one day of pointing that out to a Suffragist friend, who was an ardent feminist, and yet a member of the White Rose League; and I asked her whether it was not a little ridiculous that she should be supporting a "legitimist" descent against one which after all had its origin in female primogeniture. I saw her whiten at the gibe, but she said nothing. A few days later she wrote to tell me that at the time she had been too angry to say anything; but having since looked up the genealogy of the House of Hanover and found that what I said was correct she had resigned her membership in the White Rose League.

Ancient institutions and their encumbering relics seldom move me. I am less susceptible to their psychic influence than I am to haunted houses. I do not believe in ghosts—at least, I try not to—but I do believe in telepathy; and in a telepathic sense I believe that places can be haunted.

I was once put to sleep in a room which I hated to enter in the dark; and when I got into bed (though I was no longer a child) I used to put my head under the bedclothes till sleep got hold of me. In that same bedroom, I heard later that a friend used to burn candle-ends to go to sleep by, because he too could not face its darkness. Neither of us knew then that in that room a woman had committed suicide, and that in the neighbourhood the house was reputed to be haunted.

In another room which made me slightly uncomfortable, I used to find relief by getting up and opening the window and putting my head out; and directly my head was outside I no longer felt haunted. But one night I had a strange experience: I woke, and in the wash basin close by I heard a washing of hands going on; yet in the dim light I could see that no one was there.

The most foolish and ineffective thing to do when faced by a portent of this kind, is to lie paralyzed by fear, and next morning tell a sincere ghost story hoping to have it believed. Not adopting that course, I struck a light and investigated; and there in the basin, paddling around for dear life, was a mouse; and so—enter mouse, exit ghost.

But my best ghost of all came to me in Italy, under circumstances which did for a short time undermine my disbelief in voices coming from the dead.

I do not know Italian; we are not on speaking terms. Yet when, at the dead of night, a ghost spoke to me in Italian, I understood him well enough to switch on the light and make a leap for the dear life which is still mine, only to find that the ghost, though audible, was invisible.

I had gone to Italy, and—in Italy—to Assisi, with a friend who spoke Italian well. For which reason my ignorance of the language gave me no trouble; it was all done for me. This for preliminary: now for the case itself. And to make that case as foursquare and as watertight as I possibly can for any who are ready to accept the truth of my narrative, let me set forth all the circumstances, mental and physical, which gave me ground for believing my experience to be genuine.

As I have already said, I do not believe in ghosts; I am not the victim of hallucinations; I was not drunk. I was in my room alone; I had locked the door, the windows were closed to keep out mosquitoes, the walls of the room were not of papier-mâché, but of stone. There was no communicating door; no sounds ever came to me from the adjoining rooms, either above or below or alongside. But I had omitted—I make this admission—to look for thieves or murderers either under the bed or in the clothes cupboard.

At two o'clock in the morning I awoke, feeling hot. I took off the counterpane and composed myself again for slumber. I was drifting off into unconsciousness when a voice said in my ear, in what seemed to me an urgent and threatening tone, *"Non parlati!"*

Believing in the possibility of burglars, but not of ghosts, I cried foolishly in English, "Get out!" switched on the light, and sprang out of bed.

Nobody was there. I made swift investigation: door still locked, windows still closed, cupboard empty, floor under bed dusty, but bare.

It was not a dream. I had heard the words said; they had come to my ear from outside, and had struck my drowsing senses awake.

"Non parlati!" meant, I imagined, "Don't speak!" It seemed a reasonable and a likely thing for a thief to say. And a thief I took the thing to be, till I had found it, in the material sense, non-existent. I was then face to face with a new fact—that a voice, apparently without a body, had spoken in my ear and had said, *"Non parlati!"*—"Don't speak!" How was I to fit in with that my previous disbelief in ghosts?

It was an unnerving experience; and my only way of accounting for it was that by telepathy I had come into contact with something which had previously happened in that room and in that bed—assault, theft, or murder—and that the telepathic influence was so strong on me as to give the voice that external quality which had startled me into action.

A shaken sceptic suffers from a sense of moral downfall. I got back into bed and passed rather a miserable night. In the morning I went and asked my friend the meaning of *"Non parlati."* She told me, and I told her why I had asked.

She, an ardent believer in ghosts, was spitefully pleased that the thing should have happened. "Now," she said, "perhaps you will believe in them!"

I almost did; or in something so like, that "ghostly" if not "ghost" was the word for it; and I remained sufficiently impressed to sleep badly and wake nervously for the rest of my stay. I would have liked even to have changed my room; but the fear of seeming ridiculous to myself kept me from doing it.

When we left the hotel a week later the mystery was still unexplained: though I had not seen a ghost I had heard one.

Readers who believe in ghosts had better stop here, for within two hours of our leaving the hotel the ghost had been explained away.

We had taken food with us; and alone in our railway carriage, having eaten, we composed ourselves for an afternoon nap. I had not, I thought, really gone to sleep when something disturbed me. I roused up and opened my eyes. My friend smiled at me. "What were you dreaming about?" she inquired.

"Nothing that I know of," I replied. "I wasn't asleep."

"Indeed you were," I was told. "You were not only asleep; you were talking in your sleep, and you talked Italian—or what you supposed to be Italian. You said, '*Non parlati Italiano!*' "

As I heard those words light shone on me from Heaven. Unbelief was restored to me. "Oh, thank you very much!" I said. "Now you have explained my ghost."

Is there any reader who needs further explanation? In a forgotten dream I had tried to talk Italian; tried so hard that I actually had talked it—incorrectly, no doubt—and my own voice, sounding like another's threatening and urgent, had waked me! And had I not started to nap in the railway carriage, and done much the same thing again, I might have remained robbed of my comfortable scepticism and become a believer in ghosts.

And I wonder how many people are believers merely because they have not had my luck of lighting on the real explanation—so far-fetched and improbable that, but for proof-positive, it could not be believed?

A few years later I woke to hear what sounded like a clanking of chains. I took the trouble of getting up and investigating; I opened my window, finding that the sound came from outside. You would not think a sheep suffering from bronchial asthma could make a sound even remotely like the clanking of chains. But it did; and as long as I did not know the cause it sounded like chains; but when I did know the cause the resemblance ceased, and it sounded like what it was—a sheep coughing.

CHAPTER XVIII

TRIALS OF A PLAYWRIGHT

Prunella was produced in the winter of 1904-05, with *Peter Pan* as its contemporary; for which reason Nina Boucicault, who would have been ideal for the name-part, was making her reputation elsewhere. Both monetarily and with the critics the play failed. "Quaint, but feeble," I heard a lady say, as I came away from the first performance. The press damned it with faint praise; the general line taken by the critics was that the authors were ambitiously trying to produce a new *genre* which was scarcely worth while; Granville Barker and I were put severely in our places—in our anxiety to be original, we had merely been fantastic; most of the compliments went to Moorat's music.

The one exception was a flaming and enthusiastic notice in the *St. James' Gazette*. Of that I heard the explanation later from Miss Netta Syrett. She had written it. The critic of the *St. James' Gazette* had given her his second ticket. At the end of the middle act he said to her in gloomy despair, "Whatever *am* I to say about this play?" "Say——" replied Miss Syrett: high flights followed. He stared at her amazed. "Do you really think so?" She did. "Then I wish you would write the notice for me." It was a face-saving request. The Barker-Vedrenne Management had already exacted respect, but had not quite inspired conviction. Netta Syrett's critique took the place of the genuine conviction of the *St. James' Gazette* critic that the play was rot.

But one swallow in the press does not make a summer for theatrical management; the play trickled through three weeks, and retired on a heavy deficit. Subsequent revivals were symptomatic. In 1906 it paid its way and the critics became respectful. In 1907 it made a profit, and the critics were complimentary. In 1910, with the hearty assistance of the press, it was bringing its authors affluence when the death of King Edward brought the theatrical season to an untimely end. In 1916 it ran for a hundred nights in New York, and was put on the films.

In the planning, though not the composing of the music for *Prunella,* Granville Barker had a considerable share; the work was done against time and was accomplished not without difficulty. For another opera (if it so might be called) stood in its way, and it was still Moorat's hope to substitute *Japonel* for this later and much inferior article which was now being thrust on him.

Barker had gone down to Moorat's place at Campden, to coach him in the task of fitting his music to dramatic moments which would not brook delay (that also a difficulty) ; and every morning, in the undying hope of securing the substitution for which his soul yearned, Moorat rose fresh to the charge, and the first quarter of an hour had to be spent in luring him back from the ideal to the practical. Then real work began. Barker knew exactly how much music was wanted to accompany words and action at certain points of the play, and how much music could be allowed for atmosphere, without action, at other points. Moorat's tendency, on the other hand, was to believe that, given a worthy motif, stage and audience could be held entranced for as long as invention lasted; and when, in place of the thirty bars he desired, Barker could only allow five, the difference took some time to settle. It was wonderful that from that bed of Procrustes so much pleasantly proportioned harmony was able to emerge.

For eight hours a day they sat and hatched music together. I only came in to approve when the day's work was over, but sometimes, finding them still at a loose end, I was allowed to hear how certain portions, under repeated hammerings, "rose slowly to a music slowly breathed, a cloud that gathered shape." Barker would say, "Now, Moorat, I want a theme for the Moon;" and Moorat's fingers would stray tentatively for a while over the black notes of the piano (for he composed always, to begin with, on the scale of B sharp), and presently something like moonlight trickled out of

them, and the moon motif was jotted down. He had more difficulty when called on to bring Love's statue to life. Perhaps, had
we thought of it, a dramatic reading of Paulina's invocation to the
statue in *Winter's Tale* might have helped:

> "Music, awake her: strike,
> 'Tis time; descend: be stone no more: approach:
> Strike all that look upon with marvel. Come!"

But we didn't; and Barker's prose promptings had to do duty for
poetry which might have brought quicker inspiration. We watched
while Moorat meditated. After an indefinite stammering of notes,
something emerged—a soft chromatic run, and a low jump of re-
solving chords—charming, soothing, but not what the dramatic
situation required. But Moorat, for the moment seemed satisfied,
and he turned and gazed expectantly at Barker, waiting for him to
approve. No, it didn't do. "My dear Moorat," expostulated
Barker, "have you for a moment imagined what it would feel like
if you yourself were miraculously changed from stone into living
bread? Try again!" Moorat tried again. "Better; but remember
this is *Love* coming to life—not just anybody." And at last a theme
was discovered, majestic and moving enough to satisfy them both.

But even when the skeleton of the music had thus been planned
and laid out to the last bone, Moorat still pined for *Japonel* to
take its place; and after Barker had returned to London with the
promise that in three weeks the music should be ready and complete, a final but unavailing plea followed him. "Have you asked
Vedrenne whether he will not first consider *Japonel?*"

I doubt whether Vedrenne ever heard *Japonel* mentioned, not
unless Moorat approached him on his own account. But the ghost
of *Japonel* haunted me for years, and was laid only with difficulty.

While Moorat was composing the music of *Prunella* there was
in the house a small child, his daughter Cecily, then aged four;
and in her nursery she could hear the tunes as he composed them.
And I have seen her come into his music room, and there, standing at the piano, and looking not at the keys, but at us, pick out on

the black notes (her father's pet scale) and with perfect correctness, the tunes she had just been hearing. It is pleasant to be able to record that, with a good deal of her father's gift for melody, and with much more technical training, she is now a Bachelor of Music and well established in her profession.

It was shortly after the failure of *Prunella* in 1904, that I made the biggest mistake in my life by entering into a contract which promised commercial prosperity. Granville Barker wrote to me that he had been approached for a collaboration between Madame Liza Lehmann and ourselves for a light opera, based on the *Vicar of Wakefield*. "We ought to do it," he said, "as a demonstration of how light opera should be written."

Madame Lehmann, with her gentle voice, her distinguished presence, and her pronounced profile, attracted me; so also did the story of her domestic afflictions, which had left her for the time as the sole supporter of her family. Terms were arranged, and Barker and I set to work. But before long musical and dramatic exigencies clashed; Madame Lehmann's music required an outdoor setting for its climax in the second act; Barker's dramatic sense required an indoor; Madame insisted, and Barker retired from the collaboration, but remained friendly and helpful. With generous care he shepherded me to the completion of my task, commended it at the finish, and then said grimly, "Now see them spoil it!"

His prophecy came true. But for a time all went swimmingly; so long as Madame Lehmann and I worked alone together, with Barker advising us, things were as harmonious as one could wish. I wrote and rewrote songs till they suited her music; whenever she wanted song or chorus, if it could be wrought into the action of the scene, I devised a place for it. She wrote me letters of profuse gratitude; and when the play was finished assured me that she was more than satisfied.

Then David Bispham, her main hope for getting the play produced, arrived from America. My heart sank at the sight of him. His personality did not suit the part proposed for him to play; however fine his voice, I saw at once that the Vicar's gently whimsical character was outside his range. The event proved that it was also outside his perception. Having accepted the play he started rehearsing, and behind my back appropriated dialogue and repartee from the sarcastic Burchell to himself. All the effective bits were to be his. Here was the star actor and singer requiring every available moment of limelight to be turned on himself. A lot more songs, which had nothing to do with the plot, were suddenly required; songs already written were found unsuitable—one especially. On the authority of Goldsmith, I had written a song for the Vicar in praise of monogamy. Monogamy was not Bispham's strong point. He hummed and hawed, didn't like the song, but wouldn't say why; finally he confided to Madame Lehmann that, for domestic reasons, he could not possibly sing it. So it was ruled out, and another had to take its place.

This was the beginning of the end, for naturally I was annoyed. Presently I found, that, without consulting me, he and Madame Lehmann had started cutting the play to make room for more and more musical numbers, the words of which were not mine. She, too, had caught the infection. It was no longer a light opera that they required, it was a song sequence with a thread of story running through it. Against this combination of Composer and Star the mere writer of the libretto was at a disadvantage unless he chose to be ruthless. Had I put down my foot and asserted my legal rights, Bispham might have refused production; and as Madame Lehmann (who was carrying on with great courage under very difficult circumstances) had herself brought me the commission for her opera, I did not feel able to make a firm stand. So, protesting against further change, and saying that I had now fulfilled my part of the contract, I withdrew from upsetting discussions, hoping, I suppose, that without my collaboration, they would not be able to make any further changes of importance.

Before long I heard that things were not going well; as it was their own fault I offered no assistance. But when at Madame Lehmann's request, I went to a rehearsal shortly before production, ye gods! what did I find had been done? Burchell's part had become almost nonexistent. Bispham had suppressed two of his

songs and stolen all his best dialogue. Imagine the foolishness
of attempting to combine two such different characters into one.
Nor was this all. Forced entries and exits had been devised for the
introduction of new songs, and I heard that Isabel Jay, the com-
panion-star of the production, had refused to sing, "When lovely
woman stoops to folly," unless all the characters walked out leaving the stage to her, only to come in again when the song, and the
applause, and the expected encore were over.

The whole thing had become dramatically empty and silly.
Granville Barker joined me at the dress rehearsal to see the butch-
ery of the piece which we had spent so much time to make respectable. He dragged me out, in one of the intervals, to a restaurant. "When I'm angry," he said, "I have to eat." He munched
sandwiches. "This will do you harm," he said. "What are you
going to do about it?"

"What can I do?" I asked. (The play was going into the prov-
inces for a two months' trial.)

"Tell them they must put it back into a decent shape before it returns to London, or you will withdraw your name." And that is
what I did.

Negotiations began. Bispham and Madame Lehmann made
stipulations for the retention of certain numbers, to which I agreed
on condition that I was allowed to give them a dramatic *raison
d'être*. I also demanded that the other characters should not, without rhyme or reason, be driven off the stage for a star singer to
occupy it alone.

That eventually put all the fat in the fire; for Isabel Jay was
the prospective wife of Mr. Curzon, the lessee of the theatre where
the play was to make its London appearance. But, at the time, on
the eve of the provincial production, a sort of agreement was
reached. I presented my reconstruction of the play, which was accepted by Bispham, and while on tour the company rehearsed it.
But at our final meeting, on their return to London, explosion took
place.

Madame Lehmann had written a very charming setting of "It
was a lover and his lass," for Dick Primrose to sing in the last act

on the Vicar's return. But his way of introducing it had been something as follows: "Oh, Papa, I've learned such a pretty song while you were away. May I sing it?" This I had ruled out, and had devised instead a small Father Christmas scene, the child stealing away, and returning appropriately clad, and singing the song as part of a small performance domestically planned for the Vicar's home-coming.

For some reason or another, Madame Lehmann rejected my compromise. "It is *my* opera," she said, "and I will have it as I choose." Whereat I gathered up my revised version, and retired from the conference.

The next day I again put it into Bispham's hands, that he might take it or leave it, knowing the consequences. It was not taken, and twenty-four hours before the production of the play, I ordered my name to be withdrawn from all playbills, posters, and advertisements. I also sent notice to Messrs. Boosey, the publishers of the libretto, objecting to the inclusion of unauthorized songs in the publication of the words, for which I had a signed agreement. On this point my legal right was so clear that Messrs. Boosey dared not allow the book of the words to be sold at the opening performance. This so enraged Mr. Curzon that, soon after I had entered the box which the management had sent me, he came and ordered me out of the theatre, threatening me with personal violence if I had not gone before the end of Act I. It was unfortunate, I think, that I had, on the advice of my lawyer, gone to see the performance at all. It would have been better for me to stay away. I had two friends with me. "We can't risk a brawl," I said. "Curzon may be outside, waiting to misbehave himself. Come and see me out."

They saw me safely to the street. Mr. Curzon followed us tempestuously to the door, and shouted after me that I was never to enter his theatre again; at which I laughed.

The next day Mr. Curzon got himself interviewed by the press, and I found that my laugh had been transferred from the street entrance to the box which I had quietly quitted during the first act. I was accused of having stood up and booed at the actors while

Photo. by Vandamm Studio

Miss Hayes as Victoria in Mr. Housman's play. (The queen has just
received a visit from Disraeli at Balmoral.)

the play was proceeding. I was so guileless that, though it was a lie, I did not know that it was also (in the legal sense) a libel; and my lawyer, not having heard from me, thought that the charge must be true. But the only thing about it which then troubled me was that, at the moment when I had got up to go, Miss Edith Clegg, with whom I was on perfectly friendly terms, was singing her first song which I had written for her, and I could not allow her to suppose, on lying information, that I had done anything discourteous. I wrote to her at once and received from her a very kind reply telling me that, of course, she knew I had done nothing of the sort.

Madame Lehmann, who sat in the opposite box, must have known it equally well, and yet, years afterwards, I found—but only after her death—that in her reminiscences she had given guarded countenance to the story, without however asserting it to be true. But very shortly after the event I received from a member of her own family a testimonial to my good behaviour which touched me greatly. I was at a social gathering; the room was pretty full, and I had not noticed that Mrs. Barry Pain (née Lehmann) was among the guests. All at once I saw her coming toward me. She smiled, shook hands warmly, and went back to her seat. It was beautifully and graciously done. I knew what she meant, for she had been present at that first performance, and knew that the charge which had been made against me was baseless. I still think of that generous silent gesture with lively gratitude.

The opera had stumbled on its foolish way less than a month, when Bispham and Curzon came to loggerheads, and the unholy alliance was over. Then, somewhat belatedly, I received a letter from my agent saying that Bispham wished me to know that he had never given any credence to Mr. Curzon's lying tale, and would I be prepared to negotiate with him for the American rights? I replied that I certainly would if the play was restored to its proper version. After that I heard no more of the matter, or of Bispham till in 1916 I went to America, and there at a dinner given in honour of Masefield, Alfred Noyes, and myself, Bispham came running towards me with outstretched hand. I took it and said, "I suppose this means that the hatchet is to be buried?"

"Never mention it!" cried Bispham rapturously. This seemed very satisfactory, but when, a few days later, he found that I was still adamant over the restoration of the play to its right form, he got himself interviewed in the press, and once more trotted out the old Curzon story—quite forgetting, I suppose, that I had received his written assurance that he had "never given it any credence."

I can see now that Bispham and Madame Lehmann had some grounds for annoyance. I was not the kind of collaborator they wanted; our standards were different and incompatible; and when Madame Lehmann, in a last effort to bring me to heel over Bispham's foolish demands, cried out impatiently, "Do try for once to have the dramatic sense! Your *Prunella* is very charming, but it will never be popular," I answered with more truth than tact, "Madame Lehmann, my *Prunella* will be still playing when your *Vicar of Wakefield* is forgotten." It was an easy prophecy to make, but it did not conduce to friendly relations.

I only met her once again. It was on the platform of the Actresses' Women Suffrage Society, where I was booked to speak. She was hostess for the occasion; we met with frigid politeness, and sat side by side. It was the day when my sister was released from prison for her tax-resistance, but no one then knew of it. A telegram had reached me just before I started for the meeting, saying, "Am released." Telling nobody the news I made my speech. My sister being just then the only prisoner for "the cause," I as her brother was warmly welcomed, and listened to. I told the story, which I shall tell at more length later, of how the government had tried for more than eighteen months to extract from her the four shillings and sixpence of its claim for Inhabited House duty, and how eventually, with legal costs mounting into pounds, they had sent emissaries a week before and taken her to Holloway in a taxi, which, as it entered the prison gates, registered the exact sum of four shillings and sixpence—a fare which not she but the government had to pay.

"And there," I said, "she was supposed to stay, till the four and sixpence, plus costs, was paid. And today at one o'clock she was let out again." I made as if to finish my sentence, but was unable. My audience gave a gasp of astonishment, and then broke into rounds of applause. I waited till they were quiet again, then added, "And the four and sixpence is still not paid, and never will be." At this there was still more applause and laughter, and turning to Madame Lehmann, I whispered, "Who says I haven't got the dramatic sense now?" She gave me a smile of pained sweetness, but said nothing. I left before the meeting was over, to go and meet my liberated sister, and thus saved Madame and myself from the embarrassment of further conversation.

I should not have given this unfortunate episode in my playwriting experience at such length, had not Curzon's lie been given further life by those who should have known better. I do not choose to leave that story, which might hereafter be quoted to my discredit, any possible leg to stand on.

But while these uncomfortable things were going on, a small incident happened which may, for those who cherish the superstitions of the stage, account fully for the mess in which I finally landed myself.

It was after one of those stormy interviews I have recorded, and on a stormy night, that, having returned home late, I heard a pitiful wail at my door, and going to open it I found a small black cat, very miserable and drenched, asking admittance. I welcomed her with effusion, for I was well aware that in matters theatrical black cats are reckoned to be harbingers of good fortune. And so, taking her up in my arms, I carried an honoured but scratching guest down to the kitchen, dried her, warmed her, and set food and drink before her. She was not gracious in her manners, she alternately fed, and spat at me, and though I gave her a roof for the night, next morning she showed no intention of becoming friends. I was patient, recognising that homelessness and exposure to the weather had probably upset her nerves; anyway, accepting her as a mascot to see me through my theatrical afflictions, I offered all the comfort my house could afford, and let her stay. But presently I found her to be devoid of all domestic decency; she went from room to room and fouled it; and when, for the transgression, I chastised her—as I would any cat of my own—first mildly, and then on repeated offence, more severely—she quitted my roof with cries of rage, and climbing to the top of a laburnum, there sat and hurled down curses on one whose sense of hospitality she had found so defective. An hour later she had gone for good; but her curse stayed, and the moral of that incident is, I suppose, that if those in theatrical tribulation show charity to black cats it must be charity which "endureth all things." Of that standard my charity fell short, and as a consequence I paid the penalty.

CHAPTER XIX

MORE PLAYS—AND THE CENSOR

IT WAS a relief, after that wretched "battle of Wakefield," to get back into the hands of the Barker-Vedrenne management. When the move from the Court Theatre to the Haymarket was decided in 1908, I was commissioned to write a new play—this time by myself, but with Barker still coaching me; and *The Chinese Lantern,* (Moorat again providing the incidental music) was the result.

Barker was a wonderful coach; he knew exactly when to bully me, and when to let me alone. It had been so all through our collaboration over *Prunella.* And when I set to work on *The Chinese Lantern,* I knew that it was mainly through Barker that I was getting to know the ropes, having started too late in life to have the instinctive sense of dramatic technique, which comes early to the born playwright. Fifteen years of literary composition is a hindrance, not a help to the writing of stage dialogue. Your story-writer relies too much on the printed word, and leaves too little to the actor. Again and again Barker's cuts to my over-valuation of words left me amazed; but they also taught me; and when quite recently I sent him my last book of plays, and received in return his assurance that I had now learned my job, I was happy in being so commended by one who had never let me off lightly—or himself either.

But *The Chinese Lantern* was, in its send-off, even less of a success than *Prunella;* the actors liked it, but the critics didn't, and before a sufficient public heard about it from those who did, it died from inattention at the box office. Though a certain famous playwright said it had the same future waiting for it as *Prunella* when people got to know about it, that future has never come, and

203

except among amateurs, here and in America, it is a forgotten play.

Over the casting I had several good bits of luck, and one big disappointment. It helps greatly in the shaping of a stage character to have in mind one's ideal actor for the part. And while writing *The Chinese Lantern,* I had from the very beginning chosen O. B. Clarence for one of the principle characters; and, to my great satisfaction, I got him. But over my heroine I had less luck. I had then, and I have still, a great admiration for Sydney Fairbrother, an actress whose fine emotional powers have never been sufficiently recognised, or indeed given their chance. I believed that in the part of "Mee-mee" she would make a big success not only for herself but for the play. But alas, not Barker but Vedrenne put his veto on my choice; he did not think her young enough, or charming enough. He wanted, he said, "somebody whom all the men in the stalls would fall in love with." In the end a most difficult part was given to a very young actress, not without charm, but without sufficient experience. When Sydney Fairbrother heard of what I had wished, she said (her mother who was in the cast told me) that she would have gladly given five years of her life to do it. I can almost say that I would have paid the same price to get her, when I think of the interpretation she might have given to what I think to be my most original stage character.

The cast had in it several fine actors—Henry Ainley, Lyall Sweete, James Hearne, Michael Sherbrooke, and O. B. Clarence—and others who became so afterwards, but had not then reached their form. One of these was O. P. Heggie; it was his first London engagement. Ten years later I met him again in America where he had become something of a star, and found that he very much wished to get the play revived over there, with himself as the hero. At the Haymarket he had only had the small part of a Chinese art student. "And how bad I was in it!" he owned.

"Yes," I said, "so bad that I asked Barker to get rid of you; but he said you were a good actor, and time has proved him right."

Time had, and without long waiting; for I would say here, that it was his beautiful interpretation of "Androcles," in Shaw's play not long afterwards, which gave me my first incentive to writing

the *Little Plays of St. Francis.* When we met in America, I
had done only three or four of them; but I told him that I had
written them with him in mind, and they were waiting for him.
They are waiting still. I have since been blessed with an ideal
"Juniper," but the ideal Francis (though several have given me
satisfaction) has not yet arrived.

In my experience, the production of plays can provide an author
with livelier satisfaction than the writing of books. It is pleasant
to be told that one's books are appreciated; but it is not merely
pleasant, it is thrilling, to see one's play, or its characters, brought
to life by good production or good acting. I have had that great
happiness even over plays which have not been a success. The
three first "Pierrots" in *Prunella*—Granville Barker, Graham
Browne, and Charles Maude, all gave in that part what many of
their friends considered their finest performances. I thought Barker's was the best, but it was the least popular; it had too much
"bite" in it—the audience preferred a Pierrot whom they could
like—and forgive—more easily. Other performances, which have
brought joy to the author, I shall speak of later. As regards production I do, in one case, owe a very special debt to the producer.
About ten years ago Mr. Nugent Monck put on *The Chinese
Lantern* at the Maddermarket Theatre, Norwich, and at the very
finish he sprang on me a stage effect of darkness and long rolling
thunder (indicative of the wrath of Heaven over the foolishness
of man) which added a hundred per cent to the dramatic value of
the last curtain. I had not thought of it, but I took it over with
gratitude, and added it as a stage direction in subsequent editions
of the play; and my advice to all future producers (if any such there
be) is to make the most they can of that last long roll of thunder,
on which, invisible to the eye, the magic picture goes charioting
away through space, leaving behind it a spellbound crowd, too
frightened to move or speak—and then, curtain.

It is a curious and a pleasant fact, that my failures have so often
brought me fresh commissions. Though *Prunella* had not yet become popular, it secured for me the commission for *The Chinese
Lantern,* and when that had, for the time at all events, proved

itself a dead failure, there came from Miss Gertrude Kingston the request that I would write her a play for her management of the "Little Theatre."

I offered her *Pains and Penalties,* an historical play of four acts, and with Gertrude Kingston as Queen Caroline the theatre was to open. But on this project, even before rehearsals began, trouble fell from a fresh quarter. This time it was not the tyranny of a foolish manager but a foolish Censor which took all the market value out of the six months' hard labour I had put into it.

The play dealt with certain events in English history which had taken place ninety years before, and incidentally with the marital relations of King George IV and his wife Queen Caroline. The license was refused without, at first, any explanation, or any indication of offending passages, the removal of which would make public performance allowable. The Lord Chamberlain's office has a wily way of trying to persuade managers to withdraw their application for a license, so that the office may be relieved of the odium of performing for a fixed fee what presumably is its duty. That game was tried on my play; Miss Kingston very properly refused to provide the required camouflage; the fee was paid, and the play was refused a license.

It then became my task to extract a reason for the refusal, and to find out whether the cutting-out of anything that seemed undesirable to the official mind would save my dramatic property from ruin. It took me some time, and for several weeks I was given no reason that could be made public; letters marked "private" were no satisfaction of my claim that the refusal of a license for a public performance should be publicly explained.

Yet before a word of the play was printed, defenders of censorship supported the Lord Chamberlain's decision with blind zeal, and industriously set themselves to assert that their beloved defender of the dramatic proprieties must be right. The author had dared to pass unfavourable comment on the character of King George IV, and hostile reference upon the stage to the great-granduncle of our then present sovereign was declared incompatible with respect for the institution of monarchy.

But at last the Lord Chamberlain was persuaded to give his reason publicly—perhaps it would be more correct to say "his public
reason," and then, hey presto! the defence of our monarchy, in the
person of so bad a representative as this happily-distant relative of
our present king, was sent to the limbo of untenable foolishnesses
and a brand-new reason was fitted out for public consumption. The
Lord Chamberlain, it then appeared, had refused to license my
play, not for the supposed reasons at all—on those I had been
"misinformed"—but because it dealt with a "sad historical episode
of comparatively recent date in the life of an unhappy lady!" The
"unhappy lady," as I at once pointed out, had been dead for ninety
years, and during the whole of that period her memory had rested
under a cloud which it was the main purpose of my play to remove.
Driven to give a public reason for his action, the Lord Chamberlain decided that such an attempt to rehabilitate her character was
not to be allowed.

Those who defend a bad cause have to defend it blindly, otherwise its life would be short. Driven from one false argument to
another, they still find sufficiency in the last that is left to them. It
is the thing, not the reasonableness of the thing, that they are defending. The pro-Censor press had declared that I was "guilty
of trifling" when I asked for a public statement as to why my play
was banned. It also accused me of "not playing the game," because I had refused to submit without protest to an unexplained
veto; but my trifling had at last brought me an explanation
which, in its sublime fatuity, did satisfy me abundantly. The
tussle had been worth while, and ten years later, though it did not
recompense me for damage done, the Lord Chamberlain's Office
(having a better head to it) gave me judgment on appeal.

But the immediate situation created by the censoring of my play
was very serious. Miss Kingston had no other play ready to hand,
and the Little Theatre was waiting to be opened. She asked me if
I would do a free (but not too "free") translation of Aristophanes'
Lysistrata.

I jumped at the opportunity. The Woman Suffrage agitation
was then in full blast, and here was a play of feminist propaganda

which offered lurid possibilities. Even if this also was censored (as well it might be) it would still be good material for publication as an aid to the women's cause.

I finished my paraphrase (one could hardly call it a translation) in three weeks; Miss Kingston accepted it, and, after its production, *The Women's Press* published it. It was so discreetly *worded* that the Censor passed it; but had we chosen, we could still have made it such a hair-raising performance that the cry of "Where is the Censor?" would have resounded throughout the press.

I own that I wish we had—or that we had gone nearer to it; but Miss Kingston decided that *épater les bourgeois* was not good policy for a newly opened theatre; and though great expectations were raised at rehearsal, where certain episodes threatened to become "dangerous" if given free play, in the end prudent counsels prevailed, and Mr. Redford and the Lord Chamberlain were not made to look as ridiculous as they might have been made.

It may be remembered that before inheriting his brother's title, the then Lord Chamberlain had been familiarly known in the House of Commons as "Bobby Spencer," chiefly remarkable for the superlative cut of his clothes, and the magnificence of his collars, and, thus arrayed, had made one famous speech, the opening sentence of which had brought down the House. "I am not," he said, "an agricultural labourer." That famous sentence I had managed to introduce into the play in the chorus of old men discussing the claims of women:

> "No agricultural labourer am I:
> Yet I defy
> Woman to wield a spade as I can," etc.

And when the play came back from the Censor's office with that line undeleted, I wondered whether it had been spared knowingly, or unknowingly, by the person it was intended for, or whether the passing of the play had not this time been left entirely to Mr. Redford.

It was, I think, in the following year that the "Pioneer Players," with Miss Edith Craig as producer, put on a "private" performance at the Savoy of my banned play, *Pains and Penalties*. Gertrude Kingston played the part of Queen Caroline magnificently. Henry Ainley came just once, and rehearsed the part of George IV as to the manner born, and then disappeared, having given us a glimpse of what would, I am sure, have been a superb performance, had not unfortunate circumstances called him away. The first performance came the day after the announcement that Charles Brookfield had been appointed successor to Mr. Redford, as Censor of stage morals; and perhaps it did not help to concentrate interest upon the play that I agreed to let Granville Barker turn one of the intervals into an indignation meeting to denounce an appointment which, in view of the kind of plays Brookfield himself had written, was something of an insult to those playwrights whose banned plays were so much more decent than some of his.

The protest resolution was carried with only two dissentients; it relieved our feelings, but I don't know that it did any good otherwise.

It was not till just after the war that I succeeded in getting the ban removed (the subject matter of the play being then a hundred years old, and so, I suppose, less dangerous than when it was only ninety). I was then helped by the fact, that, under a more enlightened censorship, licenses previously refused had been granted to *The Cenci* and *Mrs. Warren's Profession*. Seizing the occasion, I wrote to the Lord Chamberlain, and suggested that as more sense had now been shown in the matter of these two plays, it should be exercised on mine also. In reply I received a letter from Sir Douglas Dawson, the State Chamberlain, asking me to go and see him. I did so. I found him very polite, and very flattering. He had re-read the play and had found it "very amusing." "I laughed and laughed," he assured me.

"Very nice of you," I said, "but I wrote it as a tragedy." But comedy or tragedy was not the point; what mattered was that the Lord Chamberlain (it was no longer Lord Spencer) authorized him to say that, if I would leave out one word and one sentence, a license would be granted to any manager who applied for it thereafter.

The sentence I was to leave out was this: "Heirs male of the last generation have not been a conspicuous success." The reference was, of course, to the sons of King George III. In the Lord Chamberlain's office there was apparently a fear that it might be applied—more recently. It seemed to me a fantastic notion, but I consented. The *word* I was to leave out was "adultery." It came in a sentence which Queen Caroline had actually spoken. "If I ever did commit adultery, it was when I married the husband of Mrs. Fitz-Herbert." It was a magnificent answer to her tormentors; it put the case in a nutshell, but—it contained the forbidden word.

"But, my dear sir," I protested, "the word 'adultery' is said in church every Sunday in the ears of men, women, and children. What does it matter?"

"Nothing at all," he said. "In church it means nothing, but on the stage it means everything."

There, of course, he was quite right, the stage being so much more alive in meaning what it says than the church. Still it was comic.

"Well," I said, "I can do this. I can make Caroline say, 'If I ever did commit . . .' and then Mr. Brougham can interrupt with an exclamation of horror, representing the mind of the Lord Chamberlain's office up-to-date, so that the word never gets spoken."

But this, I found, did not satisfy him. "No," he said, "I'm afraid that directly you say the word 'commit' everybody will know what the next word is going to be."

And so, that my play might have the possibility of life restored to it, I agreed that the word adultery should be left out, and that the sentence should run: "If ever I did *that thing,* it was when I married the husband of Mrs. Fitz-Herbert." And so, passed in its amended form, the play now has a license waiting for it, to be granted to any manager who chooses to apply.

To do Sir Douglas Dawson justice, I ought to say that he seemed thoroughly ashamed of the wholesale ban which, without giving me a chance of amending the text, had destroyed my property. He kept saying, "It was not my doing; I assure you, it was not *my* doing." But I do not think he ever came near to telling me the real reason why Lord Spencer had decided that the play must not be allowed. I thought, however, that I could make a good guess. Certain foolish tittle-tattle which had been going the round in 1910, and earlier, seemed to that court functionary sufficiently serious to make my historical play undesirable; he was afraid that false parallels might meet.

By a curious coincidence, on the very day when my play was thus released for future production, I was due to give a dramatic reading at a house in Mayfair. And I found my hostess was wearing a ring given by Queen Caroline to Lord Denman, one of her counsel in the divorce trial, as a personal recognition of his services. And I heard then, to my considerable astonishment, that Lord Denman (then Mr.) had always believed firmly in the Queen's innocence. I confess that I myself had my doubts, but Denman, as her counsel, had seen and heard the witnesses for the prosecution. That their evidence had been bought I knew; he, it seems, was convinced that it was also perjured evidence. I wonder whether Lord Brougham was of the same mind. His eloquence at the trial was magnificent, and (legally) convincing, but it has never struck me as being quite sincere.

Sir Douglas Dawson told me that, as a small boy in the company of one of Brougham's grandsons, he had hidden in the bushes of a garden at Cannes, and thrown oranges at the old man's back as he ambled past—a small unhistorical link with the Georgian era which seemed to please him; he threw it at me as a proof of how very modern, and therefore within the Censor's jurisdiction, my play really was; but he was so un-modern himself that his argument cut no ice.

My association with Miss Gertrude Kingston over the opening of the Little Theatre, gave me the assistance of a friendly management for rescuing *Bethlehem* from the censorship, under which it had been deprived of a legitimate and normal existence for ten years. To help me on my way, Miss Kingston made renewed application for a license, and was met with the old traditional answer that Holy Families could not be allowed upon the stage. But since the censoring of my play, another play called *Eager Heart* had been given a license, and in that play, also, the Holy Family appeared. When this was pointed out to the Censor, he began by denying it, but the text of the play convicted him. Inattentively he had given a passport to the Holy Family, because it had come upon the scene in peasant disguise. He then fell back for defence upon the fact that in *Eager Heart* the Holy Family did not speak. To that I nailed him. If I so arranged matters that in *Bethlehem* Our Lady should remain speechless, would he grant it a license? He could do no other than say yes. And so, for the next five years, with an "Earth-Angel" standing by as interpreter, the not-to-be-spoken words were spoken, public performance was permitted and once (I think it was at Peterborough) a Bishop came before the curtain and spoke the prologue.

Then another fortunate thing happened. Rutland Boughton took one of the old mystery plays, set it to music, and without question it was publicly performed. Apparently the old mediæval play had, like *Everyman* (in which the Deity Himself appears), commonlaw rights which the Censor could not override. But in Boughton's play, Our Lady not only spoke, but—being accused by Joseph of improper conduct—answered him back handsomely. Again I approached the Censor, and having set the facts before him had the satisfaction of making him at last climb down from an untenable position.

But the way of the forerunner is hard, and though he clears the way for those that come after, he gets more knocks than ha'pence, and his reward is not with him in his own lifetime. It would be easy enough to lay oneself out for the penalties of the censorship, by writing indecent and impossible plays, and if one did, it would be nothing to boast about. But though I have never written an indecent play, or an indecent sentence in any of them, thirty-two of my plays have been censored up to date, and only over two of them, as yet, has the censorship withdrawn its veto—without compensation or apology.

Four years ago, when the censoring of my Victorian plays began, I received a polite letter of regret from official headquarters. Though I may not quote that letter, as it was marked "private and confidential," I may give my answer, which was as follows:

"It was very kind of you to write to me personally about the censoring of my plays. Of course, I will regard your letter as private and confidential: but equally of course, I must be free to make public use of the fact that the plays have been censored. In this instance I have no doubt that you will have the support of the more conservative section of public opinion. But the Censorship has treated me so unfairly in the past, and has caused me so much financial loss, at a time when I could ill afford it, that my opposition to it is natural and will be continuous.

"May I take this opportunity of bringing to your notice the hostile acts committed by your predecessor in office against my plays in the past?" (Then followed a plain statement of the prohibition, and reluctant climb-downs already recorded— concessions which, in the case of *Pains and Penalties,* came too late to be of any value.)

"I think you must admit the gross unfairness of such treatment, especially the Lord Chamberlain's (Lord Spencer's) refusal to say what alterations would make the play possible for public performance.

"I cannot claim damages: the Crown is in a privileged position for destroying dramatic property; but I do feel that the least your Licensing Department could do to show contrition, would be to grant free license to all my plays that *can* be licensed from now on till the day of my death, or, till a death which I hope will come earlier, the death of the Censorship.

"Pardon me for this long letter. In the words of Mr. Martin Tupper, in one of the 'Palace Plays' submitted to you the other day, 'I have let my indignation carry me away.'— because really to feel indignant is one of the few compensations left to a defrauded author.

"Believe me, yours very faithfully——"

Any intelligent reader will realise that in writing that letter I enjoyed the moral indignation which prompted it. It is one of the few enjoyments which are left to the victim of injustice, but it is a very real one, especially when one is able to express it.

The censored plays above mentioned have since been collected under the common title of *Victoria Regina.* A selection of them was given "privately" at the Gate Theatre, with considerable success (and with Pamela Stanley acting the title rôle with brilliant verisimilitude) during the Silver Jubilee festivities of last year. A larger selection is now being performed publicly in New York and other places in America.

It was Mrs. Ramsbotham of *Punch,* I think, who, not liking Americans and their ways, made the historic remark, "Oh, those dreadful people! Why did Columbus discover them?" But for me, at any rate, Columbus's discovery has had its compensations.

The censoring of a play does not carry with it the same implication as the suppression of a book. A play may be legally banned merely because the Censor considers it "undesirable," but when a book is banned, by police court prosecution, it is generally on the charge of "obscenity," and though it is a larger outrage on liberty that the milder accusation should be allowed to destroy a man's property in a play, the graver charge, which causes a book to be suppressed, is often, in practice, as outrageous and silly as the other, for it frequently only means that the book conveys "undesirable" knowledge—knowledge, that is to say, which the powers-that-be desire shall not be made public. "Birth control" is an instance, but over that matter officialdom is now fighting a losing battle.

Obscenity is easier to apprehend than to define, and, when one comes to the borders of it, as hard to fix by the amount of noxious matter contained, as the term "drunk and incapable"; for what we might regard as obscenity in one man, or writer, we should pass as allowable in another who has the better head for it. The obscenity of Shakespeare we allow for the greater body of virtue that is contained in him, and the obscenity of certain passages in the Bible we have to admit because they are inextricably mixed up with the "Word of God." The obscenity of Rabelais can be tolerated, and even enjoyed, by people sufficiently educated to perceive the moral purpose lying behind it, and the fine literary ability which flavours it to better taste.

But a single word scrawled upon a wall, by a writer who remains anonymous, may strike one as obscene because of the immoral intention lying behind it; and it strikes us as more obscene if it is written very large than if it is written very small—because then the evil intent is made more obvious: the wish, namely, of the writer to shock as many as possible of one section of the community and to gratify as many as possible of another, but mainly to gratify himself with a sense of powerful publicity achieved without any mental effort. For to know that by the writing of a single word you stimulated or shocked the imagination of hundreds of your fellow creatures is a realisation of authorship on a scale which more responsible writers are never able to experience.

But why is it that a word can shock some and stimulate others, when another word meaning exactly the same thing, and known to mean exactly the same thing, would not—or not to anything like the same extent? The word "sanguinary," for instance, as a polite substitute for "bloody," had been facetiously used for years by people of good taste, until Mr. Bernard Shaw came along and made the bolder word innocuous by hurling it into the ears of delighted thousands as a gay flout to the Censor. As a result, he has taken the guts out of it, and the English language is the poorer by the loss of an expletive which meant nothing whatever, but yet managed to shock. And so, in polite society today, nobody troubles any longer to use the word "sanguinary," its figleaf usefulness having gone, since the other has lost its masculine virility.

But other words, simply because they retained their virility into an age which virility shocked—words which were once in quite reputable use—have been suppressed. And it is entirely because of their suppression into a low underground life that they now stimulate some and shock others. Just as the suppression of *The Well of Loneliness* caused an entire girls' school to read a book which they would not otherwise have troubled to read, so has the suppression of words acted as a stimulus to their use for the excitement of the sexual sense, and if only we could get rid of the shock the stimulus would go with it. The effect that words have on us is governed by habit and by association, so that to this day timid maiden ladies will sit and listen unscared to a curate reading for the first lesson of one of the Feasts of the Church a detailed account of the Jewish rite of circumcision, which elsewhere they could not hear mentioned, and perhaps some people will be shocked at my mentioning it here.

In some cases we are even more tyrannously governed in our sense of propriety by the word than by the thing itself. Custom enables us to endure the sight of certain things of which any detailed description would be thought "obscene." A dog, for instance, runs about the streets in a state of nature, and—like his great Anagram—"fulfils himself in many ways." And when one of those fulfilments takes place, one section of the community avoids looking and pretends not to see, while another section does *not* avoid looking. But if the encounter were described in *words* as plainly as it is seen—if the dog were a *book* that is to say—he would be taken up before a magistrate and ordered to be destroyed as "obscene." But the dog is spared because the dog is a more natural and a more inevitable occurrence than the supposed book would be, and being innocent of evil intent either to shock or to stimulate—being in fact one of the vicissitudes of life—we learn sensibly to put up with him.

But books dealing openly with this and similar subjects may be written with very different intentions; and is it not perfectly absurd to treat as "obscene" a scientific, or a sociological, or a religious book, or even a work of fiction, merely because it contains frank passages setting forth social or biological facts, from which timid minds might receive a shock, or depraved minds a stimulus?

But that absurd thing has actually been done in this country to certain works by Dr. Havelock Ellis, and other writers in their own line equally serious and reputable. And apparently the reason that we do so is that a certain type of mind, which can extract stimulus from anonymous writings on a wall, can also extract stimulus from certain passages in these books; and so, though the type we are protecting will most certainly find its stimulus elsewhere, we bring a lying charge of obscenity against these books and their authors, and order the books to be destroyed. And the further we extend suppression, the further shall we extend the stimulus of curiosity which suppression provokes.

From these instances of the "making of obscenity," legal or actual, I turn to a remarkable instance of the *un*-making of obscenity, due to mere use and custom, and showing how the sensible acceptance of a thing, flagrant in itself, removes its power to hurt. On a certain hillside in Dorset is an incised figure called "the Cerne Giant," occupying about an acre of land, which is rankly phallic in one of its features. But that figure has been allowed to preside for centuries, without pious mutilation, over the village lying at its feet. And one has no reason to suppose that the morals of that village are worse, or the illegitimate births higher, than in other villages. If they were, a case for mutilation might be made out.

But what, I wonder, would happen if somebody made a picture postcard of it and sent it to Whitehall. The intent might be "obscene" or merely mischievous, but surely the Home Secretary would find it very difficult—whatever the intent might be—to censure an English landscape for its indecency! As a test case it would be worth trying.

Chapter XX

FROM PLAY-WRITING TO POLITICS

My PLAY-WRITING, up to 1912, had resulted in two censored plays which had brought me no profit, one play written in happy collaboration, which had crept slowly into public favour and had then died untimely in mid-career, and two failures, *The Vicar of Wakefield* and *The Chinese Lantern.*

It was at Bernard Shaw's generous instigation, that *The Chinese Lantern* had been put on at the Haymarket, in conjunction with his *Getting Married.* But the success of his play was not sufficient to tide over the lean time which must have run while mine, in the face of adverse criticism, was finding its public. Its failure, of course, hit the Barker-Vedrenne management harder than it hit me. They were quite generous about it; and Barker was even willing to start on another collaboration, which almost came to completion, and might have been put on at His Majesty's by Beerbohm Tree, had not a new L. C. C. rule about the theatrical employment of children come into force at the very moment when negotiations were toward.

But our choice of subject was *The Pied Piper of Hamelin,* and the new regulations, excluding from the stage children under the age of ten, made impossible the adequate presentation of a play which depended for much of its dramatic effect on a whole crowd of children "as small and young as they make them"—although their appearance had only to be brief.

And so, in 1912, my efforts to write for the commercial stage ended, and have never been resumed. The fact that, in the present year of grace, the commercial stage has come to *me,* was none of

218

my seeking. For when I wrote *Victoria Regina* I knew that in England, it would be censored, and had no thought that it might have a successful run in America.

My very uncommercial standing was speedily recognised—and has been still more extensively recognised since I published the *Little Plays of St. Francis*—by those parasites of the theatrical profession, the producers of amateur performances for "charity." They pay for their halls, their stage carpenters, their costumes, their programmes, and their posters, but they expect the playwright to let them have his wares for nothing. They do not even ask him for what charity he would like them to perform. They select their own—a charity in which he may have no interest whatever, or of which he may even disapprove, since it may simply be a means of enabling a social service to be run inefficiently instead of being charged to the general community. And while seeking thus to exact from him a gratis service, which they have no right to expect, they may actually be doing him a disservice, by acting his play so badly that no one will ever wish to see it again.

I own that I am not as adamantine toward these extortioners as I ought to be; my treatment of them varies. Sometimes I say that if *I* may choose the charity, they may do my plays gratis; sometimes I say that if I can have their assurance that hall, stage carpenter, costumes, printing, and all other services are being freely rendered, they may have my play on the same terms; sometimes I say that I have no interest whatever in the proposed charity, and let it go at that. Quite recently I received a proposal that I should myself form and rehearse a company for the performance of a full programme of my *Little Plays* in a distant town for a charity of which I had never heard; in return for which, travelling expenses would be paid, and "hospitality found." To the person who made this proposal I replied with a politeness which she did not deserve, expounding to her the financial absurdity of the proposition, but saying nothing whatever about its damned cheek. But it may not be amiss that I should here put on record the sort of moral indecency of which charity-mongers are capable in their claims upon playwrights. Truly, as the Apostle Peter observes, "charity covers a multitude of sins," and because it is charity, the sinners are quite shameless about it.

Autograph-hunters are a much lesser nuisance; the demand they make has no market value to speak of, and gives little trouble. Also (though not always) they enclose a stamped and addressed envelope for the return of the favour they are asking. But the trouble they give does become appreciable, when, without permission, they plant down on one a book to be signed, and repacked and re-addressed. But there again I am not as adamantine as I ought to be, though I do draw the line at putting on stamps, when no stamps have been provided. I think it was Browning who said that he reckoned his autograph was at least worth the twopence which he left the post office to collect when applicants had not troubled to provide postage beforehand.

But it is from America that one gets the extremes of generous recognition, and arrogant presumption in the matter of autographs. I have one American devotee who sends me for every book that I autograph for him a box of preserved fruits. He is a preserved-fruit merchant, so trade advertisement may be at the back of it. I had once an applicant from America, who requested that I would copy out for his autograph collection one of my poems, about a hundred lines in length. As he had sent me a stamped envelope I replied to his request; I cannot remember the whole of my reply; only that it began, "Damn you, sir! No, I will not." In course of time I received an effusive letter of thanks for my "valuable addition" to his collection, and of course I ought to have guessed that he would value so personal a tribute to his brazen effrontery far more than any poem, however long, or however good, that I was capable of writing.

Still it is no use pretending that it is no satisfaction to an author—especially to one who for the greater part of his literary life has been what is called "a struggling author"—in finding that his autograph has acquired a sentimental, and probably even a market value. When I sign a book for a Bazaar, I find that its price has gone up sixpence or even a shilling; and when about a dozen presentation copies which I had given to a friend found their way into a second-hand bookshop, it pleased me to discover that my signatures with accompanying inscriptions had made the bookseller set a higher value on them than their original price.

It is indeed one of the most comforting things for an author's self-esteem to find in second-hand book catalogues that his books have not gone down in price, and have sometimes gone up. The highest appreciation in that quarter which I have discovered up to date, is the price of five shillings set on a penny pamphlet which I wrote during the Woman Suffrage Campaign, called *The Bawling Brotherhood.* I also found recently that my brother Alfred had kept a copy of it, which pleased me even more.

I got less satisfaction from finding my first book of poems classed as "rare" and priced a shilling above its retail value, while copies were and still are at the publishers waiting to be sold. I wrote, indeed, to protest, that "rare" was a misnomer, and that so to price it was an attempt to get money under "false pretences"; but when I last saw a catalogue emanating from that same firm, "rare" was still the lying epithet applied to *Green Arras,* and the price was still six shillings.

Apropos of second-hand copies and "rare" editions, I have a story I might tell, but shall not here, of how by artful incitement, I drove the second-hand book market to increase its bids for certain "unopened" copies of *A Shropshire Lad* (which I had bought speculatively in the early years of its career at 2/6d a copy) from five pounds to fifty pounds, and finally (for a signed copy) seventy pounds. I need hardly say that the last named sum was paid, not by an Englishman, but by an American, who, about to embark for his native land, feared that he might find its price had risen before he got to the other side of the water.

When I told Alfred of my exploit, he told me in return how the Dean of Westminster had recently thanked him for the great pleasure his *Angels and Ministers* had given him. "So," wrote Alfred, "if I bring you money, you bring me fame."

Having scored a good all-round failure with my plays, I let

play-writing go, and in 1912 wrote my first social and political satire, *John of Jingalo,* in the form of a novel. Like its sequel, *The Royal Runaway,* and the others which followed, it was a disguised commentary on certain contemporary events and public characters, as scathing as I could make it; the first named having been prompted by the Liberal Government's hanky-panky manipulation of King and Constitution, and its dishonest treatment of the Woman Suffrage Movement.

It was that movement which first brought me into active sympathy with the aims and doings of my own generation; and I date the interest which I have increasingly taken in the political problems and controversies of the present day to the request made to me a few years earlier, by the dear old lady who wore "what o'clocks" in her bonnet, that I would go to a meeting in Chelsea and hear Mrs. Pankhurst speak on Votes for Women. Until that time I had made rather a cult of being much more interested in things of the past than of the present, and had managed to escape from most of the ordinary burdens of citizenship—from income tax for a good many years, owing to the smallness of my income, and from jury service and qualification as a voter, by changes of address coming just at the right time.

I suppose being a brother, and sharing house with my sister had something to do with it; but anyway after that meeting, I became, in the eyes of some of my relatives and friends, a lost soul. My own explanation of that fall from grace would be that I then first found myself to possess that most uncomfortable thing, a social conscience. I would far rather not have had it, for it got badly in the way of my book work; and looking back on the past I can say truly and fervently that the periods of my life I would least like to live through again are those when my social conscience has been most active. Virtue may be its own reward at the time, with the prospect of release lying ahead, but one wants no repetition of the dose.

It is quite likely, I think, that the experience of those agitating years did give me better material for the future, but at the time it was a distinct hindrance. But when a kind friend expressed regret to some ardent Suffragist over the diminution of my literary output, she got for an answer, "What does his silly old work matter? Votes for women is far more important."

I thought so at the time. Yet they would have got the vote exactly when they did get it, without my help, while I, perhaps, should have written a few more of the books which I was then wanting to write. But I know of only one that definitely died for lack of the time and attention which it needed; and I don't think it would have been a very good one.

On the other hand, the Women's Movement provided me with a political antipathy which enabled me to write, a good many years later, a far better book (called *Trimblerigg*) than the one that died. So, though I would prefer not to be virtuous again, virtue has provided me with compensations.

The most devastating blow dealt me by the Suffrage Movement was the discovery it forced upon me that I could speak. Hitherto I had made only short after-dinner speeches (which I had learned by heart) at Old School-boy gatherings; and when I was first called upon to speak for the Suffrage, I learned that speech by heart also, and lay awake for two previous nights repeating it.

This happened at Hereford where we were keeping house temporarily with an old and very Victorian relative, whose attitude towards the Movement may best be summed up in her own words:

"When they speak of Votes for Women, I pretend I don't hear."

It was an Anti-Suffrage meeting held at the Town Hall, and addressed by a granddaughter of Charles Dickens, which forced us into action. Hereford, like all Cathedral cities, was backward in its politics; but it had a Dean and a Bishop who both approved of Woman Suffrage, and there were also certain ladies of social importance belonging to "the Cathedral set" who did likewise. To our great surprise the Anti-Suffrage resolution was defeated, though the Chairman declared, amid laughter, that it was carried "by a small majority." On that showing, a counter-blast became necessary, and three weeks later we held a very successful meeting—Lady Frances Balfour, Mr. Baillie-Weaver and the Bishop being our chief speakers, and our resolution was carried by a large majority.

But the happiest circumstance connected with that meeting, at which I made my first public speech, came from outside. Hereford had a large Training College for Women Teachers, with two hundred and fifty students. The Head of the College had written to inquire how many seats we could spare them. I asked how many wished to come? "All," she replied. This was a call to action; we could only allow them seventy seats for the Town Hall meeting, but I said that, as so many were interested, I was willing to go and speak at the College. I did so; I came back jubilant. "It's all right," I said to my sister. "We shall win; we've got the younger generation with us." The College had been practically unanimous.

After that early experience we never doubted, even in its darkest days, that the Cause would win; and I remember how very angry we sometimes made opponents whom we met socially with our complete assurance that victory awaited us. "I'm not arguing, I'm telling you," is always rather a provocative way of stating your case, and throughout the Suffrage Movement that note of provocation was constantly being sounded. The certainty of its supporters as to the final result was one of the main causes of the irritation which the movement continued to provoke, more especially when the militancy of the W. S. P. U. (Women's Social and Political Union) ceased to be symbolic and became violent. For then, in the estimation of many of its quite genuine supporters, the Movement was committing suicide, making further support a waste of time. Our only doubt came with the war, when it seemed at least likely that a general suspension of the agitation would mean ten years' further delay. Yet in the event, Votes for Women, on wider terms than had before seemed possible for a start, was one of the very few good things that the war brought us: that, and Daylight Saving.

Just now I used the expression "symbolic militancy," for that is how militancy began. A window was broken in Downing Street; and my first suffrage article was written to point out that glass windows might be taken as a symbol of the consent of the governed, and that if consent was withdrawn on a large scale, glass would become an expensive luxury, and shutters a necessary substitute. I did not know, when I wrote, how correctly I had prophesied.

It is probably forgotten now, except by those who were in the Movement, that the illegal use of violence began with the police. The constitutional right of the voteless to go in petition to Parliament had been overruled by police regulations; and petitioners had again and again been battered and bruised and rolled in the mud with the sanction of the Home Office, while exercising a right that had become highly inconvenient when the Government refused to receive them. Eventually that right secured recognition in a court of law; and thereafter petitioners were allowed to stand at the doors of Parliament unmolested, but unattended to, for many days in succession while the House of Commons was sitting. That waiting deputation of the Women's Freedom League set up a record of patience which lasted from July 5 to October 28, 1909.

But it was after a third or fourth attempt of the petitioners before their legal right was recognized, that symbolic militancy started in a concerted attack on the windows of Government offices in Whitehall and Downing Street. Following upon that came arrests, crowded police courts, fines which the offenders refused to pay, sentences which became more and more severe, and finally the hunger strikes which led on to the "Cat and Mouse Act."

It is not my aim here to give an account of the Militant Movement, but only to show cause why from the very first it won my sympathy—though not always, in its later developments, my approval. And having friends who were active members of the W. S. P. U. which my sister had also joined, we heard many stories of symbolic militancy practised by women of meek and retiring character, some of which make good telling.

One friend came from the north of England to stay with us for the necessary night or two, when the first large concerted breaking of Government windows had been planned. She took her little bag of stones with her, and was away for some hours. About midnight she returned trembling but triumphant. "I've done it," she said; "I'm going before the Magistrate tomorrow." And then she told us her story, which I think I can give almost in her own words.

"I went into Whitehall, and I looked about for a nice policeman. Presently I found a young one, standing on the edge of the pavement. I took a stone out of my bag, and I threw it at the smallest pane of glass I could see. It hit, and it sounded like the Heavens falling. I turned and looked at my policeman; he never moved. I went up to him and said, 'I've broken a window.' 'Oh, no, you 'aven't, Miss,' he said. 'But I *have,* and there it is,' I said pointing. 'Well, anyway, I didn't see you do it,' he said; so he wouldn't arrest me, and I thought to myself, 'Am I to go on breaking windows all night, before I get myself arrested?' So I went on, and I chose another policeman, less nice-looking; and I took out another stone, and broke another window; and he came, and arrested me. So that's done, and here I am."

She told it without laughter, her nerves very much shaken by the ordeal she had gone through, and the next day she got a six weeks' sentence, which was intended as a cure for "such foolishness," but failed to have any effect.

These acts of militancy were, if I remember rightly, always preceded by an attempt to carry a petition to Parliament. When that had been violently turned down by the police, more window-breaking followed. On one occasion, instead of the petitioners going in a single body, a scattered deputation was devised. They were to go two and two, separately and from different directions. Earlier in the day the destined victims met for future recognition, and were given their partners, with instructions to meet again at a given time and place. One of our friends found herself paired with Miss Alice Paul, an American Suffragette who had come over with missionary zeal to join (not quite constitutionally) in the hurlyburly of a political field which was not her own. They had never met before. Having taken note of each other, they parted to come together again at the chosen rendezvous on the stroke of six. When, at the appointed hour, our friend stood waiting on a certain street corner, she saw coming toward her an exceedingly stout person whom she did not recognise. The stout person stopped and spoke. She had come to keep the appointment. "But it wasn't you I met this afternoon?" our friend objected.

"Yes, it was. I'm Alice Paul. You see," she explained, "we are going to be in the hands of your police presently, and I am told they are rough about it; so I've padded myself."

She certainly had; over the protective armour which fore-thought had provided, the buttons strained like hounds on the leash, and when a few minutes later, under the excited gaze of an expectant crowd, the rough handling began, the buttons (strained beyond endurance) broke from their moorings in swift succession, and the padding like the entrails of some woolly monster emerged roll upon roll. She must have looked rather like the Michelin Tyre advertisement coming undone, for the material she had chosen for a chest-protector was an unending coil of black cottonwool, wound round and round her body, times without number; and when the outside coil slackened and gave down, the rest followed, loop upon loop. The crowd was, of course, highly diverted. "Oh! Look at the stuffing!" was the cry. Immediately she became a popular favourite; and, as she went off under arrest carrying her coils with her, opinion was in her favour, and cheers followed her.

It was things like this—these nice personal touches of courage and quaint humour, amid the vituperations of the press, and "the condemnation of all right-thinking people"—which continued to make the Suffragettes popular. They were also fulfilling their purpose.

Long before they had been driven to these later extremes, and when the militancy still came mainly from the other side, Mr. Justice Grantham had, at a dinner table in Hereford where he was holding the Sessions, passed a shrewd though adverse judgment upon their conduct. "I am entirely against giving women the vote," he said, "and I think what they are doing is very wrong. But it's the way to get it."

It may not have been the only way to get it, but it proved to be one way. Mrs. Fawcett, who was not herself a militant, admitted, at the time when it began, that militancy had brought the movement to life, and made it practical politics.

It was inevitable that it should do so, for the life in militancy, both aggregate and individual, was amazing. And when the form of its militancy became more wild and extreme, there was still in it the same extraordinary personal courage and determination, carried to the nth degree by women who had never done anything daring before, not even to the extent of being unconventional.

One of the most delightful accounts of these wild doings (when the shop-window-breaking stage had been reached) came to me at first hand from one of the perpetrators thereof. Point was given to the story by the precise and collected way in which she told it—more as if she were addressing a Mothers' Meeting than recounting an act of lawless violence.

She and a friend had pledged themselves to a shop-window-breaking expedition in Oxford Street; and, as was always the case when the W. S. P. U. went off on the warpath, they were under strict orders as to time and place. The main point was they were to break as many windows as they could before being arrested, and six o'clock was the time for it. And this is how the story was told me:

"We were going down Bond Street toward Oxford Street, and we both had our hammers under our cloaks. It was about five minutes to six. All at once my friend said to me, 'I can't do it! I can't do it!' I said, 'Do you mean to say you are going to break your word to Mrs. Pankhurst?' 'Yes,' she said, 'I can't help it; I am.' 'Then I shall never speak to you again,' I said, and I left her and went straight on, for I didn't wish to be seen with her any more. And then, suddenly, behind me, I heard a sound of breaking glass. 'I'm doing it! I'm doing it!' she cried. Well, of course, that was very wrong of her, because we'd been told not to begin till six o'clock, and it was then only five to, and it was Bond Street, not Oxford Street. But I was so afraid that, from having been seen with her, I should be stopped before I could do anything, that I didn't dare to wait any longer; so I ran on into

Oxford Street, and there were a lady and a gentleman looking into a large shop window, and I drew out my hammer from under my cloak, and I said, 'Excuse me!' and I broke it under their very eyes. And they looked at me as if they thought I was mad."

She told the whole story in character, and the telling, done with the measured precision of a sewing machine, made it doubly delightful. But when, some years later I made the mistake of saying that early Victorianism was her main characteristic, she was greatly hurt, and said that she never wished to speak to me again— and she never has: a sad cause for estrangement, seeing that I am Victorian myself, and that it is my Victorianism that has made me what I am.

For it was, I imagine, the repressions of their Victorian training which—when they did break out—made these women so aboundingly brave, while remaining so collected and self-possessed. One little old lady, aged seventy, who had volunteered for imprisonment when hunger strikes had begun, felt quite unable to promise that she would make any resistance when it came to her turn to be forcibly fed. Yet when the feeders entered her cell with their life-saving apparatus, and in answer to her inquiry told her what they had come for, she sprang to her feet, and said, "Then I will fight you to the death!"—and did so, so effectually that she had to be released within the next twenty-four hours.

A similar spirit was in an old lady, of very quiet and Victorian aspect, to whom at a Suffrage Meeting one of the stewards tried to sell literature. "No," she said; "I've read everything; a great deal has been written, and a great deal has been said, and it's no good. Something has got to be *done!* My daughter and I are both tingling to do something. I just want to go out into the street, and smash, and smash, and smash—*everything.*" And then she added in a still small voice, "And nobody, looking at me, would suspect me."

I could tell many more anecdotes of the sort of people, who, if looked at, would never be suspected. Once, on my Suffrage rounds, I was staying at the house of a rich coal magnate, who afterwards was made a peer. At dinner the increase of militancy was being discussed, and, in certain of its forms, condemned. Only that week a local letterbox had been set on fire; it was the latest form that militancy had then taken; and in that high social circle it was not approved: it was hoped that the perpetrators would be caught and punished. My host's daughter was sitting next to me. She gave me a soft nudge. "I did it," she said.

Instantaneous conversion, as a religious phenomenon, is not so popular as it once used to be; but in the political field, during the Suffrage Movement, it was constantly happening, and its victims often became terrific engines of war; once started there was no stopping them. The whole thing was infectious. There was something in the air, and I have come to think that not until the herd instinct gets hold of a movement to give it driving force does it become politically powerful. It got hold of the Women's Movement; it has not yet got hold of the Peace Movement. When it does it will produce proportionate results.

I was not myself a victim to sudden conversion, for in an indifferent lacklustre way I had been of that way of thinking for many years. But the infectious nature of the Movement did certainly alter my habits of life, and fill me with new interests right away from my literary predilections.

One day I was walking across Hyde Park, when I came upon an old man standing on a box at a railed corner, addressing a nursemaid and a perambulator. I passed without stopping to hear what cause he was advocating, but presently I turned and looked back. The nursemaid and the perambulator had moved on, but the old man was continuing his address to empty air. What a ghastly fate, I thought, for any sane human being to be landed in by faith in a cause for which others did not care! A fortnight later I was doing much the same thing myself—not quite so solitary, for generally other members of the Men's League for Women's Suffrage were with me, and we got a more hopeful audience than nursemaids and perambulators to listen to us. But often we started speaking without any one stopping to hear us, though after a while we got good crowds, and plenty of questions; and the grind went on Sunday after Sunday for two or three years.

Towards the end, when militant extremes had begun to bring reprisals on the heads of militants and constitutionals alike, we had the added interest of being occasionally mobbed—always quite mildly—and shepherded away by the police to a place of shelter—sometimes before it was at all necessary, for I think the police were always anxious for our meetings to end and release them from extra duty.

Meanwhile my studio had become the home of the Suffrage Atelier where banners were made for the Movement. Five or six of them I designed myself, and presently Clemence became chief worker. Monster processions were being organised, and banners were an important feature for the rousing of popular enthusiasm. More and more it became difficult to belittle a movement which could hold up the traffic of London with processions two or three miles long, and decked from end to end with hundreds of banners, some of them of vast size; while in the ranks the most unexpected people were to be seen testifying their support of the Movement. I think it was Jack Hobbs who one day startled the clubs of Piccadilly by joining the men's section in one of the big processions. When the hated cause had enlisted the support of a famous cricketer, matters were becoming serious.

Most of the men who had much to do with the Movement probably found the women's leaders at times exceedingly trying. They went their own way; they did not try to please, or even to conciliate; they would not take advice. On all those points I think they were generally right. To be a real movement the Movement had to think, and act, independently.

What chiefly annoyed me was the exceeding bad manners which some of them displayed—quite away from militancy—when good manners would have been such a much better policy. I remember going, one Sunday evening, to a social and non-political club to hear one of the leaders give a lecture on the Women of Shakespeare. She had not made any attempt to prepare the lecture, made no apology beyond saying she had not had time, and then proceeded to give a violent and aggressive address on Woman Suffrage, with no reference to Shakespeare at all. This was naturally resented by the audience, and protests arose. Israel Zang-will, who, like the speaker, was only a guest of the club, was in the chair. His attempts to quell the disturbance (which under the circumstances was justified) were by no means tactful; he roundly accused the members of "insulting their distinguished guest." This only caused further uproar, and an appeal for peace had to be made from the body of the hall by one of the club committee. I went away feeling angry and humiliated that anything so rude and stupid should have been done by one who, on other occasions, had shown such brilliant leadership and sound political instinct. Why, on this occasion, had she gone so gratuitously out of her way to rouse enmity and resentment?

It all boils down to this—that the outstanding reason why women should have the vote for themselves is that, even with the utmost goodwill, men cannot understand them.

But though occasionally they annoyed me, far more often was my admiration roused by the humour, courage, and resourcefulness with which the rank and file played their pranks on the enemy— more especially on members of the Government. These they dogged like private detectives, and naturally their attentions were concentrated most of all on a Prime Minister who was known to be opposed to their claim, and whose wife was even more so.

One good story came to us from Scotland where an extra big Liberal demonstration was to be held. And on the great day, the W. S. P. U. emissaries, having nothing to do before evening, chanced to visit the grounds of a large mansion noted for its fine gardens, to which somehow or another they had secured admission. And there they met a head gardener who had been com-missioned to make up a bouquet for presentation to the Prime Minister's wife. The gardener had any amount of flowers at his disposal, but he was not accustomed to making up bouquets. They offered to make it for him, and they made it most beautifully, a dream of loveliness, of great size, and in three colours only— purple, white, and green. To the majority of the present genera-tion this means nothing, but to the Liberal Government of that day purple, white, and green were as red rag to a bull; and when that bouquet was publicly presented to the Prime Minister's wife, who had not only to receive it graciously, but sit nursing it throughout the evening, the joy of the conspirators was great; and though in the course of the meeting they were thrown out violently, the delight of having seen the W. S. P. U. colours occupying a place of honour on the platform paid them for everything.

CHAPTER XXI

POLITICS CONTINUED

THOUGH the Suffrage Movement did me the doubtful service of teaching me to speak in public, so that in later years I have given up much time to speaking which might have been better employed in writing, it did one good thing for me—it made me prompt with the dentist. Hitherto I had been in the habit of putting off the more unpleasant things of life to a later day; but what I had to do for Woman Suffrage, and always on the nail, was so much more unpleasant than any of my previous recurrent duties, that I was forced, against my inclination, into a higher standard of moral courage than I had ever practised before.

Looking back on it now, I think the hardest thing one had to face was the sense of "feeling foolish." In the eyes of a sceptical, or an indifferent, public, one was constantly doing things which seemed not only extravagant but "bad form." One was also saying them. A suburban discussion group died of horror after hearing me state facts which (were I still given to extravagance) I might say would not today make a girls' school turn a hair, but which at any rate could now be said quite openly in polite society.

One day, in a London street, bowed like Issachar's ass between a double burden of paraphernalia for a Tax-Resistance Meeting, I met the surprised eyes of a top-hatted friend; he did not quite cut me, but his stare was eloquent, and the incident preyed upon my mind for days. There was also the disapproval of relatives. Having a good conscience does not always mean having a happy time.

On one occasion the members of the Men's League used the top hat themselves as an aid to publicity. Wishing to advertise an important Suffrage Meeting, the Committee decided to walk the

234

main streets of West London carrying sandwich-boards, and for the occasion all of us who had top hats were to wear them. The noble array of martyrs, led by our barrister Chairman, included Nevinson, Brailsford, Doctor Drysdale, and others. We certainly made a sensation wherever we went, but we did not march well. The carrying of sandwich-boards is a skilled trade; unable to see your own feet, you have to walk in the gutter without falling over the curb in your anxiety to escape collision with the traffic. Also, to make your advertising effective, you should keep a five yards' distance between yourself and the one in front of you. That is where we failed. Like Adam and Eve in the garden in search of fig leaves, we closed up telescopically one against another to hide our nakedness, and to get nearer to the wished-for goal—release from the awful ordeal to which we had committed ourselves; and having got through with it we felt that we had done sufficient good work for the Suffrage to last us a year.

And yet I recall that, while we were doing things like that, the W. S. P. U. was persistently belittling our efforts and occasionally resenting our aid. On one occasion when it was confidently expected that Mr. Asquith would refuse to receive a deputation of the militants, who were planning to follow up his refusal with a glorious riot all on their own, the Men's League benevolently intervened; Mr. Asquith seized his chance, told the League that he was willing to receive a deputation of *all* the Suffrage Societies together—and did so. The W. S. P. U. was furious. We, poor innocents, had entirely spoiled their pitch for them.

But there were plenty of other occasions left for refusal to be followed by riot, and riot by imprisonment. Before things were over the Movement had used up its most heroic material almost literally "to the death"; and however much we differed over tactics, we never ceased from admiration of the heroism, which the Government (wedged in a cleft stick between its Liberal principles and its illiberal opportunism) met with ever-increasing brutality, culminating in the "Cat and Mouse Act."

One of the dirtiest instances of its attempt to break the women's spirit was on the occasion of a large deputation at the opening of

Parliament. The Home Secretary imported for the occasion police from the East End, accustomed to dealing with the roughest types. What instructions they were given remained, of course, an official secret; what actually transpired was assault and battery accompanied by a persistent refusal to arrest. In spite of this devious avoidance of police duty, seventy of the battered women got themselves arrested; then, by what looked like corrupt collusion between the Home Office and the police, next day at the police court, all the charges were withdrawn, and no evidence taken. An inquiry into the conduct of the police was refused, though the demand for it was voiced by as constitutional a supporter of Woman Suffrage as Lord Robert Cecil.

This and other incidents in the history of militancy, I recall in justification of my warm sympathy for that side of the Movement, even when I wished greatly that a less headlong and more constitutional form of opposition to unrepresentative government might be adopted. I believed that Tax-Resistance, so organised that the Government would be forced to seize not the goods but the persons of the resisters, was the best and most constitutional line for militancy to adopt. But it required time—about eighteen months in my sister's case—to materialise effectively. And the militant leaders, always assuming that they were going to get the vote in a shorter time than that, though they did not discountenance it, refused to make it a plank in their organised policy. They preferred the more spectacular and provocative course of deputations, election fights, and interruption at meetings.

It was only gradually that the anti-Government policy of the W. S. P. U. began to have any noticeable effect on bye-elections. The first decisive turnover took place at Newton Abbot, where Mrs. Pankhurst's activities secured the defeat of the Government candidate, and she was rolled in the mud for it. On the day that brought the news, I met H. W. Nevinson, already a brother-in-arms for the Cause. "That's all right, isn't it?" I said, referring to the lost seat.

"Yes," he said, in his slow, sad voice, "and I'm on my way to the *Daily News* office to write an article saying that it's all wrong."

But very soon after, the paper lost its three best leader-writers on that very point. Nevinson was one of them, H. N. Brailsford another. The anti-Government policy was winning recruits; and I am sure, had all the Suffrage Societies agreed in taking up that attitude, the Vote would have been won before the war started. Unfortunately policies were divided; and though eventually the Liberal Party lost many of its best women supporters, never to return, the bulk of them still clung to party, and let themselves be used by politicians, who, in the words of Mr. Lloyd George, were only ready to give their support "in their own time, and in their own way."

There was, however, one variation of the anti-Government policy, on which Brailsford succeeded in bringing the constitutionals into line, and which I gladly supported, but which the W. S. P. U. resolutely turned down. Labour was, at that time, closely allied to the Government over its policy for curbing the House of Lords, but was far more in favour of Woman Suffrage than any Government supporter dared to be; and often at bye-elections three candidates were in the field. It seemed then good policy to drive a wedge into the alliance between Liberal and Labour by giving Suffrage support to the candidate of the more forward party. In many cases it presented the best chances of securing a Government defeat. As I was supposed (quite mistakenly) to have influence with the W. S. P. U., I was asked to join the committee which Brailsford had formed, of which Mrs. Fawcett was Chairman, and Zangwill, also a member. I did my best, asking the W. S. P. U. to stay their hand in all bye-elections where Suffrage support for Labour was the best means for defeating the Government. But because Labour was not then prepared to throw out the Government bodily, the hand of the W. S. P. U. was against it; and at bye-election after bye-election, where three candidates were standing, the voices for Woman Suffrage were hopelessly divided. Nevertheless, the Government became gravely alarmed; and maybe an attempt was made to arrange that there should, for the time being, be no more triangular elections, for in answer to one of my appeals, Mrs. Pankhurst assured me that such a pact had been made, and that there would be no more of them. Within the next three months there were three; whereupon I returned to the charge, after which my letters ceased to be answered, and presently I was no longer allowed to speak at W. S. P. U. meetings.

It was perhaps as well, for about that time there came a phase of militancy which I could no longer approve. The stab in the back given to the Rokeby Venus hurt my artistic feelings, though I quite understood that it was no personal dislike towards Venus, or any disapproval of the nude, which had prompted the deed. After that came the burning of churches, and I felt myself obliged to cease subscribing to the W. S. P. U. funds. But when a public prosecutor, named Bodkin, threatened with legal proceedings any one who contributed to the support of that law-breaking association, I renewed my subscription as a "gesture," sending notice to Mr. Bodkin that I had done so. Others did the same, but nothing happened to us.

There was, of course, a good deal of coat-trailing of that sort, at a time when "law and order" were setting themselves up against constitutional right; and together with other supporters of the Movement, I did once make a definite attempt to get into prison, but failed. "Interfering with the police in the execution of their duty" was the charge brought against us. But we were only standing on the four sides of Richard Cœur de Lion's statue, making a simultaneous protest against the Government's denial of the right of petition; and the police came running twenty or thirty yards to secure the "interference" for which we became chargeable. When my own particular policeman tried to remove me, hurling me this way and that, I clung for safety to his belt. Whereupon I heard a sergeant say, "Arrest him!" and I said, "Thank God!"— and to my policeman, "I am very much obliged to you." This so puzzled him that when he gave his evidence at Bow Street next day, he altered it, and reported me as having said, "I expected this," which, though I had not said it, was true to fact.

But we were far too respectable a lot—being all first offenders—to be sent to prison without option, for this particular batch of embryo militants included a famous war correspondent, a Liberal candidate for Parliament and the wife of the future Lord Rhondda. We were not even to be fined, only to be "bound over for six months." This we all refused, and in consequence we were remanded in custody for a couple of hours; then, when the court had emptied for luncheon the Magistrate surreptitiously called us back, scolded us and let us go.

This leniency had not the bad effect which leniency is sometimes supposed to have; it did not make us become habitual criminals. But it did give us very good material for pro-militant propaganda, we having got off scot-free for doing what others were being given three months for.

It was on that occasion that I first had my photograph taken for "publicity" purposes. While we were awaiting our summons outside the police court, the press photographers came along. I tried to escape. Nevinson caught me and held me fast. "They've got to make their living," he said.

My own effort to get into prison on a "respectable" charge was easily made and soon over. It took my sister Clemence eighteen months and more to get the matter so arranged that, in her own words, she might give her vote against the Government "at the Holloway polling booth." It was not much satisfaction to her militant mind to refuse to pay taxes, if in the end they could be distrained for. A good many of the Tax-Resisters were content with that form of protest; it did not content her. But the other and better way needed some planning; it also took time. She rented a holiday cottage, stocked it with furniture *not* her own, went occasionally to stay in it, and, when the time came, refused to pay inhabited house duty which amounted to 4/6d. In course of time, after repeated application, she was summoned, and law costs were added. As there was nothing on which the court could distrain, the legal process went slowly on, and the Government in its vain attempt to extract 4/6d from a pocket which could not be picked, ran up a bill which amounted to several pounds. When this enlargement of the debt failed to bring her to reason, arrest and imprisonment were threatened as the only alternative. A polite emissary from Somerset House came and interviewed her; and we heard afterwards that he reported her as being "such a lady," that it would only need the actual presentation of the warrant for arrest to bring about submission.

So the next day the warrant was presented, and, failing to take effect, the warrant officer retired for fresh instructions, and a day later did come with a reinforcement, and actually arrested her. Like all good comedy there was in it an element of pain; but it was very funny. My sister said, "Are you going to walk me to Holloway?"

"Oh, no!" she was assured. "We shall take you in a taxi."

"I shall not pay for it," she said.

"Oh, no, of course not; we shall pay for it."

I said, "I will pay the extra sixpence, if I may come too." They were most kind about it; one of them, to make room for me, went and sat by the driver; and so we all drove to Holloway, and, as I have already told, as we passed through the gates, the taxi, for which the Government was paying, registered the exact amount of the original debt—4/6d.

A week later she was out again, and I heard then some of her experiences during that eventful week of enforced idleness. Knowing her rapacity for work, "What did you *do* all the time?" I asked. "I sat and bubbled," she said; and I realized that triumphant mental satisfaction might be, for a week at any rate, a good substitute for industry.

She was interviewed by the Governor. "How long are you in for?" he inquired.

"For life," she told him. What did she mean by that? She explained. "I am here until I pay; and I am never going to pay." She never did, either then or afterwards, until she got the Vote.

The Chaplain paid her an early call. "Are you," he asked, "any relation of Mrs. Housman of Perry Hall, Bromsgrove?" She was, very much so.

"I was once Curate at Bromsgrove," he explained.

"What a good thing," she replied, "that she is now where she can't get word of our meeting *here* of all places."

The medical officer came to see her twice; it was soon evident they wanted to release her on the score of health. "You are eating too little," he said.

"I am not a big eater," she told him, "even though I lead an active life. Here I am doing nothing, so I eat less. But I am perfectly well, thank you." That excuse having failed, after a week they let her out for no reason stated.

I heard shortly after from a mutual acquaintance that the Governor had said to him, "What did those fools mean by sending us a person like Miss Housman?" It is pleasant to know that officialdom sometimes looks foolish even to its own officials.

It so chanced that my sister's imprisonment took place during the lull in militancy which for six months accompanied our hopes over the Conciliation Bill. For which reason some of the too trustful ones in the Movement thought that she should have postponed operations to a more suitable time. With the militants, however, happening at a time when enforced waiting had become a trial, it was exceedingly popular, and Clemence, who loathed speaking, had to speak on one or two occasions.

A few months later, Mr. Lloyd George, in his own words, "torpedoed the Conciliation Bill," (which would, for the time being, have satisfied the leaders as a first step towards the equal Franchise), without securing any alternative, and at once the fight was resumed more grimly than ever.

Before the much darker days that followed, there was one happy and successful interlude, in which I took an active part. This was the Census-Resistance of 1911, one of the very few things in the way of militancy which the Woman Suffragists did on so large a scale that the Government was unable to touch them. It was the only act of defiance to imperfectly constituted authority which that authority—in spite of much threatening beforehand—did not attempt to punish. From which fact one may deduce the moral that had women combined and organised on as large a scale in other forms of passive resistance—Tax-Resistance for instance—they might have reduced the Government to similar impotence, demonstrated their case to the world on a more constitutional basis, and so won their battle with far less individual suffering and more general sympathy than by way of more extreme forms of militancy.

Before the census began, I drew up a scheme for organised resistance, and offered it first to the W. S. P. U., which rejected it, then to the Women's Freedom League, which had already, I found, started a similar scheme of its own. In a very short time the idea "caught on"; even among the constitutionals it found a certain amount of favour, especially perhaps when the size of the demonstration made legal penalties become less likely.

But the main reason why Census-Resistance succeeded so well, while other forms of resistance hung fire, was that it was an act thoroughly representative of the feelings of the rank and file, and of the amount of risk they were prepared to take to express those feelings in a concrete form. Tax-Resistance took too much trouble, involved too much risk of loss, and was too long in coming to a head to be attractive to the more impatient spirits who formed the circumference of the wonderful patience of spirit which, in certain of the leaders, kept the Movement strong. Census-Resistance was well-suited to the mentality of the non-heroic many; thus it insured numbers. It was also good principle, and as such could not be despised by the heroic ones who preferred to get their shock of battle in more active form. It proved, indeed, so representative, that the W. S. P. U., which had at first been held back by its leaders from organised participation, was forced by the restiveness of its own rank and file to come in, give the protest its official blessing, and as a result make it doubly effective, and safe. Honest John Burns, when informed by his enumerators that he was against resisters to the tune of many tens of thousands, amounting quite possibly to figures in the hundred thousands, climbed down in a night, and announced in the Commons that as he had been able to circumvent and count the lot he would be magnanimous and let the offenders off. Those who were behind the scenes of that midnight orgy of resistance did not trouble to wonder how he managed to count them; they knew that he did not. To this day I do not know whether my own house contained ten, twenty, or thirty resisters; for though I slept in the studio adjoining, I found my door barred to me in the morning when I presented myself with the forms which the law required me to fill; and when finally I obtained entry the house was empty.

A few hours later I informed an official collector that my house had been full of women, ages and numbers uncertain, who had refused me all information (though through the keyhole I begged for it), and had then decamped, leaving me by way of recompense a nicely prepared breakfast. He took it all lying down, as one already inured to the tale; and the paper he carried away had nothing on it but my own name and particulars, with the additional note, "A quantity of females, names, numbers, and ages unknown"—or words to that effect. Nor were any later questions asked. If Mr. John Burns got his numbers, he did it by second sight with the aid of the all-seeing eye of Heaven. And if he was satisfied with the amount of aid Heaven gave him, so were we.

It is not to be pretended that the census protest had a devastating effect upon the Government, but it had its uses none the less. It was good argument, and it got—if not a good press—plenty of publicity; it was not only the converted who heard of it—which was the main drawback of meetings and the other constitutional devices which used up so much time and energy without, so far as we could see, making history. As a rule, the Suffrage propaganda cost Suffragists more than it cost their opponents (in which term, of course, I include the Government). But in this case, with comparatively little wear to themselves, the Woman Suffragists were able to undo the accuracy, and therefore the efficiency, of a very elaborate and costly piece of Government machinery. A census, I believe, costs well over a million pounds; it is the pet of many important departments, and its increasing accuracy in each succeeding decade has been to those departments an affair of *amour propre*. I well remember the consternation of an official high up in a Government department—personally friendly to the Suffrage—whom I met in Manchester about six months before the event, when, in answer to his question "what the women were going to do next," I answered, "Resist the census." He was deeply concerned, and asked me to use my influence. I said I would, if I had any. He said that the census depended for its value to the departments "on fractions." I said I was very glad to hear it; for I knew that the direct actionists of the Suffrage Movement, if they could not make hay of the tens and hundreds of census statistics, could do so with the fractions; and I have no doubt that they did, and that quite a lot of important department officials had it brought home to them that the value of that particular census had, for their own special departmental purposes, been reduced in value owing to the refusal of the vote for women. It was a very useful bit of peaceful penetration into skulls which had hitherto remained offensively impervious to argument.

In the Suffrage camp it did a great deal of good. It gave the women a sense of numbers and solidarity which heartened all, and an opportunity for action to many who had previously done nothing. It was also a distinct score in another direction, at that time rather rare—the women had come off victors from the field, without any rough handling or bruises from the mob or the police, or any subsequent imprisonment from the Government; they had had a thoroughly enjoyable time seeing friends, keeping late hours, sleeping in strange beds. They had had a virtuous "night out," and were none the worse for it. Taking it all round it remains, I think, one of the happiest memories of the Suffrage Movement; it gave all concerned in it a good time and a good laugh.

After it was all over, "I'm glad you forced our hand," said Pethick-Lawrence, who had, I suppose, been in favour of the move when others were for rejecting it. And the W. S. P. U. was so unaccustomed to yielding to pressure or to accepting outside advice, that it did constitute rather a score for co-operation versus the "splendid isolation" on which they usually prided themselves.

As a souvenir of my part in the business, the law-breakers gave me a library chair, with a brass plate on it recording the event; and it is in that chair that I am now writing, and have written nearly all my work from that day to this.

In comparison with what the women went through in those years up to 1914, my own experiences were easy and humdrum, and even when adverse rather amusing. Once outside Brixton Prison, where a man was being imprisoned for his wife's taxes which he could not pay, I was continuously shouted down by a mob of young Liberals, under the impression that I was George Lansbury, who, without permission, had consented to speak in another M. P.'s constituency—this being (while Liberal and Labour were in alliance) a breach of Parliamentary etiquette. Lansbury was unable to come, so I got the knocks intended for him.

The only time I was really mobbed was when speaking not for the militants but for the constitutionals. This was at an open-air meeting at East Grinstead. Luckily not rotten eggs but tomatoes were the chosen missile. One, missing me, struck a woman standing beside me in the eye. I pointed out the assailant to the policeman who was in charge of us. "I shan't do nothing," he said stolidly. "You oughtn't to be here at all."

One of my heresies, which came out sometimes in answer to questions, was approval of women as M. P.'s. The question would be asked in triumphant tone as "a corker." "Do you approve, etc.?" "Yes, decidedly," I would say. And I remember how once at Winchester my questioner, on receiving my answer, turned and walked contemptuously out of the meeting, while our chairwoman got up in haste to explain that, though I had a right to my opinion, that was *not* what the women were asking for. At another quite friendly meeting, where the same question was asked, and the same answer given, a supporter came up to me afterwards and congratulated me on my "courage!" How ludicrous it all sounds today.

But I never really enjoyed question time. I was afraid of not being able at the moment to give the right or the best answer. Only once do I remember making an enjoyable score. I had been speaking of equal opportunity for women in education and in business. At question time a young man got up to ask how, if women were allowed a free run of so many alternatives, were they to be persuaded into the bliss of matrimony! "That," I replied, "is your job. You must make yourself a more blissful object." That answer was the only good hit I can ever remember making. One definite impression I got from question time was that the most sensible questions were asked by the working class— more especially in the North—and the silliest by the so-called upper and educated class, whose whole mentality revealed itself as a concern for the maintenance of existing privilege.

Sometimes in the Anti-Suffrage camp the border-line was amusingly crossed, and they talked Suffrage without knowing it. A male opponent of Woman Suffrage came away from an "Anti" meeting horrified. "They are just as bad," he declared, "as the others. I heard one of them say, 'We don't wish women to have the vote, but if we *did* wish it, we would have it, and nobody could prevent us.'" Where was virtue to be found, when even opponents said things like that?

I must have been a considerable nuisance in those days to authors, actors, and others of my acquaintance, who were friendly to the Cause but did not want to be bothered by it. It wasn't their job, any more than it was mine, and though most of our leading authors signed a declaration in favour, few of them did more. I did on one occasion get Bernard Shaw to speak at a protest meeting over the imprisonment of Mr. Wilks for his wife's taxes, which she conscientiously had refused to pay. That secured us a big meeting. He was genially brutal in his treatment of the situation, and made the unfortunate Mrs. Wilks cry by declaring that, were she his wife, he would take all possible steps to divorce her for so callously allowing him to be imprisoned for her debts. I had to speak after him, and I said, untruthfully, that I was sure he had not meant to be unkind. I think he had meant to be, and thought that she thoroughly deserved it. Mr. Wilks was, in fact, a willing victim: though it was perfectly true that, with only a working-man's wage, he was unable to pay the income tax of a wife who was a successful medical practitioner.

Chapter XXII

FROM PEACE INTO WAR

THE note of comedy, which helped so much in the carrying on of the struggle, during those first four years, became rarer towards the end. The last two years before the war were a nightmare to which I look back with a memory of wearing anxiety almost as constant as what one experienced during the four years of war that followed. It had then become literally a fight to the death; in their hunger-strikes under the "Cat and Mouse Act," there were women who were not only willing but determined to die rather than give in. Foremost among these was Mrs. Pankhurst; and each time that she released herself, frail and broken in body but indomitable in spirit, we feared that the end was near. And a dreadful whisper went about in the Suffrage ranks that if Mrs. Pankhurst died, a cabinet minister would die too. It was known that one at least (and she was named to us) of Mrs. Pankhurst's devoted following, had made a vow to do what she regarded as the right and necessary thing in that event, and hang for it.

In comparison with that dark dread which hung over us, the desperate heroism of Emily Davidson came almost as a relief. In a strange way her act of self-immolation in stopping the King's horse at the Derby was popular; it caught the public imagination. I was speaking to a large crowd in Hyde Park, a day or two after, when news came to us of her death; and as it was announced, all through the crowd hats went off, and one heard a low murmur of sympathy over the price that had been paid for that most astonishing act of courage, coolness, and resolution combined. In the minds of many thousands, hitherto careless or indifferent, it made the demand for Woman Suffrage a serious thing.

A week later came the great funeral procession two miles long organised by the W. S. P. U. through the main streets of London—a procession of triumph, not of mourning. I did not see it myself for I was at the far end with the men's societies which brought up the rear; but I was told, and saw later at the cinema, what a wonderful and beautiful sight it was. During its course a very quiet and significant thing happened. Once again, as often before, the police and the W. S. P. U. were of different minds. The W. S. P. U. had announced that the procession was to go along Piccadilly; the police had decided that it was to go up Park Lane. A young girl in white—Charlotte Marsh, I think—was leading the procession; by her side rode a superintendent of police—who had his instructions. At the corner where ways branched, he gave the order he had been charged with: "Park Lane."

"No," was the reply, "Piccadilly." And Piccadilly it was.

Just that once, hands down, without the police daring to oppose, the women won. And, there can be no doubt of it, that power had been put into their hands by a dead woman.

Two years later I saw another procession of women, which, though organised under a cabinet minister's patronage and with financial assistance from the Government, gave one less cause for pride. It was a procession of women workers for war. As propaganda it was effective, as a demonstration of the national part played by women in war it bore out the Suffrage argument; and yet it was made to look foolish; for the Suffrage leader who had come back from abroad to organise it, had determined in her own mind, that the one and only statesman necessary for winning the war was Mr. W. Hughes, of Australia; and so, without any special knowledge of Mr. Hughes themselves, or any special wish for him, these thousands of women workers were bearing banners, scores and scores of them with the strange device, "Give us Hughes!" "We want Hughes!" "We *must* have Hughes!" And I wonder if those who financed that sham demonstration of unanimity knew beforehand that it was a demonstration for the recall of Mr. William Hughes of Australia to take up the reins of power to which they were giving countenance and pecuniary assistance?

We had moved by then into a very different world of ideas from that for which the Suffrage Movement had previously seemed to stand. For all along the Movement had been of an international character—a break from nationalism. Voteless women, we were told, were not responsible for the mess men had made of things in a man-governed world, and would, when political power was given them, guide our feet into the way of peace. Until the responsibility of full citizenship was granted to them, they were guiltless of the social and international crimes perpetrated by their respective countries.

All that went in a day. In the first week, after the declaration of war, there was a meeting at the Franchise Club to decide what Suffragists should do—what special work they should undertake, as Suffragists, in a world which had suddenly become divided up between allied and hostile nations.

At that meeting I found myself almost alone in pleading that we should offer considerate treatment to the women of enemy countries who found themselves stranded in our midst. But no, they were no longer to be held guiltless of what their rulers had done. To be born a German had become a crime, hatred a virtue. One trembling old woman, born a German, but naturalised by marriage and a staunch worker for the Suffrage, rose to speak and, while admitting that her native country was in the wrong, pleaded for a tolerant spirit toward those who could not help themselves. She was listened to in stony silence; a younger speaker followed, and asked passionately—was she to associate with the sisters of the men who were fighting against her brothers? The sense of the meeting was with her; the spirit of the Suffrage Movement had died a sudden death.

Sick at heart I resigned from the club, and turned to look for some better work to do in more congenial surroundings. A small body of Suffragists was still carrying on; and, kept together by the devoted service of Evelyn Sharp, who continued to edit *Votes for Women* till the vote was won, the "United Suffragists" remained to the end a symbol, if not a very influential expression, of what the Movement had stood for. But those who remained thus active for the cause were nearly all pacifists or of pacifist tendency, and were suspect to the rest.

I did not myself go into those years of war a pacifist, and my change of conviction was only gradual; but everything that happened from then on pointed the way, and five years later, the peace lost at Versailles brought final conviction that out of war, however righteous its intention and origin might be, no good could come. "The knockout blow," to which we dedicated a final year of slaughter, made things worse not better. Of all the poisons of war complete victory proved the most deadly and the most lasting in its evil results.

The work which almost immediately came my way, and which kept me occupied during the greater part of the war, was the post of secretary to a large Home for Belgian Refugees set up at Ealing under the management of Mrs. Blaker, the wife of a local doctor. In the first flush of indignant sympathy which we all felt for violated Belgium, her refugees were received with enthusiasm; and during the first few months, and indeed for more than a year after, the Home throve exceedingly. One large house was given to us rent free; at a very low rental we extended into two others. Our numbers rose to over one hundred and fifty; butchers gave us more meat than we could eat; free bread and free groceries, though in gradually diminishing quantities, saved us for nearly six months from any serious inroad upon our funds; contributions in money went up into the thousands. As for clothes, we lost count entirely; in spite of lavish distribution there was (or *should* have been) enough for all. Of that more presently.

At the first send-off it seemed that everything in the garden was lovely, and that we should be able to carry on during the six months' war (which was all that we then expected), free from care or any kind of serious embarrassment.

But before long we found that the Belgian Refugees were themselves the problem. It was not the pick of the nation that we were housing, though we had all sorts and degrees, from a Princess (of Russian origin) to dockworkers and scavengers. They arrived,

very tired and dirty, with large bundles of salvaged articles, and
(quite naturally) a larger sense of grievance at having been sacri-
ficed in a cause which was not their own. Many of them greatly
resented the fact that Germany had not been allowed a peaceful
walk-over; for they suspected that if Germany had not done it
first, France would have done it later. What then were they fighting about? So while some of them were exceedingly grateful and
eager to help in the emergency, others were not. It is perhaps
unfair to estimate the characteristics of a nation under adverse
circumstances, but even when we were well settled and had secured employment for most of our able-bodied inmates, we found
our Belgians difficult, and throughout the locality their popularity
diminished. Some of them seemed to combine the acquisitiveness
of the Scotch with the cunning of the Red Indian; we did not
understand their ways, they did not understand ours; and constantly they were trying to get round us by means which we
thought shady.

Take clothes for instance. Our clothing store was served by
voluntary workers who came on different days. During the second
month, on stock-taking, we found that we had distributed some
three hundred complete outfits, among only about a hundred of
our casuals. This must mean that some had secured more changes
of raiment than they were entitled to. On examining the books
we also discovered that names had been entered which were not
in the office register; this was due to the fact that in Belgium
married women keep their maiden names for alternative use. In
visiting the clothes store some of them had entered their names
twice—but differently, and had by that means secured double portions for themselves and their families. Having discovered the
leakage, we raided the dormitories. As there were no wardrobes
in which the ill-gotten superfluities could be concealed, our search
turned to the beds of which they had the making themselves.
Under some of the mattresses as many as six suits were found
neatly stacked; five of them we carried back to the storeroom, and
between us and the re-impoverished ones relations became
strained. On that matter, however, we were able to strike a bal-

ance, by securing the goodwill of the newcomers for whom the returned suits made better provision. The quarrel then transferred itself to the wearers of the clothes; they were not a harmonious family.

For this there were several reasons; the two races, Walloon and Flemish, did not mix well; class distinctions also remained stiff. One family in particular was so disagreeable to its neighbours that we put it to dine at a table separate from the rest; and the office received a polite letter of thanks for thus recognising its social superiority, a compliment which we had certainly not intended.

For acquisitiveness our finest example was a very handsome upstanding sergeant who, invalided out of the army in the first months of the war, had brought his refugee family, a wife and two small children, to the Home. They came carrying a few bundles tied up in handkerchiefs; when they left us a year later their baggage train, comprised of twenty-eight pieces, required two four-wheelers to carry it to the station. The sergeant had come wearing his uniform, he was six feet tall and very upright, and whenever the Belgian National Anthem was played (which was done whenever a newspaper "victory" was reported) he stood stiffly at salute, a symbol of proud patriotism. Presently we heard that out-of-doors his salutes were bestowed more promiscuously. He went about the streets of Ealing, saluting and collecting tips; he saluted everybody he passed; I followed him up from the station one morning and saw him saluting small errand-boys. When told that it was not seemly for a sergeant in uniform so to demean himself, he promised amendment; but the thing had become a habit and a profitable one, he could not break himself of it, though to make it less noticeable he took his daily walks through back streets where we were less likely to catch him. And so, we found him a job elsewhere, one at which he would have to discard that bait for tips, his sergeant's uniform. When it came to the time of his departure he made it quite clear to us that we were not going to be rid of him unless we provided a second four-wheeler for the estate which he had accumulated. It was an amazing sight—those twenty-eight pieces. They filled the passage, and lined the stairs up to the first landing of the lodging-house to which we had recently transferred him. He was very dignified, but no longer friendly; we were paying for everything—his two four-wheelers, his railway fare of two whole and two half tickets; we had found him another job; but he was an exile in a strange land, and we had not treated him well. He refused to shake hands with us— with me at any rate.

Another cause for friction was that the Continental habits of our refugees—their less highly developed instinct for privacy— shocked some of us badly, and we expressed ourselves forcibly. One day into the office our lady housekeeper came running, with uplifted hands, expressive of a horror which she could not explain. "Oh, those dreadful Belgians!" was all that she could say.

"What has happened?" I inquired.

She shook her head. "I can't tell you."

And then the door opened, and a portly and very respectable Belgian gentleman entered to explain the mystery in slow broken English. "Meesis Hahrees," he began, "I haf com to apowlogise." ("I don't want to hear a word!" interjected the distressed lady.) "I deed not know zat ze door was not lockit. Had I known zat it was not lockit, I would haf lockit it." He was allowed to say no more. She rushed away. He stood and looked at me in forlorn contrition. "I am sorry, Monsieur, zat zis should have happened," he said.

"It doesn't matter," I assured him. "She'll get over it."

But it took her a long time to do so; and it was to the credit of her real kindness of heart that she did not resign a position which exposed her to such encounters.

On another occasion, I was interviewed by a member of the staff who showed much more self-possession over the shock she had experienced. She began by inquiring whether ten o'clock was not the hour at which all our inmates were supposed to be indoors for the night. Yes, that was the rule. "Last night," she said, "at half-past ten, I saw Monsieur Sirou, with a woman, coming out of the garden tent. The side door was then locked; I let them in."

Clearly this was a serious matter which must be looked into, for Monsieur Sirou was a married man, he had a wife and children on the premises. "Could you," I asked, "recognise the woman? You don't know her name, I suppose?"

"No, not her name, but I should know her again."

I led the way to the large room where the refugees congregated when their domestic duties were over, and had the woman pointed out to me. Then, inviting my informant back to the office, "Miss B——," I said, "the matter is not quite so serious as you suppose. You know that on account of numbers we have had to divide our inmates male from female, married and unmarried alike, into dormitories. The woman you saw with Monsieur Sirou last night was Madame Sirou. The tent was the Garden of Eden."

The lady was quite as much shocked at having her case explained away, as she had been at the supposed discovery. With an exclamation of horror, she flew out of the room. I am not sure that she did not report me to Mrs. Blaker for indecency; but I had already reported myself, and Mrs. Blaker had only laughed.

Our refugees were, as I have said, a mixed lot; in the first few weeks we had, I believe, unwittingly housed a spy—of Belgian origin but in German employ, who had come camouflaged by numbers—a wife, two sons, and a daughter. One day, on receipt of a letter, they all disappeared, and we never heard of them again.

Another, an ex-soldier, received a permit to return to Belgium, to look for the wife and family he had left behind. He came back with a tale of outrage and wholesale massacre, which we had reason presently to believe to be quite untrue, for we discovered its facsimile (only of different date) in a newspaper, where probably he had read it; and the newspaper story may equally have been fiction.

I was very soon given good reason for doubting the atrocity stories which, true or false, helped so greatly to bring the war mind to the necessary concert pitch of blind hatred.

We had hardly opened the Home a week, when word went round Ealing that we had in our charge a two-year-old child whose hands had been cut off by the Germans. Hot on the scent, a reporter from one of the papers came to inspect the Home. Naturally, in search of good copy, he asked to see the child. I told him that it did not exist. In the report he wrote for his paper, he said that he had seen it. I wrote to his editor to protest. His editor did not print my letter. It was typical of what the war spirit required—untruth piled upon untruth. For four years this game went on. No doubt there were atrocities (not on one side only)—war makes them inevitable, but before long those who dared to doubt them were labelled "pro-German"; lifelong friendships were broken between those who wished to believe everything evil of the enemy and those who refused to believe without better evidence.

And as there may still be those who think that atrocities were the perquisite of the Hun, here is a verbatim extract from a lecture which was given by a sergeant-major to an Officers Training Corps, presided over by the commanding officer himself, and afterwards printed for distribution, with the approval of the authorities:

"If you see a wounded German, shove him out and have no nonsense about it. What is the use of a wounded German anyway? He goes into hospital, and the next thing is that you meet him again in some other part of the line. . . . The only time that a German can find pluck to kill with the bayonet is when he comes across one of our own wounded. He will plunge the steel into their hearts as they lie unable to defend themselves. When you see this done, can you have any sympathy for them?"

Surely as good a specimen of "pot and kettle" as could well be found! And then further: "I remember a corporal saying to me, pointing to some German prisoners close by, 'Can I do those blokes in, Sir?' I said, 'Please yourself.' He did."

And when the address was over the commanding officer said, "I wish to express my very cordial thanks to Sergeant-Major F—— for his speech. I hope you will all bear in mind what he has said to you, and that you will all try to act up to it, not only in his department, but in all other departments while you are here. I call for three cheers for Sergeant-Major F——."

It should in fairness be said that the speech I have quoted was made not at the beginning of the war, when idealism had still room in which to breathe, but towards the end, when all idealism had been crushed out of existence. But even at the beginning the joy of hatred had become a patriotic virtue. Just when the campaign had got itself well started, I happened to be speaking at a meeting held by the United Suffragists; and I said something which was mere ordinary common sense about people of alien birth landed in our midst—some of them naturalised, who happened to have been born Germans. The wife of my once next-door neighbour chanced to be there; she came to me and said, "Do you really feel like that?" I assured her that I did. She asked me if I would go and see her husband; he had been naturalised for eight years, she was English, they had three children; life had become a hell to him.

We met then on speaking terms for the first time, and became friends. Later I was able to do him some service. When conscription came, he, like others of military age, was conscripted to risk his life for his adopted country. The military authorities, with more bowels of compassion than some of our stay-at-homes, did not indeed call on him to fight against those of his own blood; but he was given military work to do which brought him within the danger zone, and in that work he did his duty. But it so happened that just as the war was ending, his lease of the house, into which he had moved on the increase of his family, came to an end; and because he had a German name he was not allowed to renew it, nor could he obtain any other. I was then myself meditating a move out of London, and had once or twice had my house occupied by friends. He asked me if I would sublet it to him, or allow him to take over the lease. This suited me well, and I wrote to the house agents informing them of the transfer that I wished to make. They replied that they had no objection to my making a transfer of my lease, but they wished first to know the nationality of the person I had named, as they were unwilling to have a German tenant. As names were to count, I took advantage of my own, which is more usually met with in Germany than in England. I said, what was strictly true, that Mr. A.——'s nationality was the same as my own, but that in any case, even if they did not allow me to transfer the lease, I should exercise my right under our agreement to sublet, so it would come practically to the same thing. At that they capitulated, and the transfer was made.

But their explanation was an amusing one. To my friend's wife who, as time pressed, had gone anxiously to inquire whether the matter had been arranged, they said they had not quite decided, but as Mr. Housman himself was a German they would probably allow the transfer. "Oh, but he isn't!" she exclaimed with patriotic horror.

"Well," was the reply, "we have his own word for it." And they showed her my letter, which took her in just as it had taken in them. And I had to reassure her that I was really and truly English, but that the word "nationality" had more than one meaning.

Conscription produced another incident, in which I became personally concerned. I had a friend in the London police who, without any conscientious objection to war, became for all practical purposes a conscientious objector. It came about thus: He had served during the Boer War in a crack regiment, and had left it to join the police. Directly war was declared he went to see his old Colonel, and asked if he might be taken on again; he was a fine rider, and his Colonel was only too ready to have him. Accordingly he applied to Headquarters for temporary release from the Force with reinstatement and pension rights unimpaired. His application was refused; at that time he was too much wanted at home. Having done his duty in trying to volunteer, he accepted the decision of the authorities and went on with his job. But presently he began to take an active part in the movement for a Police Force Union organised by ex-Inspector Sime, and when Sime was arrested and sent to prison, my friend became secretary in his place. One day, while a committee was being held, it was raided from Headquarters; names were taken, all were told to report themselves at Scotland Yard the next day, and were then given the alternative of abandoning the Union or being dismissed from the Force. My friend chose dismissal and remained secretary.

Then came conscription, and in due course he received notice to present himself for enlistment. But though quite willing to be a volunteer for service in his old regiment, he was not going to be conscripted into any other that was "no class." After stating his claim, he ignored the order, was arrested and placed under detention for refusal to obey military orders. I went with a permit to see him; he emerged from a large barnlike structure in a military camp at Wimbledon, somewhat dusty and dishevelled but quite cheerful. I asked how he was getting on. "All right," he said. "There are twelve damned 'conchies' in there, a good sort all of them. If I'm there much longer they'll have converted me."

What happened next I heard from his wife. She, also, had applied for permission to see him, and was told that this could only be allowed if she would promise to do her best to make him obey orders. As an added inducement, the suit in which he had left home was returned to her, torn to ribbons. This indication of how her man was being treated had not the effect on her which presumably it was meant to have. In a voice trembling with anger she said to me, "I'd rather see him dead at my feet than that he should give in to them now."

He did not give in; but it is only fair to say that what they had done to his suit, was only the same as he had done to theirs when, by overpowering numbers, khaki had been forcibly thrust on him, from which, when left alone, he had emerged to sit quite comfortably in his underwear (for it was warm weather) till with a six months' sentence he was passed on to Wormwood Scrubbs. Before the end of his first sentence, he got a second for again refusing to put on khaki; and the tussle of opposing obstinacies might have gone on still longer, had not Sir Edward Henry, the Chief Commissioner of Police, just then retired from office. His successor, coming upon the official record of the case, sent for my friend's wife and questioned her. She told him the whole story, and apparently won his sympathy; he swore heartily, but not at her or at her husband.

"Look here," he said, "we can't take him back into the Force straight out of prison. D'you think he'd be willing to go into the Military Police for a bit?" Yes, she thought he would, if it didn't mean conscripting him abroad. Reassured on that point, she received a special after-hours permit to visit the prison, saw her husband the same night, and he was out the next day. Three months later he had quelled an incipient mutiny at Aldershot, and not long after was reinstated in the London police without loss of rank or pension.

Chapter XXIII

A VISIT TO AMERICA

AFTER two years of wartime employment without pay it became necessary for me to make a quick income. At that time the United States was still good hunting-ground for indigent English authors who could put up readings or lectures. By good luck *Prunella* had been produced at the Little Theatre, New York, in the spring of 1914 and had run for a hundred nights. On this windfall I was able to keep going till 1916. Then, on the supposition that New York might provide audiences for the part-author of a successful play, I fell in with the proposition made to me by C. R. Ashbee that I should go out with him and G. Lowes Dickenson, and give lectures advocating what had not then been officially adopted in either country, the setting up of a League of Nations.

As a preliminary we made a call by appointment upon Sir Edward Grey at the Foreign Office. He was kind and sympathetic, but warned us on no account to let it be supposed that we had come as emissaries of the British Government; anything so sponsored would, he told us, be suspect. He advised us, when speaking about the war, to concentrate on the violation of Belgium, as being the matter on which we should find America most sympathetically interested. It was that alone, he added, which had brought Britain into the war a united nation, though he himself was convinced that we must have gone in anyway. As regards a League of Nations, he said that if the United States would come in, he would be ready to advocate our acceptance of the American doctrine of the freedom of the seas, but added that without America the League would not be strong enough to work effectively and impose its will on recalcitrant nations. Events have proved this to be a true prophecy.

260

I started for New York at the end of January. Escorted by a French warship for the first two days, we encountered no submarines; but because of my sister's tender fears for me, I suffered in that connection a humiliation which enraged me. I had been lent by a friend an extra superfine life-saving apparatus—a waistcoat of a vivid orange which, on the turn of a screw, inflated itself to balloon-like proportions. This she made me promise to wear in my bunk for the first two nights of the voyage. I wore it, cursing myself for a conscientious fool, and so lay exposed—a yellow terror—to the astonished eyes of my cabin steward when he came to call me in the morning. Curiously enough, on the first night out, there came one loud clap of thunder, and I started awake, thinking that here was the real thing; it proved a false alarm, and the rest of the voyage was without incident. But before the end of the war the boat I went out in and the boat in which I returned were both sunk by submarines, the latter with heavy loss of life.

It was on my second voyage out, four years later, that an incident happened which has stuck hard in my mind ever since. One evening a fellow passenger, with whom I was on nodding acquaintance, a stalwart-looking fellow in the early thirties, went past me into his cabin saying, "Good evening." Five minutes later I heard that he had died of heart attack; and at ten o'clock that night I saw a sea burial for the first time. Very few had been told of his death, only four or five who were his friends came to see the last of him. On the upper deck there had been dancing from nine o'clock on. At ten o'clock the dancing was stopped without explanation for half an hour, then went on again. It was explained to me that travellers by sea dislike hearing of a death having taken place on board, and so, for the repose of their souls, nothing is said, and the dancing stops for only half an hour. It's a good parable of the way the world wags on, quite easy and comfortable so long as it does not know what it does not wish to know.

New York is the most upstanding city in the world; it is also beautiful, so long as you look at it only from outside; but except at certain moments its beauty is hard as nails. My first sight of it was against sunset, its skyscrapers dark upon the west, till, as lights sprang stage by stage from basement to roof, they became a pile of golden honeycombs—a melting loveliness of halfway lights and shades; then, character reasserting itself, they hardened into night, sharp-eyed and glittering amid their huge black walls, and once more the fairy palaces became prisons.

Met by the usual inquiry from reporters as to what I thought of America, I replied that it struck me as very large, and that I expected to find it larger when I had seen more than its nose. The eagerness of Americans to know what we think of them is a compliment which Englishmen laugh at but enjoy. We are quite aware that we are not half so anxious to know what they think of us. But I did put the question to an American friend during that first visit, and learned that they thought us arrogant. I asked for an instance, and was told how a certain famous author, coming on a lecture tour, had found it sufficient, on more than one occasion, to read to a two-dollar-a-seat audience a couple of chapters from a book which they could get at half the price. I had to admit that, in that case, the charge was justified.

My own inquiry had followed the more usual one made to me. Asked what struck me most about Americans—their politeness, I said; and my astonished friend replied, "You are the first Englishman I have ever heard say that." But I was pleased recently to find that H. W. Nevinson has, in his reminiscences, said exactly the same thing. And it is perfectly true. Their ways and manners are not the same as ours, but to the stranger in their midst they are overwhelmingly kind and polite; and though the flattering things they say may strike one as excessive (as indeed they are) they do not strike one as insincere.

During the first week of my stay, at the dinner where I once more met Bispham, I found myself along with Masefield and Noyes in the company of a group of American poets, of whom the most prominent was Amy Lowell. We were all photographed together; she, and one or two others seated, the rest standing around. I said to her, "What you would really like, Miss Lowell, would be a symbolic group—you with your foot on the necks of at least two of us—myself for one." Her answer, "I would love it!" was delivered with the literary vindictiveness which was one of her chief attractions. I remember that in the speech she made at that dinner she invited her audience to hiss her, which, for the fun of it, they did heartily. But the best speech of the evening was Masefield's, beautifully spoken in his deep rich voice; simple, sincere, and humorous, it won the hearts of his audience.

Shortly after, as a guest of the National Arts Club, I met no fewer than a hundred and twenty American poets, all domiciled in New York, at their monthly gathering, where poems were submitted anonymously, first for criticism and then for members to vote on.

I had put in a poem of my own; it only got two votes, the prize-winner got forty; and there was plenty of laughter when my low standing was revealed, and when, in the speech which I had to make, I said how good it was for me to find my true level among the hundred and twenty poets whom New York was able to produce.

It was on that occasion that I first met and most improperly became friends with a young German married to one of my American hostesses, herself a poet of some repute. America had not then come into the war, and to show sympathy in a still neutral country towards one who was almost as much a pacifist as myself seemed to me only right and natural. But there were, at that time in America, certain people who, owing to President Wilson's delay in declaring for the Allies, were suffering from repressed war fever and were far more violently anti-German than the average Englishman; and when at the table of a professor of Columbia University I owned to a friendship which had sprung warmly from a common detestation of war and of hatred that had become a virtue, I was cut by my hostess. Not another word would she speak to one whom she regarded as a traitor to his country. And maybe there are some who still think that she was right.

But sometimes, in unexpected ways, America had lovely things to show. One day as I walked along Broadway I came on a sight that delighted me. I was on my way to lunch with some friends;

as I entered, I said, "I've just seen the most beautiful thing in America!"

"What? The Aquarium?" inquired one of them.

"No," I said, "more beautiful than the Aquarium. I saw that yesterday. What I saw just now was a street pillar box, and piled up against it parcels waiting to be collected—by anyone."

"Well, why not?"

"We couldn't do that in England. We are not honest enough."

"Oh, well, but you see we are a prosperous people; and we shouldn't send our diamonds like that anyway."

So, what seemed to me wonderful was to them quite ordinary.

And the next most beautiful thing that I saw in America was Thomas Mott Osborne's Sing Sing experiment in prison self-government, which under an organisation called the Mutual Welfare League had then been running some six or seven years.

Sing Sing, the biggest prison in New York State, was one of the oldest, and one of the worst in America, combining bad buildings, bad sanitation, bad ventilation, and (up to the time of the Osborne experiment) a bad system and a thoroughly bad record. The system was so unreforming that seventy per cent who entered returned as second or third offenders. It was so provocative of bitterness that the warders went armed, never alone, and when they stopped stood back to back or against a wall. When I went there, the governor (in America he is called the warden) handed me over to the prisoners to be shown everything. I was with them for three hours, and during the whole of that time not a warder came in sight. I was safe of course; there were warders somewhere, but they no longer went armed; they no longer went in couples; they no longer stood back to back, or against a wall to avoid attack from the rear. No amount of hostile theorising about the necessity for repression and punishment can get rid of such a fact or of its significance. The prisoners were no longer, as in former days, shut up in a negation of society to learn how they could do without it; they had been given a society of their own— to tend, to develop, to improve, and it had made all the difference. Under the supervision of the warden, to whom they had the right of appeal, they held their own courts of discipline, administered punishment to offenders, organised their own workshops, maintaining a standard of output considerably higher than had been extracted under the old system, arranged their own concerts and other recreations, managed their own library, and edited their own paper without censorship. I was asked to write for it, and did. The warden told me that I might say anything I liked; he would not see it till it was in print.

At the time of my visit Mott Osborne was away, and another was acting for him. He was away for grave reasons. Charges had been brought against him of acting beyond the powers given him by law; of breach of discipline by absenting himself from the prison when capital punishments took place (that charge he admitted to be true) and other serious offences. The trial was going on at the time.

The acting warden took me first into the large hall where the prisoners (six hundred of them) were having their midday meal. They supplied their own staff of waiters; there were no warders. As we came into the room we took off our hats—one of the rules of the new system (American politeness had got itself to prison). The warden carried a slip of paper in his hand; he called for silence. "You will be glad to hear," he said, "that the first count in the charges against Mr. Osborne has broken down; on that count he has been acquitted." Instantly all the men were on their feet, cheering like mad. The cheering went on unchecked for about two minutes.

At the warden's lunch table we were waited upon by a butler of dignified deportment. When he had left the room the warden said to me, "That is a life-sentence man; one of our best. The other day I had a guest dining with me; the next day this note was brought to my office: 'Dear Warden, yesterday your guest left a dollar for the waiter. The butler donates it to the Mutual Welfare League.' "

When luncheon was over the warden handed me over to the prisoners. "Do you mind," he said, "if I send you round with a German?" And hearing that I was already guilty of association with certain harmless specimens of the race, he introduced me to my conductor. On hearing my name, the man's face brightened; he hoped he was meeting a compatriot. I had to undeceive him. "Ah, well," he said, "it's all the same in here. Nationality doesn't count with us." And if, under those friendly circumstances, it counted little with me also, I was but following the example set by our own soldiers in the trenches, who, on the invitation of the enemy, accepted the Christmas truce in the first year of the war, and so scared the authorities by the cordiality of the relations thus established that great precautions had to be taken lest it should ever happen again. If true representatives of those men could have had the making of the Peace of Versailles, what a different, and what a much better peace it would have been.

The peace of Sing Sing was itself a remarkable demonstration of what human nature, under sane treatment, can do to get itself out of the mess into which insane treatment has landed it. But even though the Mutual Welfare League, under the guidance of a dominating personality, was a proved success, vested interests were against it; and when Osborne, acquitted of the charges brought against him, went back to carry his work to completion by securing for it less inhuman accommodation than old Sing Sing could provide, he found himself faced with such persistent opposition that he resigned his post, in order that he might be free to put up a political fight for fundamental reform not only in the system but in the building of the prisons which were to contain it.

He did not live long enough to complete the work on which his heart was set; but when America entered the war, official recognition was accorded him, and he was given charge of a large military prison camp to manage in his own way. On my second visit in 1920 I heard him give some account of it. When he went to take over as warden, great debate was going on as to whether the camp should be enclosed by a high wall or by barbed-wire entanglement. He vetoed both. "Run up a fence," he said, "that a man can put his leg over. Any man of pluck and intelligence wants to show that he can escape if you try to stop him."

Under his government (it might not have succeeded so well under others) the fence proved sufficient; there were some escapes, but they were well below the average; probably it was the less intelligent ones who went and had to be brought back again.

I met Osborne only once; he impressed me more than any other American I have seen either then or since. Shortly before his death he came to England, and spoke, I think at Dick Sheppard's invitation, to the congregation of St. Martin's. Very gradually what he stood for is finding acceptance in a tentative revision of the prison system both here and in America; but neither here nor there has it yet got more than halfway; and in Sing Sing, I am told, the scope and the efficiency of the Mutual Welfare League have been greatly reduced. *E pur si muove.*

Just before I left for home, I got an amusing example of the informal functioning of American law in relation to summonses for small offences. I was being motored by a friend's chauffeur to a speaking engagement in Chicago. At that time the twenty-mile speed limit was the disregarded law. I asked the chauffeur if he always exceeded it, as he was doing then.

"When I've got my employer with me, yes," said the man. "When I'm alone, no. I did once though, and got caught. A policeman stopped me, and told me I was to be summoned, and I got my summons the next day for that week Saturday. On the Friday, when I got back from work, I was called to the phone. 'Who's that?' says I. 'I'm Judge Raymond,' says he. 'Oh, how d'you do, Judge?' says I. 'What can I do for you?' 'You are up before me tomorrow,' says he, 'for exceeding the speed limit.' 'I am.' 'Do you admit it?' 'How much does your man say I was going?' 'Thirty-three.' 'It's a lie,' I says; 'I was only doing twenty-seven.' 'Well, that's more than the law allows,' says he; and I owned it was. Then he said, 'Look here, I want to go fishing tomorrow. Can we settle this now? If I fine you two dollars straight away now, it'll save your time and mine. What d'you say to it?' 'Right you are, Judge,' says I. 'You can go fishing.' "

Due to make landing at Liverpool on our return, we heard by wireless that a submarine was waiting to give us a welcome. Before we sighted the coast of Ireland, fog enveloped us; our captain was delighted, it made for safety. We crept northward in its soft

clinging embrace, and blew our foghorn gently and sparingly. A
day late we entered the mouth of the Clyde, making for Glasgow.
It was an inspiriting return. We were welcomed loudly; all the
shipbuilders along the banks stopped work, waved and cheered
lustily. Another boat had got safely through from the tale of
wreckage which before it ended had come near to losing us the
war.

I had been away twelve weeks, and the experiment had been
worth while. It had given me enough to go on with for another
year, and three friendships which were to last much longer. But
though I had gone out for the special purpose of advocating a
League of Nations, there was at that time so little interest in the
subject that I was asked to speak on it only twice. American
audiences much preferred that I should give readings from my own
plays. So, though they did not make as good a use of me as I
hoped, I had to oblige them.

CHAPTER XXIV

BACK TO THE WAR ZONE

I CAME back just after the Dublin rising was over. The news of it in America had been received with mixed feelings, for England's Irish policy had always been a sore point with Americans, especially in New York, where the Irish bulked large and made their bitterness felt. Dining at a friend's house, I was asked not to mention Ireland lest I should give offence; she had Irish servants, who were quite capable, she said, of letting me know what they thought about it, and flinging something at my head if I expressed the opinions of the average Englishman on this latest "trouble," and how it ought to be put down. My views, however, were sufficiently away from the average to make such caution unnecessary, and the potatoes were not thrown at my head. I think it was from W. B. Yeats that I stole the phrase which I afterwards put into John Morley's mouth in my play *The Comforter:* "The English mean well by the Irish, but they don't mean it much." During those war years we seemed to mean it less and less, and H. G. Wells's petulant outburst in reply to a plea that the Irish should be trusted, "Damn it all, we *have* trusted them!" was a grotesque perversion of the truth. Had John Redmond's offer of Irish support at the beginning of the war been sympathetically met, the Easter rising might never have occurred, and Redmond need not have died of a broken heart.

When I got back to London, I found my work at the Refugee Home reduced to a minimum. There was then no lack of employment for men or women. The bulk of our refugees—all but the mothers of young children and a few of the old or infirm—were out earning their keep, and were contributing to the maintenance of the Home. The Hospital which we had run for wounded Belgian soldiers was closed, for other reasons; all our Flemish dockworkers, whom we had been obliged to place under a separate roof for fear of domestic war, had found in the East End and elsewhere a more congenial environment than that provided by their hated compatriots. My whole-time job had thus become a matter of only a few hours weekly, and I was able to get back to my work.

By that time my reaction from all that war stood for had become decided, and in that reaction I wrote the first of my *Little Plays of St. Francis, Sister Gold.* I had no idea when I wrote it that it would form the first of a long series, only to be finished nearly twenty years later. But in the serene sanity of St. Francis I found such blessed escape from a world gone mad, that before long others followed, though I think only four had been written when the war ended. The idea of presenting St. Francis in a play-cycle only came gradually, and my work on it was interrupted by the theme which suddenly presented itself to me of a novel, based somewhat distantly on the life of Mrs. Girling, the Mother of the Shakers.

The Sheepfold: the story of a shepherdess and her sheep, and how she lost them was the result. Over my plays I have had frequent trouble with the Censor; but *The Sheepfold,* which is certainly the most moral of all my stories that can be called novels, is the only one over which, on the score of morals, I have had trouble with a publisher. As I was writing it against time, my agent asked for the first part as soon as it was finished, as a sample for the publisher to whom he had offered it. In that part my heroine, who was to grow up one of the best of women, had been violently seduced at the age of fifteen, and a few months later had killed her man with a fairly good conscience. It was rather strong meat, but as nothing stronger was to follow I reckoned that it was an honest sample. Anyway the publisher (through his reader) accepted it, and offered good terms. But when the complete script reached him, the reader took fright; he asked me to go and see him, told me that if the book were published as it then stood there would probably be a police prosecution and said that, unless I would modify it, his firm must cancel the agreement. It looked then as though a year's work must go begging were I to hold out, for if this expert adviser to the firm was right, I had little chance of getting the book published elsewhere. Nevertheless I did hold out, and my anxious but conscientious agent said nothing to dissuade me. Within a few weeks he had found me an equally respectable but less timorous publisher; the book had quite a fair success, reviewers were kind to it, and we had no trouble from the police. On present-day standards, no publisher would have turned a hair over it, but it was not till after the war that the decisive change took place which has made literary fig leaves a superfluous mark of respectability. It is a far cry to the day when Messrs. Mudie refused to circulate a book of mine because it contained the sentence, " 'Tis Molly, the bad wench; she's big, to her shame be it said." The book suffered badly in consequence—died after a sale of about five hundred, but has since been reissued.

Of that book—*All-Fellows*—I used to say that I should take it with me up to the Judgment seat, and if then I found sentence of damnation about to be passed on me, I should hold it up and say, "You can't damn me. I wrote this." But the assumption that a book can have in it such redeeming virtue is based on the notion that the book and its author are one. Having written some sixty or seventy, I have come to realise that there is no such close relationship, and though an author's books may be regarded as his children, they are by no means himself. They cannot "make agreement unto God for him"; if they could, a book of impeccable moral emblems might provide an easy pass into Heaven for the worst of sinners.

I once heard Yeats make the perverse suggestion that the more abominable a man's life, the more liable he was to produce works of an exalted character; and when one of his hearers, who had written a work which aimed at such exaltation, angrily protested, he added, "Yes, now it's very interesting that I should suddenly have discovered such a profound truth." It was probably only said to annoy his rather foolish opponent; but there is often undoubtedly a very wide separation between the character of a writer, and the character of his writings. It is not what he is but what interests him, which decides an author's choice of subject. No doubt my liveliest interest which has found literary expression has been St. Francis of Assisi, though Queen Victoria runs him a good second, and there is also a person whom I have called "Trimblerigg." But what most attracted me to St. Francis was not his exalted piety or his practice of holy poverty, but his artistry in human nature, and the extraordinarily effective use he made of it, whereof Juniper the fool is the standing example.

In the winter of 1916-17, in order that I might get back to my writing without interruption, we exchanged places for three months with our friends the Elliott Seabrookes, and at their house in Great Langdale endured the rigours of a Lake winter unusually deep in snow, and saw a series of sunsets which changed the whiteness of the surrounding peaks to a deep rosy glow which lasted long into twilight. In that remote corner of the world the war became a distant murmur; so far as appearances went, all was peace. Yet hidden in a wood two miles away was a large gunpowder factory; and the clock of the neighbouring church through all its quarters and hours remained mute so as to give no landmark of sound to an air-raiding enemy. That precaution, in so remote a district, was more ominously expressive of war's grip on the whole life of the country than all the anti-air-raid paraphernalia with which one was familiar in London.

I forget whether it was before or after our stay in the Lake district that I had one experience in connection with an air raid which is pleasant to remember. Somewhere in the Waterloo district of South London, Evelyn Sharp was helping to run a club for working women. She asked me to go and give them a lecture, or a dramatic reading, I forget which. It so happened that my lecture synchronized with a rather severe air raid, the one which managed to drop a bomb on Waterloo Station. On my way to the club, warning of the coming raid having just been sounded, I met parents running for shelter to the Elephant-and-Castle Tube station with small children in their arms; and I had hardly begun my lecture when the banging of anti-air-craft guns started. We had got to know by then that nearly all the noise caused by an air raid was defensive—nothing therefore to be frightened about. But suddenly in the middle of it all came a much louder bang (probably from the bomb which fell on Waterloo Station) and one of the women in my audience gave a squeal. Whereat Evelyn Sharp, as chairman of the meeting, lifted a corrective finger. "Now, now, you mustn't interrupt Mr. Housman!" she said, and nerves were calm again. It was a simple instance of that manipulative skill in dealing with human nature, which was so attractive in St. Francis, and even more delightful to meet with in actual life. Fear is very infectious; but absence of fear when so serenely and genially expressed is equally efficacious in the other direction.

The last event which I connect with my stay in the Lake district was the news of the Russian Revolution. It came one morning just as I was starting for my day's walk, and I remember well, as I tramped the dales, laughing aloud for joy over the one good thing that had emerged from the welter of evil into which the nations had been plunged. The downfall of Czarism did suggest, at that time, that the world was going to be made safer for democracy than had before seemed possible. And when the exposure of the secret treaties followed, and the call for the Allies to clean up their war aims so that New Russia might have something honest to fight for, it looked as though the abomination of desolations sitting in high places had received a knockout blow from which recovery would be difficult. But when I returned to London shortly after, I was surprised to find among most of my friends far more perturbation than joy over the great event; and when the refusal of the Allies to make clean the inside of the platter, whose outside they had made so polished and bright, brought about the fall of Kerensky and paved the way for the Second Revolution, I saw that my friends had good reason for their fears. From that time on the war became more sordid, more useless, and more abominable.

But while hope was still young, some time in the first half of that year we had a glorious meeting at the Albert Hall to welcome the Russian Revolution. The right people came and spoke, and said the right things, and Madame Clara Butt, rising to her full height, physical and vocal, sang to us a hymn with the refrain,

"Give peace to Thy people," for which indiscretion we heard afterwards she was taken roundly to task by some of the Czar's royal connections, who were also her personal friends or patrons.

I have not set down in these random notes any of my deeper impressions of the war. The deaths of relatives and friends, lovely and pleasant in their lives, remain matters of private concern. They were but part of a huge commonplace occurrence which was going on week by week, day by day, hour by hour. In some of the illustrated weeklies one saw pages of portraits of young men, like gods, but all prematurely mortal; and more and more, as our politicians manipulated the war to its desperate and wasteful end, did the doubt grow strong whether the outcome could ever be worth the sacrifice. At Versailles they took a year to settle that for us; but they did settle it—abysmally well.

But if I set down nothing here of my own more intimate and personal contact with the waste of war, I will give instead one short extract from a recorded experience, which of the many I read revealing the heartless horror of war, impressed me most. The story was told to a Danish Red Cross nurse by a young French corporal who had come into hospital minus an arm, of what took place on the night of February 24, 1916, during the siege of Verdun. There had been a terrific bombardment, and the Germans had attacked en masse, time after time, only to be mown down by the French guns. Both sides had suffered terrible losses. There were heaps of killed and wounded lying about, but the firing continued.

"To help the wounded was impossible, and night came on. It was freezing, and snow began to fall. Whether it was the darkness and the snow that caused it, or whether the thousands of wounded realised that help was impossible, nobody can know. The phenomenon cannot be explained. But suddenly it was as if madness had seized all of them. . . . It began like a kind of deep murmuring, gurgling and wailing, which spread over the whole battlefield, and a moment after it changed to screaming, screams wild and piercing that spread as a contagion. At last it became like one single scream from thousands of despairing throats—a bellowing, a sobbing, a wail of the soul's agony and fear of death.

"And we who listened to it were nearly going mad. We screamed too, we cried that we could not endure it any longer. We wanted to run out, to go out there and help, or to kill to stop those screams—to murder or die. It will hardly be believed possible, but the screams almost drowned the roar of the shells.

"The officers felt that there was danger afoot. Everyone who ran out of cover was certain to fall. The demoralisation of the men had to be avoided. And so orders were given that music should play! Forward all the regimental bands! Music, more music—patriotic songs and merry melodies without ever a pause, drums and trumpets right into our ears, all through the night, to drown the appalling screams."

That was the story; and so all through that night the dying heard the music that was being played to drown their screams—by their own comrades.

And when I hear of our War Office sending their bright military tattoos round the country to stimulate recruiting, and fetching children from their schools to be given a lying picture of war made attractive, I think of those bands playing at Verdun, to blot out the true reality of war. And just as those bands played to drown the screams of dying men whose agony is now over, so does our War Office play its bright music to drown from the minds of unthinking thousands the dying screams of a generation which it is training to believe in war.

CHAPTER XXV

WE GO WEST

AT THE end of the war, we gave up our house in Kensington, and retiring to a holiday cottage which we had rented for some years at New Milton, between the New Forest and the sea, made it our whole-time residence until such time as we could decide where our permanent country home was to be.

That question took more than three years to settle; and when we did settle it, our choice was as much influenced by personal attraction as by the attraction of locality. Somerset is a very beautiful county, and in visits to our friends, the Clarks of Street, we had got to know parts of it well. But what had drawn me more strongly, during the last years of the war, was Quakerism. In 1919 I joined the I. L. P. mainly because it was the one political party which had no use for war; and away from politics association with the Society of Friends, some of whom had become personally dear to us, seemed to offer a more sympathetic milieu for our declining years than we were likely to find elsewhere. So one day, when staying at Street with my friend Roger Clark, I asked if he could find me a building site or a house. As we were passing one on the road, "That would do for us," I said.

"Well," was the reply, "if you don't mind waiting for it ten years or so, you can have it. But Cousin Joseph lives there, and he is only eighty-six."

The Quakers are a long-lived community, but this estimate seemed a little excessive. Nevertheless, we should have had to wait six years had our choice so fallen. In the event, I bought the corner of a large field, without even troubling to cross the hedge, and find what a beautiful view it would provide for us to look out on. And there a house was built for us, which we called "Long-meadow," almost upon the road, along which I had tramped forty years before, with a homing instinct already in my heart, though unconscious of what it meant.

Our few years of waiting in our New Milton cottage before that final settlement were uneventful; but release from the interruptions of London life made me more productive, and my interest turned to the writing of one-act plays of which I have written since then more than a hundred. It was especially as the means to a play-cycle—chapters of dramatic biography, with one character as the main subject—that the form of the one-act play began more and more to attract me. This involved a certain diminution of high lights in the treatment, since the climax of a one-act play can seldom be as poignantly dramatic, or be led up to with such excitement of sustained interest as that of a three-act or four-act play. The curtains, being but punctuation marks in a whole series of scenes, are never quite final in their effect; for which reason the plays become more a commentary on life and character than a mere plot effectively staged to a definite finish. On the other hand the slower and more gradual treatment makes truth to life and intimacy of touch more possible. The crude demand on time made by an historical three-act play almost necessarily involves exaggeration and overemphasis; and though these things make for dramatic effectiveness, they are biographically untrue; and it has been my aim in my two play-cycles—the Franciscan and the Victorian—to show that one can get dramatic interest without exaggeration.

The first series of my *Little Plays of St. Francis,* finished in 1921, was published in 1922, by which time my Victorian series had, in *Angels and Ministers,* already begun.

Curiously enough, this latter series owed its origin, not to my interest in the personality of Queen Victoria, but in that of Benjamin Disraeli. I had written *His Favourite Flower* first, not as a play but as a narrative. I then turned it into a dramatic monologue, and with Disraeli still as my main interest, followed this up with *The Queen: God Bless Her.* So, with *Angels and Ministers* as a send-off, the rest followed.

In basing the plot of *His Favourite Flower* on an interpretation of dreams which was Freudian in character, I had by sheer accident been more true to life than I had any idea of at the time. When the play was published, an intelligent reviewer took me to task, as I thought justly, for giving the scientific and Freudian interpretation of dreams so early a date. But a few years ago, when I was giving a reading of the play at a summer school, a lady came to me and said, "You must have known my father—Doctor Kidd." I said I had never heard of him: who was he? He was Lord Beaconsfield's medical attendant in his last illness. He was also the first English doctor to interest himself in the science of dreams, and had translated two foreign treatises on the subject. And there, in that play, I had introduced a doctor, whose name I did not know, to explain to Lord Beaconsfield that his dream was the outcome of a thought-repression.

"Primroses," explained the Doctor, "had become associated for you—in a way which you have forgotten—with something you wished to avoid. And so they became the image, or symbol of your aversion; and as such found a place in your dream." And then, before the play ends, the reason for the aversion is discovered.

On one or two occasions in my life my guardian angel has given me prophetic promptings, which I have sometimes obeyed, and sometimes, unfortunately, have disregarded, but never have I been so divinely guided in a matter over which I was completely ignorant, as in this bit of play-writing.

My first encounter with the Freudian theory was about twenty years ago, when I heard what may have been one of the first lectures on the subject given in England. The lecturer was Dr. Constance Long, who had been abroad studying under Doctor Jung for some years. She asked me to be one of her audience. "I am going to get well laughed at," she said. It was quite true; a perfectly ignorant audience regarded the theory as a mere subject for mirth, held it up to ridicule, tore it to tatters, and thoroughly enjoyed itself in assuring her that the whole notion was childish.

It was a good example of how new knowledge gets treated by the demi-semi-educated members of what is called polite society—

who, when the thing becomes a fashion, come tumbling after it
with the same ignorant avidity which they showed first in holding
it up to ridicule.

In choosing St. Francis of Assisi as a dramatic subject, I have
already owned that I was more interested in him as an artist in
human nature, than as an ecstatic visionary, or as a lover of "holy
poverty." It was the Franciscan method of dealing with fools and
sinners which attracted me; and though I am not at all Franciscan
in temperament, it was largely through him that I became a
pacifist, convinced that, if rightly treated, human nature would
respond to conciliation and non-violence.

And thereby hangs a tale. In our garden at New Milton was a
large pear tree which bore good fruit; it grew on one side of the
hedge, but its roots went into a neighbour's garden. Now the law
says, quite unfairly, that, though your tree draws sustenance from
land which is not yours, all the fruit on it is yours by right; your
neighbour's remedy is to call upon you to lop off the boughs which
infringe on his territory, and, if you refuse, to do it himself. But
he has no further right. Our neighbour took the reasonable view
that he had a claim on the fruit which overhung his garden, and
with that I was quite ready to agree. But when one morning he got
up early and picked, before they were ripe, not only all the pears
on his side of the hedge, but all, as far as he could reach, on the
other side also, then I did not agree. And when he put the unripe
pears to ripen in a window facing south, where I could see them, I
felt not only defrauded but slapped in the eye. And therefore, in a
quite un-Franciscan spirit, I determined that it should not happen
again. So the next year, when the pears approached ripeness, I
kept a sharp watch on them, and up as early as my neighbour, saw
to it that he should never have the two gardens all to himself.
Then one day, when he was out wage-earning, I climbed the tree
and gathered all the pears that were lawfully mine, gathered them
so thoroughly that I left him only two which I could not reach.

In the evening, when he returned from work, he came down the
garden, and saw what had happened. I heard him growling to
himself; his sense of injury was great. For that I had waited. And

then I brought in St. Francis. I admit that I did so with no real charity of heart, but merely experimentally, impishly, curiously, to see how it would work. I got a large basket, and filled it with pears—his rightful share—and sent it round with a polite note asking him to accept them from the tree which "encroached upon his garden."

It did the trick. A grateful message of thanks came back, and if there was anything in *his* garden which we would like to have, would we say so.

Thenceforth, for the rest of our stay, our crop of pears was safe. But I knew well that St. Francis would have gone further, and in a far different spirit; for St. Francis (had he owned a pear tree) would have waited, and allowed himself once more to be robbed, and, after the robbery, would still have sent the basket of pears just as I did; and it would have had the same effect, only St. Francis would have contentedly gone without the crop which I took steps to save.

Life in our New Milton cottage was so uneventful that the above incident is the only one I can remember of local occurrence which seems worth telling. But one day I got a letter which led me to a fresh venture—not there, but in London—and to a friendship which has given me continual satisfaction and amusement ever since.

The letter was from a total stranger, asking whether he and Mr. Dick Sheppard (another total stranger) might come down from London and call on me with a view to my writing a "spiritual pageant" for them. I replied forbidding them to do anything so harumscarum and foolish, but said that I should be in London myself shortly, and would then come and look at them, and judge for myself how far they were in their right minds. We met a week later; one of them, the writer of the letter, was fairly sane; the other I found had that kind of madness which cannot be certified for legal restraint. He has it still.

What he wanted to get out of me was my *Saint Martin's Pageant,* of which subsequently there were two productions—one at the Church House, Westminster, in 1921, the other at the Lyceum

Theatre, a year later. It was not then written or thought of. I protested my disqualification—that the Church of England and I were no longer on friendly terms; we had parted. But that, I was assured, was an additional reason why I should write the Pageant. I might say anything I liked about the Church and its past behaviour—not only the Church of England, but the whole Church, primitive and mediæval, so long as I did not attack Christianity. Finding the distinction quite easy, I accepted the commission, and said just what I thought; and with Christianity to the fore, and the Church making a bad second all down the ages, the Pageant found a public for itself, and compassed a profit. What the Bishop of London thought of it, I don't know; it puzzled a good many people, perhaps it puzzled him. Bernard Shaw, I was told, said that he had never expected to see the Church put on the white sheet so publicly, and confess its sins so wholeheartedly as, through the mouths of piously performing curates, it did in some of those scenes. And that, at any rate, was something to have accomplished. I don't much care for pageants myself; I don't think the right dramatic form has been found for them. As an outdoor spectacle they are pleasant to the eye, but too diffuse for real dramatic effect; and I have seen only two single episodes in a whole series of pageants which have really moved me, and those *not* in the *Pageant of St. Martin*. Of recent years loudspeakers have made the writing of pageants more possible. Till then, the more they depended on action and the less on speech, the better they were. My Pageant had the advantage of indoor performance, which made the combination of speech with action more possible. But it probably contributed more than anything else to Dick Sheppard's breakdown of health which came immediately after, and lasted for years.

Before we moved from New Milton to Street, I had already become linked to a theatrical venture which gave me fuller satisfaction, and which in the following years, enabled my *Little Plays of St. Francis* to become better known, and under more ideal conditions than would otherwise have been possible.

Rutland Boughton, in 1914 or thereabouts, had founded "The

Glastonbury Festival." During the war, when he himself was called to active service, it had to be discontinued; but in 1921 when performances of *The Immortal Hour* and other operas and plays were resumed, he invited me to contribute a one-act play to the Festival programme, and the next year generously offered me an equal share in the time over which the Festival extended, for a full programme of my *Little Plays,* an arrangement which continued up to the last year before the brave experiment was abandoned, when—Boughton having left Glastonbury—I took on the whole of the Festival with an alternative programme of the *Little Plays* and *Prunella.* But running the Festival by myself was beyond my capacity, nor had I, standing alone, the reputation to make so ambitious an annual event pay its way. With Boughton gone, the whole of the musical public drawn by his operas was gone also; and it would have been a whole-time job to rake in a second public at the high prices which were necessary to make the Festival pay its way.

By good luck we managed to make a small profit on the final performances, and in the autumn we sent a small travelling company on tour, with a programme of the *Little Plays,* to about a dozen large towns, ending up for a week at the Polytechnic in London. This left us with a profit of a few hundred pounds for the depleted treasury of the rather nominal Glastonbury Festival Company. Six months later the whole of that profit had been swallowed up in the victory of artistic conviction over commercial prudence. Boughton's *Bethlehem* in modern dress had failed to win public support at the Church House, Westminster; we died without committing an act of bankruptcy, but we died thoroughly and well.

But though that venture ended as much on the bad side financially as some of my previous theatrical ventures had done, it was of all to me the most worth while, and on the whole the most pleasant in its memories and associations.

I was too nervous and anxious a producer, in that first year of the *Little Plays,* for my company to find me other than trying; I wanted to get things done too exactly in my own way, which a

Laurence Housman at the door of "Elbow-room," "Longmeadow," Street, Somerset.

producer of technical experience may do if he is given time. But we had only about a week in which to do it, and when I remember how much I worried some of the company with my trepidation and my inexperience, I must admit that they came through the ordeal wonderfully well; and those whom I tried most remained friendly, and returned each year to take part in a fresh programme. George Holloway, the Bristol amateur, made an excellent St. Francis, and Frederick Woodhouse a jolly Juniper, with an interpretation which quite satisfied me as true to type, so far as the Juniper of the earlier plays was concerned. In later years a new conception of Juniper was thrust upon me from an unexpected quarter. How I succumbed to it I shall tell later.

Year by year Rutland Boughton ran the Festival with terrifying energy; if he was not able to exhaust himself, he exhausted others— sometimes their patience as well as their physical endurance. He had a devoted following in which rows and reconciliations played a natural part and gave daily stimulus to the rush of a production against time which had wonderful results out of material that was largely amateur.

He had also reciprocal aversions which he seemed rather to enjoy, having sometimes mischievously provoked them. It was on that score that I was obliged to explain to him one day why I had to seem inhospitable. My housemate, I told him, had a distaste for his company. To which, with the sweetest smile, he replied, "Mutual, my dear." And that disarming assurance, so helpful to me in its frankness, gave satisfaction also in the reciprocating quarter. If people have to be enemies it is better that they should be honest about it, and—if they can—see the humour of it without loss of temper.

It was not, I think, to the first but to the second production of my *Little Plays* at Glastonbury that I got Alfred to come, rather doubting whether he would like them, for he had never cared much for my religious affinities. When I published *Spikenard*, a book of devotional poems, he had gone unkindly out of his way to describe it as nonsense verse, and over *The Sheepfold* had written to say that he preferred its moral impropriety to its theology. After seeing the *Little Plays,* he said to me quite kindly, "Not so bad as I expected," which was as much in the direction of praise as I could have hoped to get from him.

When, years later, he published his *Name and Nature of Poetry,* I found that for him nonsense in poetry was no drawback; indeed, he had by then told me that though *Spikenard* was nonsense, he thought it about the cleverest thing that I had done. I had not meant it to be "clever," yet the imputation consoled feelings that had been wounded.

One of the features of the Glastonbury Festival year by year, was the inclusion of lectures, or dramatic readings, by distinguished authors. On one occasion John Drinkwater came down, under promise to read us his then unpublished play on Oliver Cromwell. Only as we were starting for Glastonbury did he discover that he had brought the wrong manuscript.

As there was no help for it, he read us two narrative poems instead, the first of which, called *The Old Mill,* was a quite beautiful modern version of the story of *Paolo and Francesca,* in this case the lovers coming to their tragic end when the old mill, struck by lightning, falls and buries them in its ruins. The applause that followed the reading was scarcely over when an old clergyman rose from the body of the hall, and said solemnly, "In the name of Jesus Christ, I protest against this glorification of fornication and adultery." Having said it, he sat down, and the audience gasped, waiting for what would follow. Drinkwater stood, not thunderstruck but thunderous of expression; then he said, "Who is in charge of this meeting?" and up the gangway ran Boughton, and stood at Drinkwater's feet below the platform, gesticulating. At the time I thought foolishly that he was begging Drinkwater not to take up the challenge, but to hold his peace. On the contrary, he was urging him to battle. "Have his blood! Have his blood!" he was saying in effect. It was a curious situation; Drinkwater had, no doubt, the sympathy of most of his audience, but there was sympathy also for the old man, who was obviously sincere and conscientious, and had spoken with a certain dignity of demeanour which impressed. Drinkwater's treatment of the situation was admirable. He said very quietly, "I don't think this is the proper place and occasion for a debate on morals; elsewhere I should be quite ready to take up the challenge. Whatever else may be thought about their story, I think most of you will agree that those two unhappy lovers were to be pitied. But you will notice that in my story there was one important character which had *no* pity for them; and that was—*the Old Mill!*" On that he finished, and there was loud applause; the representative of "the Old Mill" had been answered in the best possible way.

When the Glastonbury Festival was held for the last time, we transferred the performances from Glastonbury to Street, which had a larger and a better hall. On that occasion the part of St. Francis was taken by Maurice Evans for part of the week, in order to relieve George Holloway who was also acting Pierrot in *Prunella*. It was not for the first time that Evans had taken the part; he had done so in the previous year at the St. Pancras People's Theatre; and it was his outstanding performance as St. Francis, which, having won the praise of discerning critics, decided him to make acting his profession. In the tour which followed in the autumn, Francis was played by Denis Barry, while I took over from Woodhouse the part of Juniper when other engagements called him away. I was not good as Juniper, for though I can play the complicated fool, I cannot play the simple fool; unfortunately I had to take it on in London. It is the only character I have ever played on the professional stage, and though it is the character I most enjoyed writing, it is the one I least enjoyed acting.

CHAPTER XXVI

MY SECOND VISIT TO AMERICA

SOON after the publication of *Little Plays of St. Francis,* I received from M. Paul Sabatier (who had asked through a mutual friend that I would send him a copy) a letter of which this is a translation.

"Dear Sir,
"It is a long, a very long time indeed, since I have read any book which has given me so much pleasure as this which you have so kindly sent me. I have read it from cover to cover with ever-increasing delight.
"I am not competent to pass judgment on verse, or play-writing; but after having spent all my life in trying to reconstruct the life of the Poverello, I feel that I have the right to give an opinion on the historic side of your work; and it seems to me that your insight into the Franciscan effort is marvellous. Your little plays show us the milieu in which Francis lived, and bring it to life for us once more with an accuracy which is unique; while it also reveals to us his interior life with a delicacy of touch which I have never found elsewhere. You have avoided an error which took from the official legends and from the later biographies a great part of the reality which they should have emphasized; for you have not separated Francis from his companions. The important place which you have given to Brother Juniper, for example, conforms perfectly with strict historical truth. . . . That you have been able to write your plays without having been to Assisi is something of a miracle, and I wish all the more that you could make its closer acquaintance. You would find there people of sympathy, appreciation, and understanding, who would also be able to talk with you in English.

"There is one other point which interests me greatly—that is what practical effect your *Little Plays* will have in England. I hope some Guitrys will arise to give them representation, and that we shall thus have a sort of resurrection of the 'Joculatores Domini' organised by St. Francis, and reconstituted to his memory, thanks to your *chef d'œuvre. Votre bien reconnaissant et devoué.*

"PAUL SABATIER"

Such a testimonial from the greatest living authority on St. Francis would have made me impervious to any amount of adverse criticism from other quarters. But I had nothing to complain of; the reviews were almost uniformly kind and appreciative; only one morning paper, which had consistently knifed me year after year, remarked what a pity it was that the writer had so little sense of humour. If adverse criticism can ever give an author amusement and joy, I think that did so to me.

Subsequent correspondence with Sabatier took me to Assisi in the following year. I went specially to meet him, only to receive news on my arrival that he was too ill to come, and we did not meet until a few years later, when, at the Septuacentenary Commemoration of the coming of the Grey Friars to England, Sabatier gave a discourse in French, and I a reading of two of the *Little Plays,* in the nave of the Canterbury Cathedral. In order that Sabatier might be better understood, a printed translation had been supplied to every member of the audience; and the rustling of turned-over pages made a loud accompaniment at intervals to an address beautifully delivered in French, so clear to the ear that I wondered whether it could be in the true Parisian accent which has always been the most difficult for me to understand. Belgian French I had found so much easier; perhaps Sabatier's was Alsatian.

I have said that holy relics do not appeal to me; perhaps a doubt as to their authenticity is what gets in the way. But at Assisi there was one relic which I greatly wished to see, and was prepared to venerate. That was the autographed parchment given by St. Francis to Brother Leo, his beloved disciple, as a cure for his spiritual desolation. Had Sabatier been with me access to this relic would have been easy; but I was too shy to make application for myself, and I gave up all hope of seeing it until one day in the lower church (during the great Festival week early in October), I saw a side door open, and out came a procession of priests, friars, and a cardinal with, at their head, one who carried what looked like a square of parchment enclosed in a gold frame. Here, then, was my relic; at a side altar the priest who bore it took up his station, a crowd gathered, the formal process of veneration began, and very joyfully and fervently I took my place in the long waiting line, and watched the kisses which the faithful were bestowing upon the relic, each in turn as they passed.

In my devotion I had been prepared to take the risk of infection; nevertheless it was a relief to see that after each kiss, a disinfecting wipe was given to the glass covering the relic. Presently I drew near to my turn; and then, looking ahead, I saw upon the frame Latin words, which informed me that what I was about to kiss was a piece of "the true robe of Our Lady." There was no help for it— there I was pinned into line, unable to escape; the deed had to be done. And so, without any belief in it at all, I gave the kiss which the situation required, respectfully—or politely, at any rate—but with no real satisfaction. I felt I had been sold.

But Assisi itself satisfied me abundantly, far more, indeed, than I had expected, and towards one of its features I experienced an unaccountable sense of affinity. The white wagon-oxen that I met in the streets became special objects for my devotion. I could not help it; when I met them standing still, I went up to them, and embraced them, and said loving words to them, while their owners looked on puzzled but pleased. I cannot account for it; I have a general liking for cows, I prefer them to horses, and I had met and admired draught-oxen before at Cercina near Florence, and elsewhere. But nowhere else has my heart gone out in such abject devotion to any animal (except occasionally to cats), as it did to the white oxen of Assisi; and if I ever do go back to Assisi it will be quite as much to see them, or their successors, as to see San Francesco, or St. Damien's, or the Portiuncula, or the Carceri.

At the Carceri when I went there, with my friend and guide Mrs. Elliott Seabrooke, an amusing incident happened. The Brother concièrge, who showed us round (speaking French for my benefit), was telling us the old story of the mountain torrent which had kept St. Francis awake and had gone underground at his bidding to remain there ever since. When he had finished I told him that the *signora,* being a water-diviner, could herself indicate to us the course which the stream now followed. He expressed polite incredulity, but having secured a forked twig from the adjacent wood, the *signora* proceeded to demonstrate. As she crossed the dried gully which had once formed the stream's bed, the twig gave no sign—the water was not where one might have expected it; but halfway across the paved courtyard, up went her hands with a sharp jerk. "The water is there," she said.

"The signora is right," said the friar.

It was not the first time that I had known her make the experiment. She had discovered, while staying at my house in London, that a stream ran diagonally under the basement. As quite recently a water main had been sunk alongside the premises, I asked the local turncock whether he knew anything about it. Oh, yes, it was quite true; the stream was there and had given them a lot of trouble at the very spot which Mrs. Seabrooke had indicated.

She had discovered her power quite by accident some years previously. Needing water for her garden in Great Langdale, she had observed the course of a small stream which disappeared into the hillside above the house. On the chance that its track lay under some part of her garden, she made the "dowsing" experiment; it answered; she hit the exact spot at first trial, and secured, at only a few feet below the surface, the water supply she required.

It is a fascinating gift; next, I think, to the power of attracting bird and beast, I would like to possess this personal affinity to water. Not having it myself I gave it to the hero of my first novel, *A Modern Antaeus,* the only one of all my books which has in it some odds and ends of autobiography.

Of that same book its American publisher told me when I recently met him in New York, "You killed it by giving it a bad title."

"It was a good title," I said, "for those who could understand it."

"But how many did?" he answered. He was quite right; a title that only a few can understand is not a good title, however apposite it may be.

I was writing my *Little Plays of St. Francis* when I paid my second visit to America in the early months of 1920; and I have a vivid memory of composing a large part of the scene called *The Bride Feast,* while wandering in deep snow late at night among the hills at Katonah on my return from giving a lecture in New York. I was then staying at the Community School at Brookwood, a place of delightful friendships, austere in its principles, merry in its practice. I had not asked to be met at the station, and when I started to find my way home I had no thought that I should get into difficulties, for the distance was not above three miles. But a deep fall of snow had obliterated landmarks; and when, doubtful of the road, I knocked at a door, and rather pleadingly begged to be directed, hoping that I might be offered a shakedown for the night (for it was then close on midnight), I was encouragingly told that the way (though it was now nearer four miles than three) was all quite easy and simple. I had only to go along and I should find it.

To one living in the locality it was, no doubt, as simple as was said; and with other houses in sight it was ridiculous for me to say that I was lost; but I knew that in order to get to my destination, those houses had to be left behind; and when I left them I *was* lost. I had a warm overcoat, but underneath it I was in evening dress, I had already lost one of my rubbers in the snow, and presently I lost the other. In such circumstances patent leather shoes do not make good travelling. I began to be sorry for myself, but my main feeling was not fear, but how very much ashamed of myself I should be if I had to go back to one of those houses and beg shelter for the night. It was in such circumstances that inspiration of a kind descended on me, and for the next hour or so I was busily composing blank verse which the curious may find in the first two and the last four pages of the *Little Play* called *The Bride Feast,* and when presently, very wet and bedraggled about the ankles, and beginning also to be tired, I saw a light ahead of me, I decided that I had had enough of it; and coming to a strange door I knocked, and when it was opened, found I was being anxiously expected, for this was the back door of Brookwood, which I had not seen before; and I had come to it by unknown ways, which I could not describe; but there I was, very happy though rather shamefaced over my blundering sense of locality; and with another of my *Little Plays* near to completion—a good night's work accomplished under very incongruous conditions: winter snow as the setting for a scene of midsummer night's madness, jealousy and passion, and of young love lying dead.

Some years later I composed the *Death of Juniper* while climbing the Malvern Hills; that is the only other setting to a *Little Play* that I can remember; but obviously there need be no relation between subject and environment when the writing mood takes possession.

Inspiration comes in such different ways, but always—whether its quality be good, bad, or indifferent—with determination. When the idea starts, however much it may be in the rough, it is quite sure of itself. There is your story or play—egg in shell—waiting to be hatched.

I had an amusing instance of this one day, when I was saying good-bye to an American friend at New Milton station. We were talking of my pet aversion; I was saying what I thought of him; and without much intending it, I said, "Some day I shall write his life, from the point of view of the God who created him."

"Oh, but you can't do *that!*" my friend protested.

"Then I will," I replied; and there and then, out of my mouth came, almost word for word, the first sentence of the book which that same day I went home and began writing. The sentence as I then composed it was this: "Of course when I made Mr. Trimblerigg, having shaped him I will not say to my liking, but at least to my satisfaction—I knew that I had made a very clever man. But I did not foresee how he would turn out."

The sentence got slightly altered before publication, but the whole idea was there. That was the beginning of *Trimblerigg,* and my American friend, who pins her faith to *In Memoriam* and tries not to have any views more modern than are contained in that poem, found herself the startled godmother of a book which ought to have shocked her, but which with kindly inconsistence she managed to enjoy.

My second visit to America brought me more friends than money. In friends I came back rich, having picked them up all the way along—three on the return voyage, of whom the American friend just mentioned was one. But in pocket I should have fared badly, had it not been for two fortunate happenings which made things easier. The first was the starting at the very moment of my arrival of a new left-wing weekly called *The Freeman.* The editor, who, during my stay in Chicago, was my part-time host, invited me to send him as many articles as I had time to write. And then, most opportunely to make writing easier, Brookwood Community School opened its friendly doors to me; and for some three weeks as a P. G. among students ranging in age from ten to twenty-three, I got all the peace and quiet I needed for literary work in place of the lecturing I had expected.

Brookwood was a charming example of naïve American idealism. It had been started by a capitalist with a conscience; his income came from coal mines, and having seen the conditions under which the miners worked, he was unable to spend money so derived on himself. So he devised this curious and very easy-going institution—half school, half farm. It aimed at being self-supporting, so far at least as bread, milk, butter, cereals and fuel were concerned. It did its own housework. Its students were those who for various reasons, financial or domestic, had been let and hindered in their education; they paid what they liked—that is to say what they could afford, which sometimes was nothing at all; the staff was largely voluntary; the curriculum was vagarious and experimental. They came from what in England we should call "all classes," and were a very happy, vivacious, disputatious, and introspective lot. Once a week, called together for self-examination, they pulled themselves up by the roots to see how they were getting on, amended the rules to make growth better, planted themselves again more firmly than before, and then went gaily on for another week to the next uprooting. Morning prayer one was free to attend or to avoid. Those who had a concern to pray or preach, to curse or to bless, put their names on the notice-board the day before; you knew whom you were to expect. One day the hour of prayer was taken by a charming young Russian Communist who attacked us for having any religion at all; another day we had from a member of the staff one of the most moving and quietly impassioned addresses I have ever heard. This was my friend Bill Simpson, a man of good university training, once but now no longer a free-church minister, having been cast out by his congregation for preaching pacifism during the war.

More recently, while the Victory blockade, which followed the Armistice, was keeping Germany helpless in preparation for the dictated peace which has been the root cause of all the evils that have come since, he had gone out, stood at street corners in midwinter, barefoot, saying to the passers-by, "This is what we are doing to the women and children of Germany." For that he was arrested, taken to the police court and charged with being a vagrant of unsound mind. The magistrates having examined his mind, dismissed the case, and he was set free. But that practical demonstration of what was happening to the helpless victims of war enabled him to collect and send funds to their aid which would not otherwise have been forthcoming.

The Brookwood experiment has not lasted; one day it pulled itself up by the roots, examined them, and turned into something else—true to character in its end as in its beginning. It was childlike in its ways, and typically American, alternately very pleased with itself, or—faced by its failures—deeply downcast and disappointed. The spirits of Americans are seldom level in their running.

At that time, the experiment having only just started, America was very pleased with itself over Prohibition; and when (asked what I thought about it) I said that it was a characteristic sample of American impatience plus optimism, my criticism was impatiently received. Only in the men's clubs, which had suddenly ceased to be social, was there any note of disapproval.

I found Americans very sensitive over their failures—not to be joked about them. While I was in New York there was a big police parade—an annual event, but this one on an exceptionally grand scale. Police-dogs had lately been introduced for the pursuit and hauling down of runaway criminals. And so, in Madison Square, a stunt-demonstration had been devised as a surprise feature for the assembled crowd. By pre-arrangement, a woman's handbag was snatched by a paid emissary of the police. The man made off; loud cries of "Stop Thief!" were raised, and the dogs were unleashed for a show-off of the utmost publicity. But before they could reach their quarry, a policeman, not in the know, hearing the cries, and catching sight of the runaway, plugged him neatly in the back; for in America, be it understood—to run away from the police is a crime which may involve capital punishment. In this case it was only injury for life. The next day New York was very sore about it—not so much concerned over the injury done to the man, as over the ridicule in which a foolish publicity stunt had involved its police. I found that the subject had better not be mentioned.

One lives and learns, and sometimes the lessons are entertaining. One day in a New York restaurant, I watched a coloured waiter expeditiously clearing an adjoining table, and laying it afresh. Presently he came along with a basket of bread, and a packet of triangular paper bags. He licked his thumb and started separating them in the flat. "What are those for?" I asked.

"Oh! sanitary, sah, sanitary," he said, in a tone of superior reproach to English ignorance. And so saying, he picked up a bag, blew it open with a blast of his breath, and inserted a roll of bread. This he did till, the relaying complete, the table had become an altar to American sanitation.

Chapter XXVII

THINGS UNEXPECTED

BETWEEN my second visit to America and my last, from which I have but lately returned, little has happened to me which seems worth telling except the writing of my books, and—in two instances at least—their acceptance by a larger public than I have been accustomed to for most of my life. Unexpectedly I am now able to live in comfort on my writings alone—most unexpectedly of all, a play censored in this country has brought me a windfall elsewhere, which more than makes up for the official veto imposed at home.

But though the listing of an author's books does not make interesting reading for the general public, they are in the main what he himself has lived for; and the years during which he has produced most of his best are for him the most eventful.

Judged by results, departure from the noise and dust of London was the wisest move of my life, for since I did so, I have written more, and I think better, or at any rate more completely to my own satisfaction, than in any previous years.

There is a familiar hymn, beginning with the words "O sweet and blessed country," known, I suppose, to most of my readers. Those words refer to man's hope for a better life in a better world. But after forty years of a working life spent in London, I can apply them very wholeheartedly to this world also; and during the last twelve years, (since my escape from the captivity of Town) it is not only "O sweet and blessed country" which expresses my thankfulness, but "O sweet and blessed county"—the county of Somerset. Over forty years ago I found myself looking into the very heart of Somerset almost without knowing it; for I had not realised what an embracing view of Somerset looked like, till from the top of Mendip above the Cheddar Gorge I gazed westward on such a delectable stretch of country as, till then, I had never seen.

At that time I had no notion that I should ever come to live in Somerset—to live actually within the range of what then lay before me. But as I caught sight of Glastonbury Tor for the first time, with a flow of wooded hills to right and to left, and here and there crowning columns—memorials to what men or what events, I did not know—a sudden thrill took hold of me; I felt as one standing on Pisgah, gazing into a Promised Land which might never be mine; and as my arms had embraced the white oxen of Assisi, so did my heart embrace the hills of Somerset. A few days later, passing over Glastonbury Moor after an evening storm of rain, I saw the Tor encircled by a double rainbow against a dark leaden sky; and again the Pisgah sense came to me that this was the land where I would love to be. Half an hour later I passed within a stone's throw of the spot where Longmeadow, my home, has now been built for me.

A while back I heard, with great contentment, somebody say that Somerset was the most beautiful county in England; and when somebody else (controverting that statement) named some other wretched county as more beautiful, I in my infatuation said that, if so, I did not wish to see it. And though that may seem a perverse sort of thing to say, there is this truth in it—that when one is well-rooted, one does not want to change one's roots. Beauty grows by association; nothing, when a thing is good for one, has so endearing an influence as association and familiarity.

That is a deep-down truth of human nature; it takes unexpected forms. There are men who love a coal mine, and prefer greatly to work in the dark bowels of the earth than in field or garden. A friend once took me into the engine-room of an Atlantic liner. To me it was like a glimpse of hell, to him it was Heaven; being an engineer by training, for him machinery was the most beautiful thing in the world. For me, as a place of domicile, Somerset with its accompaniments is as near Heaven as I am ever likely to get.

Longmeadow was designed for me (an improvement on the pattern I sent him) by the Quaker friend from whom I bought the land. The garden we designed ourselves. And in these quiet surroundings I have written the greater part of the two works which give me most hope of leaving behind me something which will remain of interest to another generation of readers. It was not through clever calculation, but through lively interest in two remarkable historical characters, unique in their personality, that I came to write my play-cycles of St. Francis and Queen Victoria. But though I had no clever reasons for writing them, the fact that my interest was so drawn has done me good service. I might have written plays as good, or better, of other characters famous in history; but they would not have "caught on," and secured for themselves the faithful and the fortunate backing which my happy choice of subject has brought me. And how greatly I am indebted to that outside help for the wider recognition of my two dramatic biographies—*Little Plays* and *Victoria Regina*—I make full acknowledgment. That help came to me in the first place from amateur companies, later from professionals.

As already told, it was "The Glastonbury Festival" which gave the *Little Plays* their first send-off. Then, in January, 1925, they won a new following, which has lasted ever since; for, at the beginning of each year, the University College, London, Dramatic Society has given a week's performance of a double programme of *Little Plays,* which, after the third year reached, and from then on has maintained, a high dramatic standard.

How those performances led to the doubling in number of the plays, owing to the beautiful interpretation of the part of "Brother Juniper" by one of the students named Frank Heath, the following account, which I wrote two years ago for the College Magazine, gives the full story:

"It never entered my head that I should at any time in my life receive a University training—least of all in such a subject as play-writing. Yet that, in effect, is what has happened to me, owing to the dogged persistence with which University

College, London, Dramatic Society has continued performing my *Little Plays,* and incidentally, with equal doggedness, pestering me to write more. Any reasonable Dramatic Society, with its appetite decently controlled by a sense of its many imperfections and deficiencies, would have found eighteen plays enough for it to bite on. But when, with a morbidly stimulated appetite, this Society made those plays an annual event, in the form of a double meal lasting for a week, eighteen were not enough. And so it was that—after the third year—I began to write more.

"I do not think I should have done so had not one bright particular star shone out of the murk of those early performances. It was the 'blasted Heath' that led me on to my doom of having to write what eventually became a whole second series of equal length, and—so Granville Barker has assured me—of greater merit.

"So it was that, in my sixtieth year, under Heath's tuition I began my University training in the writing of religious plays for a very non-religious company to perform. In that process Juniper became my main subject, making his appearance in all but three of the eighteen plays that followed—in eleven of them as the chief character. It was when I found what a debt I was under to the University College Dramatic Society for providing me with Heath—not merely as a perfect interpreter of the character of Juniper in the plays already written, but as the inspiration for a further development, that I granted it the free run of my *Little Plays* so long as it might choose to perform them.*

"But even then my University training had not ended; for even thirty-six plays proved insufficient for the Society's re-

---

* The following is the text of the said grant or "Indulgence." "Granted to the Students of University College, London, by the Author of the *Little Plays of St. Francis.* The Indulgence to be known as the Indulgence of the *Little Plays of St. Francis.* The terms of the Indulgence are as follows:

Henceforth we grant to the University College, London, Dramatic Society, that whensoever it comes to perform these Plays, soberly and in its right mind, having duly rehearsed the same, submissively and obediently to its chosen Producer, it shall be absolved henceforth from all payment of Author's fees, both in this world and in the next, from the day of the present performance of the Plays unto the day when copyright expires. And we ordain that this Indulgence shall hold good every year, and for ever, during the week of the said Plays' performances, from the evening of the Monday when they begin, to the evening of the Saturday following. *Auctor locutus, causa finita.*"

quirements, because they provided so few parts for what my
brother A. E. H. describes as 'the deplorable sex.' So I was
obliged to add four *Plays of St. Clare* with Juniper in two
of them. And then, by special request, an Epilogue. And
there—Heaven helping me (by expeditious death, if in no
other way)—I did mean to stop. Forty plays and an Epilogue
were really enough; and even if the Horse-leech's Daughters
were to come to University College for their training, I hoped
that I might hold out against them. But before the Society
had done with me, it extracted five more; after which, to
make a finish of the matter I brought out a "complete and
final" edition in three volumes, and made a solemn promise
to my long-suffering publisher that I would write no more."

That, roughly, is the history of how the forty-five *Little Plays*
came to be written. But there is this further to be said, for I think
it is worth saying, since in these days the circumstance so seldom
occurs: there is very real value for a playwright to be in intimate
and continuous touch with his players—for the writing of the
plays and the tradition of how they should be acted to grow up
together; for the playwright to receive inspiration from the players
of his characters, and for the players to know exactly what the
playwright meant them to be and do at certain points where stage
directions are inadequate, and where even the character intended
does not quite explain itself in speech.

That has been my good fortune at any rate, even if to producer
and players the other side of the arrangement may have seemed
a more mixed blessing; and it is quite literally true that had the
University College Dramatic Society not continued so faithfully
to produce my plays from year to year, some at least—perhaps
most of the second series—and all that came after, would never
have been written.

It is a pleasant irony of history that London University College
should have become a training-ground for religious drama. What,
I wonder, would some of its pious Founders (if pious they can
be called) have thought about it, could they have looked forward
to the centenary with prophetic eyes, and in that year of com-

memoration seen "the glorious poor little one of Assisi" taking part—under the approving eyes of the College authorities?

The above-mentioned Epilogue was a separate affair. It stands by itself, and only the University College Dramatic Society has the right to publish or to perform it. I was persuaded to write it with Bernard Shaw held up to me as a model; he had written an epilogue to St. Joan, so why should not I write one to my St. Francis? And as about that time I had been asked by a newspaper to write my own obituary notice, it struck me that I might go a step further and write my own death scene; which accordingly I did, and two years running acted the dying author to full houses. I was more popular in my death than in my life.

I sent word of it to Alfred at Cambridge, and asked him to come and see me perform. He replied that, though my death had attraction for him, he could not face the journey to London in the cold of winter, or tear himself from the College feasts which were taking place at that season.

Bernard Shaw was asked by the producer to come and act the Doctor; his reply was that if he did he would be mistaken for God Himself, which would hurt the play, making me no longer the principal person. I had already written to tell him that he, along with John Drinkwater, was irreverently mentioned; so also was the performing society, and here, by its permission, are the two passages in which the dying author does his last bit of leg-pulling.

> *The Author, for stage purposes, is lying in bed, preparing to die. The Doctor, no longer of any use, has gone. The Author and the Nurse are talking:*

Nurse: You have written quite a lot of books, someone told me.

Author: In my life more than I ought. My brother used to say that I wrote faster than he could read. He wrote two books—of poems—better than all mine put together.

Nurse: But you wrote plays, too, sir.

Author: Oh, you know that, do you?

Nurse: Why, yes. Last year I saw six of them, done by the students at University College.

Author: Yes, poor dears! It's become a habit with them. They can't break themselves of it. What did you think of them?

Nurse: Oh, very nice, sir . . . very beautiful.

Author: The *students,* I meant.

Nurse: Oh, well, sir, of course they did their best.

Author: They did; they always do—they are excellent in parts, like the curate's egg.

Nurse: Oh, not as bad as that, sir!

Author: No? Well, I suppose it takes an author, or a God, to put all the blame on others and none on himself.

And having thus intentionally shocked the Nurse, the Author sends her off to get his beef-tea. And then presently, in answer to the Author's call, St. Francis enters, and after a few preliminaries comes the following:

Francis: So you think you are not one of my sheep, eh? Then what made you write plays about me? Did you do it for mischief?

Author: No, Father—I'll tell you. There are (or were when I wrote them) two monsters going to and fro in the world seeking whom they might devour.

Francis: Monsters?

Author: Yes, Father. Not bad monsters, good monsters; but with a terrible appetite for getting hold of people and writing plays about them. One of them was called "Drinkwater"—but didn't, except sometimes. And the other wasn't called Drinkwater, but did. And Drinkwater was always looking for real people—great and good people—to write plays about; because he thought that if the people were good and great, the plays would be good and great also. And the other person, who wasn't *called* Drinkwater, but did——

Francis: What was his name, my son?

Author: Shaw, Bernard Shaw, Father. He was afraid that Drinkwater would try to write a play about Joan of Arc. So to save her from Drinkwater, he wrote it instead.

Francis: Yes, well?

Author: Well, Father, that play about Joan was such a success that he began looking for some other saint to write about. And so, for fear he should choose *you,* I wrote my *Little Plays of St. Francis* to save you from Bernard Shaw.

Francis: Well?

Author: And I *did,* Father.

Francis: And why should not Bernard Shaw have written plays about me?

Author: Because, Father, had *he* written them, he would have made *you* Bernard Shaw.

Francis: Even as Bonaventura made me Benedict. Why not?

Author: Ah, Father, you know Benedict, but you don't know Bernard Shaw.

Francis: What's the matter with him?

Author: Matter? Nothing. He's a wonderful man. I love him. But he doesn't like fools—hasn't any use for them. So how could he have written plays about you and Brother Juniper?

In writing that, and all that went before and that followed, I had done my best to make a cheerful scene of departure, banish tears, and evoke smiles. But some of my friends are so obstinately sentimental about me that instead of laughing they cried; and some even stayed away, unable to believe in such a thing as a happy death.

I wonder if I am wrong in thinking that Epilogue my most original bit of work. Original need not mean good; but has anyone else written his own death scene, and has he acted it in public? I have made a bargain with the University Players that some day they will again stage it with another (I have chosen my man) to act the principal part; and when I sit in the audience and gaze on that vicarious performance, I shall feel again that here is something original which has not been done before, and that I have really got hold of a new dramatic situation—an author watching his own death—which is all my own, and not likely to be stolen by others.

That plays celebrating the life and teaching of "the Poverello," the lover of Holy Poverty, should have brought me more profit than any of my other books up to date, though one of "life's little ironies," did not give me a bad conscience, and when a piously critical friend hoped I was "not making money out of it," I replied that her own clergy got paid for preaching the Gospel of Christ, and that the Roman Church made money out of Masses for the dead; and with two such good examples before me, I did not mind being helped by St. Francis to make an honest living.

Many years ago when I told Alfred that *Prunella* had done more for me than *An Englishwoman's Love-letters,* he smiled approvingly. "I'm glad," he said; "it was the better thing." As I guessed he would not repeat that remark if I told him that *Little Plays* had beaten *Prunella,* I kept quiet about it. I had not sent him the *Little Plays* on publication, for I sent him only those of my books in which I thought he might find something to please him; but when I went through his library after his death, I found that he had got all of them in their sequent editions, that he had, in fact, got a more complete collection of my books than I had myself; and I learned from friends in Cambridge that he said kinder things about them behind my back than he did to my face.

It did not exactly hurt my feelings when I learned also that he and I were supposed to be enemies; for I happened to know how that idea had got about, and that it was his own doing, though done entirely without malice. A few years ago I was staying a couple of nights with a friend in Cambridge; on the second day I said that I was going round to see my brother. He looked at me amazed. "I thought you were not on speaking terms," he said. I asked why, and this was the explanation:

One day my friend, meeting Alfred for the first time, and sitting beside him in Hall at Trinity College high table, made the mistake of introducing himself with the remark, "I have the pleasure of knowing your brother, Mr. Laurence Housman." To which Alfred stiffly replied, "Knowing my brother Laurence is no introduction to *me.*"

I laughed; it was so characteristic of him. "It only meant," I said, "that the poor man didn't want to have the trouble of talking to you; or else, possibly, he disliked you at first sight, and chose that as the most direct way of avoiding conversation."

It was probably when I told Alfred what he had done, that I quoted to him Wilfrid Scawen Blunt's comment on him in his reminiscences, after they also had met in Hall at Trinity. He said that Alfred struck him as a man who did not wish to open his mouth unless obliged. "That," said Alfred, "is absolutely true." And considering how often, in spite of that wish, he did open his mouth and make himself quite pleasant to comparative strangers, he ought to be regarded if not as one of the most genial, at least as one of the most self-sacrificing of men.

He greatly disliked having to make speeches, though he made them well; I think I heard him only once, when he spoke, as best man, at my brother Basil's wedding, and commended the custom of a certain African tribe, which, he said, made a religious practice of eating the mother-in-law at the wedding feast. It was a good instance of his humour, which had always "a bite" in it. One of the mothers-in-law was present, the other was absent; he was on friendly terms with both.

A story was told me by Professor Chambers (which I think has been enlarged in the telling) of how on one occasion at a dinner where speeches were not expected, but where the wine had been good, Alfred rose slowly to his feet and, to the amazement of all, began speaking. And this, I am told, is what he said:

"There were two things it was very difficult to meet in Cambridge a hundred and twenty years ago; the one was Wordsworth drunk, the other was Porson sober. I am a better scholar than Wordsworth; I am a better poet than Porson. Here I stand, halfway between Wordsworth and Porson."

He sat down again. It was a short speech, but it was a great success.

All this, however, has nothing to do with what I started to tell of my own two nearest approaches to popular success. *Victoria Regina* (to give it its collected title) my second essay in dramatic biography, had a send-off similar to that of *Little Plays*.

It began with amateurs. Actually the first performance, some years ahead of any other, was that given by the Glastonbury Players of *His Favourite Flower,* in 1927 or 1928, when, with the aid of a marvellous make-up by one more skilled than myself, I took the part of Lord Beaconsfield, and was completely disguised in it, so far as appearance went.

In 1931 I produced for the Street Players the five scenes which had then been published in *Palace Plays* under the title of *The Revolting Daughter,* followed by *The Queen: God Bless Her,* and in 1932 seven scenes, mostly drawn from *The Queen's Progress* (which was the second of the series), for which out of our village community, we managed to get together a cast of over forty. The part of Queen Victoria was created with extraordinary *vraisemblance* and very good characterization by Mrs. Date, one of our local players, and that of Prince Albert by Mr. Anthony Clark, whose likeness to the original was equally good, both in appearance and character. It was, taking it all round, a very competent show, but the greatest hit of the performance (independent of the acting) was the entry of five or six of our best-known local Quakers, garbed as Bishops of the Church of England in *Promotion Cometh.* That was an entry which the Street audience uproariously enjoyed.

Owing to the censorship, we had to give free admission, but collections were taken in aid of the Street Library book fund; and it fell to me, in the part of Lord Beaconsfield, which I played on both occasions, to make the necessary appeal for the money which was to cover our expenses and bring a profit to the library. The speech, made in character before the curtain during the mid-interval, ran partly as follows:

"I am here, not of my own will, but at the unscrupulous dictates of an Author who makes the historic past his game, and, in the historic present, causes its old ghosts to walk—his stage, because he wants money for your Library.

"The question is—do you want to give money to your Library? What is your Library for? What there do you read?

Do you read—any of you, today—the speeches of my great rival, Mr. Gladstone? I devoutly hope you do not. Or do you read—do you prefer—my own novels? I hope so; they are better.

"As I lay dying, fifty years ago, a new game was started in the press: the choosing of the hundred best books. And I had followers then, who placed one of my books among them. That little attention, in the downfall of my political hopes, helped me to feel that I had not lived in vain.

"Today your Librarian wants to buy for you a hundred of to-day's best books. That requires only Twenty Pounds. Half-a-crown for seeing a great Queen brought back to life, is surely not too much. Sixpence for seeing me again as Prime Minister (as you are about to do) is surely too little!

"Ladies and Gentlemen, for the sake of my August Mistress, give your half-crowns lavishly, abundantly, reduplicatively! For my poor sake, keep your sixpences in your pockets, for sixpence will no longer buy a book; and you are here to give books to your Library."

The response to that appeal brought to the collection plates (along with other sums of larger amount) a lavish shower of thoughtfully provided threepenny bits. This reverent selection of coins usually only given to God sufficiently indicated that Queen Victoria was still locally regarded as a sacred character, and not as a fit subject for commercial exploitation. The next year threepenny bits were even more in the ascendant, yet on each occasion we managed (thanks to our less pious supporters) not only to pay our way, but to hand over a surplus to the Library Book fund.

After the Street Players, "the Unnamed Society" gave performances in Manchester. Then the professionals took up the running. Marie Löhr, wearing a garden hat which had belonged to the original, gave a gracious interpretation at the Arts Theatre of *The Queen: God Bless Her;* and as it was a sitting-down part throughout, the actress's stature—so much greater than old Royalty's—did not matter.

I met Miss Löhr at the dress rehearsal for the first time. She

whispered to me a secret which ought to have kept her altogether
away. "It's so lucky," she murmured mischievously, "I've got the
mumps, and it does make me so much more like her!"

After that nothing more happened theatrically till last year. I
suppose it was the collected edition, lavishly illustrated, by E. H.
Shepard of *Punch,* which drew more attention to the plays, and
resulted in the Gate Theatre putting up a selection of ten, which
ran for five weeks to crowded houses in celebration of the King's
Silver Jubilee. Then, six months later, sumptuously produced by
Mr. Gilbert Miller, with scenes and costumes designed by Mr. Rex
Whistler, the play broke into luxuriant flower at the Broadhurst
Theatre, New York, where it is still running.

The embarrassment of riches has not overtaken me yet; but
the embarrassment of affection and gratitude has; for within the
space of less than a year I have been presented by the producers
of the plays in England and America with two most beautiful
interpretations of the title role: Pamela Stanley's at the Gate
Theatre, and that of Helen Hayes in New York. And in each case,
if each only stood alone, my natural inclination would be to let
nobody else play the part, so long as that bright particular star
was still available. But the fact that the play went over to America, largely upon the insistence of Helen Hayes after she had read
it, has resulted in my being equally in debt to a young actress of
rising reputation, whose performance at the Gate made Mr. Miller
see in it the possibilities of a popular success, and a famous actress
with laurels already won, who has turned possible success into a
reality.

There was, in the American press generally, and in that of New
York in particular, sufficient criticism of the play, as regards its
dramatic quality, to make it quite probable that only the great
popularity of Helen Hayes combined with her beautiful acting,
enabled it to get past the barrage of polite depreciation with which
it was first received, and reach that larger public which for over
six months since last Christmas has filled the theatre to capacity,
and given to the play a record success.

On the question of dramatic form, which was the main point

of criticism—speaking to a New York audience during my recent visit to America, I made the following remarks:

"When I first visited New York twenty years ago, I ascribed the kindness and warmth of my welcome largely to the fact that I was brother to the *Shropshire Lad.* I hope that is still to some extent true. But I have to recognize now that there is an added reason, in that I am the fortunate author of a play which has provided Helen Hayes with what she assures me is her favourite part, and what you, her public, assure her is her best up to date. I am the happy pedestal of that not too statuesque Queen Victoria which she has brought so vividly to life.

"To me that is a peculiar satisfaction; for though I would not claim to be one of Lytton Strachey's *Eminent Victorians,* I am eminently a Victorian. Beneath the shadow of her throne this saint had dwelt secure up to his thirty-fifth year, and only the year before she died, I published anonymously a book—my worst and my most popular—the authorship of which was ascribed in varying degrees of foolishness to about forty eminent Englishwomen, including Queen Victoria herself!

"You will realise, then, how very truly I am a survival of the Victorian age; and you will realise it still more when I tell you that I wrote my first composition (I will not repeat it to you, though I remember it) sixty-five years ago; and that my first published composition appeared sixty-three years ago. And I confess that I was far, far more excited—though not more pleased—over that first of my publications than I was when I heard that Helen Hayes had agreed to play my Queen Victoria. Such is youth.

"But next to that first and most exciting event in my literary career, is certainly this that has happened in my seventy-first year, and has brought me three thousand miles just to see a play, and then go home again. It seems an extravagant thing to do: I will only say that it was worth it, and—that I can now afford it.

"And now may I say a few words about the play itself from the point of view of the author, in answer to certain critics

Photo. by Vandamm Studio

A scene from *Victoria Regina*.

(Helen Hayes as Victoria and Lewis Casson as Lord Melbourne.)

who have questioned its rightness of form, or whether it is, indeed, a play at all. They have praised it very kindly as a literary production, but they say that it is not dramatic; and they say this mainly because it does not conform to the accepted rules of a three-act or four-act play, based on a consecutively constructed plot.

"Now there we differ. The most dramatic thing about Queen Victoria was her duration: in the moving age, to which she gave her name, she remained static; and no three-act play conventionally constructed could have conveyed that dramatic quality. It is true that the first nine scenes in the whole series as published are closely consecutive; and, had they been chosen, might have gone nearer to satisfying your fundamentalists. But Mr. Gilbert Miller was quite right to break up the sequence, and make a more extended selection in order to emphasise the duration.

"There is also, I think, this to be said: the three-act or four-act play has become the vogue because the popular interest in drama exhausts itself in performances of not more than two and a half hours; it cannot stand more. The finer dramatic taste and interest of the Chinese public extends to plays lasting for seven days. Bernard Shaw's *Back to Methuselah* requires four or five—not days—performances. My *Victoria Regina* requires three. And anyone who reads those plays as a whole will see that the plot is not a plot of incident, but of character; and what happens to that character is truly dramatic. A self-willed, obstinate, imperious and passionate little person is taken in hand by the man whom she meant to make her adorable puppet, and he, wisely and patiently, tames her, trains her, and rules her for her own and for her country's good; and that he manages to do it through a series of every-day incidents—some of them quite trivial on the surface—makes, I maintain, a thoroughly good plot; and I think that in spite of my critics, I have found a public here which agrees with me."

It seems quite likely that what happened over the *Little Plays of St. Francis* (over the writing of them, I mean) is going also to happen over my Little Plays of Queen Victoria; for when I was in New York, spurred on by Helen Hayes, I wrote two new scenes for her, and since I returned I have written three more; and I have a feeling that there are still others to come.

This form of dramatic biography, which I think I have invented, seems to interest people, for I have repeatedly been requested to extend the experiment to other historical characters; St. Cuthbert, Napoleon, Lenin, the Tichborne Claimant, and King Edward VII *(Victoria and Bertie* was the title suggested for this last) are some of them. And quite recently I was sent the name of an American heroine of whom I had never heard, and was asked to write a play-cycle about her. From that I excused myself saying that I was too old to read up chapters of history with which I was totally unfamiliar, or to acquire that ingrained sense of things American which even naturalisation at so late a stage might fail to secure for me. But there is just one play which I would like to write as a neat finish to my two dramatic biographies—though I don't think I shall ever do so; a play of St. Francis and Queen Victoria meeting in the next world; though what they would say to each other, I cannot imagine.

Chapter XXVIII

CONCERNING COMPLIMENTS

POPULAR success in a New York theatre is as solid a compliment as any author could wish for. It may pass; for the American public loves novelty more than merit, and goes on quickly to the next, whatever it may happen to be; but when it does so it leaves material reward behind. Yet I must say this for the warm-hearted American people, that I received as much personal kindness, and compliments as generous, on my first coming to America, when I was hardly known there, as I did when *Victoria Regina* and Helen Hayes between them had made me a temporary success.

Americans pay terrific compliments; they like doing it, and in the main they are sincere; but one must not take them too seriously—their literary appreciations are apt to be more jubilant than judicious.

I have a dear American friend who thinks that I am a greater poet than my brother. I know she is wrong; I should be a fool if I did not; but she is not a fool for thinking so; it only so happens that she prefers my philosophy of life to his, and knows less about poetry than I do.

Once while I was away from home—a good many years ago— two American ladies walked in on the chance of finding me, and cured their disappointment by carrying away, as a memento, two flowers out of my garden—which was really my sister's garden. It was laughable, yet it was pleasant to be told of it. No author dislikes being appreciated, and next to the appreciation of cats, I enjoy the appreciation of human beings.

There is a curious variety of flavour in the compliments paid by the people of different nations. The compliments of a Frenchman

311

only strike me as a polish of words; he is doing the honours of his race courteously to one whose culture he knows to be inferior to his own. The compliments of a German I have not been able to analyse, for I have never received any. Compliments coming from the East are beautiful ornaments of speech which, spoken in English, one feels to be merely translations from a mentality about which one knows too little to form a true opinion. The compliments I like best are Irish compliments, because it is so impossible to take them seriously: and if you do, the Irishman thinks you a fool, which you probably are. An Irishman's compliments are paid entirely to satisfy his own sense of humour. I will give two instances, which I should not have the face to do if I took them seriously.

During the Suffrage campaign, I went over to speak in Dublin, and at the end of one of the meetings, an Irish author got up to propose a vote of thanks. I had recently written a parody of Kipling's "Tommy this and Tommy that," which, with the altered refrain "Woman this and Woman that," had become popular on Suffrage platforms. Kipling, being a pronounced Anti-Suffragist had become a subject for belittlement; and so the proposer of the vote took that eminent author in hand and thus disposed of him:

"Mr. Kipling—who, I venture to say, will only be remembered by posterity for having given occasion for the most brilliant parody in the English language——"

I need not complete the sentence; I am not sure that I heard it: that magnificent pronouncement was followed by loud Irish laughter, in which English laughter joined heartily.

Another Irish compliment, which I did not take more seriously, even though it greatly delighted me, was paid me by Bernard Shaw at his own luncheon-table. He was talking to Lawrence of Arabia who sat next him, and presently, from further away, I heard the shrill voice of the oracle saying: "What Housman suffers from is the British public's dislike of intellect."

With joy in my spine I sat up and said, "What's that, Shaw?"

"Well," he replied, "don't you know it yourself? You've got

all Barrie's qualities, but unfortunately you've got intellect as well."

With that stroke of his two-edged sword Shaw was merely enjoying himself; and was no more serious about Barrie than he was serious about me. But it told me quite plainly—and that surely was a great compliment—that of the two authors I was the one he preferred.

Half an hour later, I was paid a much more genuine compliment, followed by a disappointment which I still remember as one of the most unkind strokes fate ever dealt me. When luncheon was over, Lawrence said to me, "Have you an hour to spare?" I certainly had, for the wish so indicated.

"I want to talk to you about your poems," he said. My spirits fell.

"You mean my brother's," I said.

"No, I don't; I want to talk to you about your first book, *Green Arras*."

And then, just as we were about to go off together, our hostess intervened and said to him, "Have you forgotten that you've promised to come and help us to choose a new car?" He had—quite; and so I never knew what Lawrence of Arabia wanted to say to me about *Green Arras;* for we did not meet again.

And as I have been telling of compliments, and the grains of salt with which they must be taken, here is just one more which it would be indecent for me to tell, even as a joke, were it not for the terrific wipe-out which followed and left me nowhere.

Here, in the Elementary School at Street, a teacher one day gave her class a set of questions in general knowledge; and one of the questions was, "Who is the greatest man in Somerset?" The children who, like those of other schools, had been taught dead but not living history, had not a notion whether any great men existed in Somerset, but they had to name somebody; and one of them, because her mother happened to work for us, and because she knew that I was a writer, and that writers were sometimes famous, named me as the greatest man in Somerset. And when the teacher began to read out the various names of the chosen great ones and

came to mine, she—God bless her dear heart!—said it was a better choice than some of the others. But my one swallow did make
a summer, for then all the other children cried, "Who *is* Laurence Housman?"

I had lived in Street for ten years, had produced plays, had given
lectures, had spoken at meetings; but the children of Street had
never heard of me.

This is the best cautionary story, with a personal application,
that has ever come my way: the Lord bless and increase it to me!
"Out of the mouths of babes and sucklings Thou hast ordained"—
not only praise—but other things as well.

It is, I suppose, a compliment, though one that I seldom welcome, when people—without asking permission—send me their
plays or poems, requesting my criticism or my advice about placing
them. On one occasion I made the mistake of criticising a set of
uninvited poems when I had only been asked to advise as to the
placing of them. I made my criticism as mild and as conciliatory as
possible; and this is the answer which I received:

"Sir,
"Thank you for your personal note which I appreciate,
though you have not even thanked me for the privilege you
have had in seeing my writing. I do not think I asked for
criticism when I sent it to you. Personally I consider it pre-
sumptuous to adversely criticise the work of another writer,
even if I am requested to do so. The spirit bloweth where it listeth, and it is not for any man or woman to dictate as to when,
where, or how the spirit *shall* blow. I see by the whole tenor
of what you say that it would be quite impossible for me to
write verse that would satisfy you. After all, God is my
Judge, and no individual man.
"May I say, in all humility, that I think perhaps the only
verse agreeable to you is that written by yourself. I suppose
that is what you have described as 'good poetry'?
"Please do not think that I wish to say anything unpleasant
in this letter—No—I am simply writing as the spirit moves
me, and of this I am certain you will not disapprove.

"It is rather tempting for an established writer to assume an attitude of patronage and condescension to one who is as yet unknown to the public, and particularly is this so when the subject in question is a woman and a poet. Very few men can resist the instinctive masculine inclination to immediately put her in her place *and keep her there!* Now, isn't this all quite true?

"I shall not attempt to pass judgment upon any of your writing—not because I consider myself incompetent to do so, but first, for this reason, that as I have said previously—'the spirit bloweth where it listeth,' and secondly because by nature I am too courteous to do so. I have found that generally speaking women are far more courteous and considerate than men.

"May I close with your own words, 'I hope this frankness does not offend.'

"Yours faithfully,

"_____ _____."

I liked her letter so much better than her poems; but it was no use writing to tell her so. I knew that, after my uncalled-for criticism, it would be impossible to please her.

CHAPTER XXIX

UNFINISHED CONCLUSIONS

TWENTY-EIGHT years ago, when I first strayed from my true job of authorship, and forced myself to become a speaker, a friend—more foreseeing than myself—warned me that I should never again be able to escape from the entanglement of politics and the social problem. I thought then that Woman Suffrage was the only thing about which I should have to let my conscience trouble me; but from that day on, the trouble has been persistently recurring, and has increased rather than diminished. And though I have not again given up so much of my time to speaking as I did between 1908 and 1914, my concern over two of our greatest political problems (India and Peace) and other social matters depending thereon, has never set me as free from the disturbances of controversy as the author in me would wish. And again, I have to admit, that a clear conscience does not always make for happiness in personal or in other relations. I have friends who choose to be alienated by political differences, as for instance, when I presided at the meeting of welcome given to Mahatma Gandhi when he came to London for the Round Table Conference, and in my remarks as chairman said that our attitude toward India should be that of "unconditional goodwill" not dependent on good behaviour, or on meek submission, officially described as "loyalty," to a form of government which had not the free consent of the people.

It happened rather amusingly that just when two friends had given me a patriotic scolding for keeping such bad company, Gandhi had gone by invitation to Buckingham Palace to meet the King; and I suggested that it was rather absurd to tell me that company which was good enough for the King was not good enough for me. It was a short way for shutting two foolish mouths, but I knew, as a matter of fact, that Gandhi had only gone reluctantly, and as an act of courtesy, and that his acceptance of the invitation did not mean either loyalty or allegiance.

I think in nearly every case where I have taken sides in matters controversial my attitude has been decided for me, not by supporters of the cause, to which I joined myself, but by opponents. When in 1925 Sir Joynson-Hicks (afterwards Lord Brentford), member of the Tory Cabinet, made the damning but quite honest pronouncement which I am about to quote, and made it without provoking any disclaimer from his political associates, I recognised that it stated an historical truth, as regards the past, and was fairly representative of the official mind toward India in the present.

"We did not," he said, "conquer India for the benefit of the Indians. I know in missionary meetings it is said that we conquered India to raise the level of the Indians. That is cant. We conquered India as an outlet for the goods of Great Britain. We conquered India by the sword, and by the sword we shall hold it—I am stating facts."

That representative statement of facts which leaves the average Englishman quite unashamed, and which even has his general approval, quite decided me on which side I must align myself. To the fundamental claim of India for self-government and independence, sporadic or even organised terrorism makes no difference. It did not in the case of Ireland; it cannot in the case of India. The doctrine of racial superiority as a justification for racial dominance and the imposing our own ideas of government on races which would far rather govern themselves, becomes more and more a superstition in proportion to the standard of civilization to which we apply it.

In Germany today its more local and logical application, under far more homogeneous conditions rouses our anger and indignation; but in India we regard it as a virtue and the keystone of that corner in vested interests which Kipling described as "the white man's burden," and which Lord Brentford would have us defend to the death for the profit which it still brings us.

As regards the Peace Movement, I have come to see that it is no use saying you believe in peace, unless you cease to believe in war. Any belief in war as an ultimate remedy vitiates the whole process of peace preparation—reduces it indeed to foolishness. It is no use advocating vegetarianism while you still run a butcher's shop: your advocacy fails to win conviction. If you really believe that meat is a poison to the system you will close your butcher's shop without waiting for others. Similarly, if you believe that by supplying oil to an aggressor nation, you are supplying it with the means to commit murder, you will *not* call it "humbug" to refuse to supply it (as Mr. Baldwin did recently) merely because others are continuing to do so. It is surely the most elementary morality that to aid and abet murder does not become an innocent act if done in company. Yet that is the standard of morality to which our Government reduced this country during the last year or so, and now tells us that it would have been "humbug" to do otherwise.

The Peace Movement is becoming troublesome. So troublesome that the Secretary of State for War, finding that his recruiting campaign was failing to bring in sufficient number, has appealed to the Church to declare pacifism to be a heresy. One archbishop and two bishops have hastened to oblige; one, more recently, has declared that it is blasphemy against God, because pacifism refuses to accept the good means which God provides us for defending ourselves from evil.

As Mr. Baldwin has rightly told us that from now on the only defence in war is counter-attack, and as that involves the bombing of women and children—sooner, and on a larger scale if possible, than the bombing to which war makes our own women and children liable; and as we are invited to do that in Christ's Name, and as a demonstration of the goodness of God in the means He has provided us for defending ourselves from evil, it seems to me at least, that the blasphemy is rather on the other side and that a bishop has made himself its loud-speaker.

Mr. Baldwin has said that when our young men decide for us that the thing is evil, the evil will have to cease. He waits for the young men, whom we tell off to do the accursed thing for us, to give us the moral lead which he and the bishops of the Established Church refuse.

It was my entanglement in politics which, reacting upon the author, caused me to write *Trimblerigg*. It is not my favourite book; the writing of it left me with a bitter taste; for even to pose as the victim of verbal inspiration is not good for one's soul. All the same, I feel that it is as useful and as truthful a book as I have ever written. For though in form it is a mass of "inspired" fiction, it seeks to drive home a whole set of truths against which the body politic—wherein Nation-worship masquerades under the guise of Christianity—is still fighting tooth and claw. And the salvation of the world during the next few decades does quite literally depend on the assertion of those truths in men's minds against the racial illusion which is steadily hurling civilisation to destruction.

Mr. Trimblerigg, as the symbolic representative of that racial state of mind which we have to get rid of, was, at the time of writing, my main standby for a hopeful outlook on an immediate future which otherwise seemed dark. For, by all appearances, Mr. Trimblerigg's counterpart in real life had then come to a humiliating and timely end. It looks even now as though power has effectively oozed out of him, and that he will never again be in a position to talk through his hat to a world which is prepared to take that headpiece seriously. It is true that lip-service of a kind is still given him, that he is still the diminished leader of a diminished crew; but his piracies on the high seas seem likely in the future to be limited to fishing for sprats in the off season in places where sprats do not abound; and we shall have the amusement of seeing him fish for them with all the tackle which he used to employ to catch whales. That in itself is a form of poetic justice which inclines me to believe that there is a streak of design underlying that great work of Improvidence which we call Creation, and that the blind forces which swing man's destiny this way and that are not devoid of a sense of humour even though their practical jokes are played in the dark.

That Mr. Trimblerigg should in his own lifetime become little in man's eyes—and even in the eyes of men who once believed him great—is a conspicuous work of mercy expeditiously achieved, very largely by himself: the Lord bless and continue it to him! And if my Book of Revelation has, in any degree however small, contributed to that work of mercy, then may the reward promised to those who are merciful be mine, and may I also obtain mercy when the Book of Judgment is opened and names are called.

CHAPTER XXX

PRESENT ENDING

I BEGAN these reminiscences with the story of our family life, and of the home years when, in that process of self-education which is the best education of all, Alfred was our leader, and—in a very quarrelsome family—the only one with whom we never quarrelled.

I cannot end without saying something about his death, which came while the last few of these chapters were being written. Three years ago his health began rapidly to decline, and his walking powers, which all his life had given him that quiet companionship of nature which suited him best, had considerably diminished. For some years he had been taking holidays abroad, generally in France; two years ago, after a slight accident, he decided not to go abroad again; and I think it was then that he wrote telling me that he had begun to obey his doctor's orders to the extent of only walking twice as far as what was medically permitted him. At that time his rooms in Trinity College were on the second floor, forty steps up. "I go up," he wrote, "two steps at a time, hoping to drop dead at the top." It was the expression (merely verbal then, I think) of a wish, which from that time on became more definite, not to outlive his physical enjoyment of life.

Fortunately, during those last two years I was able to propose that we should take holiday together; and in the summer of 1934 staying at Droitwich, only six miles from our old home, we made long motor rounds daily through Worcestershire, Gloucestershire, Herefordshire and Shropshire. Last year he elected to stay in Cambridge, and with that as our centre we visited more places, churches, abbeys and cathedrals than I can count. He knew them nearly all, and had a marvellous memory for their main points of interest, and their style of architecture—even for those which he had not seen for a score of years. There was hardly a cathedral in England that he did not remember better than I did; architecture was an interest which we shared deeply; and our only difference was that I preferred Norman, and he Early English. "Of course," he said drily, as if to discount the genuineness of my preference, "to extol Norman is now the fashion." But he himself considered that one of the duties of architecture, and especially of windows, was to let in light. Monastic gloom did not please him as it pleased me.

His memory of poetry was as extraordinary as his memory of architecture. One day we were discussing Keble, a poet for whom naturally he had no great liking, though in his lecture on *The Name and Nature of Poetry,* he had taken the trouble to say which of his poems he considered to be his best. I happened to have mentioned the hymn which begins "Sun of my Soul," saying that it formed only part of a whole poem, the first verse of which I was unable to remember. Immediately he quoted it with unhesitating correctness. It is just possible that this was due to the fact which in an autobiographical note stands thus recorded. "I was brought up in the Church of England, and in the High Church Party, which is much the best religion I have ever come across. But Lemprière's Classical Dictionary, read when I was eight, made me prefer paganism to Christianity." Possibly it was early reading, or perhaps learning by heart things which his mother chose for him that gave that verse from Keble its long hold on his memory. Yet I could give other instances not limited to poetry. He did not care much for Landor, and said that he had read him but little; yet when I sent him a quotation I could not identify, he placed it for me at once in one of the *Imaginary Conversations.*

Last November I went to speak at a Peace Meeting in Cambridge; he was then staying temporarily at the Nursing Home which had by that time become his accustomed place of refuge whenever his health failed him. I went to see him; he knew what I was there for; the evening before there had been a torchlight procession to advertise the meeting. "Last night," he said, "your people were making a great noise outside, disturbing everyone. If that is what you call 'a Peace Movement,' I would prefer that it should remain sedentary."

After his death I came to stay in his rooms at Trinity, a new set of rooms on the ground floor, to which without any trouble to himself he and his belongings had been moved through the devoted service of his friend and co-Fellow, Mr. Andrew Gow. His bedmaker said to me, "I loved your brother. When I first began to do for him I used to be afraid to go into the room; but it was all right when I got to know him." The assistant matron at the Nursing Home said much the same. Many others, whom he kept rigidly at arm's length, had a great affection for him, over and above their deep respect for his power of scholarship.

I asked his doctor how long before his death he was fully conscious. Just about two days I was told. And this, as far as I can remember it in his own words is the doctor's account of their last meeting.

"You know," he said, "how silent and reserved he always was; but this time he talked quite a lot, and very affectionately. He held my hand for nearly half an hour. 'You have been a good friend to me,' he said. 'I know you have brought me here so that I may not commit suicide, and I know that you may not help me to it more than the law allows. But I do ask you not to let me have any more unnecessary suffering than you can help.' I told him that he should not suffer any more; and from that time on he did not. Then, to cheer him just before I left, I told him a thoroughly naughty story. He was very weak, but he threw his head back on the pillow, laughing heartily. 'Yes, that's a good one,' he said, 'and tomorrow I shall be telling it again on the Golden Floor.' "

I hope that no pious friend will try to force from that characteristic remark an interpretation implying belief in a future life which it was most certainly not intended to convey.

And now, though there are many more things that I remember

about him and about others, which some day I may wish to record, for the present I have finished.

Of all the strange oppositions of life the two strangest are what we remember and what we forget. How many great and important things—important in their influence upon one's after-life—has one not perhaps utterly forgotten? Strange that one should if they made one what one has become today. And yet as one knows nothing of one's first begetting, out of which came life and breath, so of these sequent begettings there is no outward expression that one can take hold of and recognise and trace to its source in things said or things done.

And then, on the other side, the things that one remembers: the little things that come stepping into life so quietly, to remain so unexpectedly permanent—not so unexpected in their happening as in their effect. Why does one remember certain intonations, gestures, actions—one's own or other people's, so trivial in character, so empty of all practical result that one can see: they were of no importance at the time, or beauty or interest, but there— minute particles of a past life inseparable from memory—they stick, beautiful in their mysterious tenacity, though with no other beauty for which we could desire them; insignificant essentials in a life which we call our own but cannot control or isolate from that web of life into which everything is spun—nothing we can do will away with them.

THE END

INDEX

INDEX

Peter Pan, 192
Peter the Great, 88
Peterborough, 212
Pethick-Lawrence, 244
Phillips, Stephen, 171
Piccadilly, 231, 248
Pickwick Papers, 69
Pied Piper of Hamelin, The, 218
Pinker, 138, 139, 170
"Pioneer Players," 209
Pissaro, Lucien, 171
Pius IX, Pope, 46
Plymouth, 50
Pollard, A, W., 97-98, 100, 128
Pont Street, 68
Pope, Alexander, 91, 170
Popes, 46, 125
Portiuncula, 288
Portman Square, 183
Potter, Mrs. Brown, 127
Poynter, 104
Pre-Raphaelites, 100
Prohibition, 294
Protestantism, 126
Prunella, 89, 104, 114, 183, 185, 186,
    192-193, 194, 195, 200, 203, 205,
    260, 282, 285, 303
Public School System, 72-74
Punch, 94, 214, 307

Quakers, 118, 276
Queen, The: God Bless Her, 305
Queen's College, 83
Queen's Progress, The, 305
Quilter, Harry, 100, 101

Rabelais, 215
Radicals, 41
"Ravenhill" of Punch, 94
Raymond, Judge, 267
Redford, Mr., 158-159, 208, 209
    see Censor
Redmond, John, 269
Reform Bill of 1832, 41
Reform Bill of 1867, 41
Refugee Home, 270
Revolting Daughter, The, 305
Rhondda, Lord, 239
Richards, Grant, 179
Ricketts, Charles, 94, 99, 100, 101, 109,
    171
Rivals, The, 69
Robert Elsmere, 115

Roberts, Lord, 185
Rokeby Venus, the, 238
Roman Catholic Church, 33, 50, 121-127,
    163, 173-174
Rome, 123, 124
Romney, 71
Rose, 67
Rossetti, Christina
    Goblin Market, 103
Rossetti, Dante Gabriel, 100
Rothenstein, Augustus John, 164
Rothenstein, Will, 172-173
    The Doll's House, 164
Rothenstein, Mrs. Will, 164, 173
Royal Academy, 129, 131
Royal Runaway, The, 143, 166, 222
Ruprecht of Bavaria, Prince, 187
Ruskin, John, 60, 109
Russia, 42
Russian Revolution, 273-274

Sabatier, Paul, 287, 288
    quoted, 286-287
Sabrina Warham, 178
St. Cuthbert, 310
St. Damien's, 288
St. Francis, 165, 166, 205, 272, 279, 280,
    287, 289, 297
St, James' Gazette, 192
St. James Theatre, 99
St. John's College, 50, 83
St. Martin's, 267
St. Martin's Pageant, 110, 280-281
St. Pancras People's Theatre, 285
St. Peter, 124, 125, 219
San Francisco, 288
Sandro, 176, 177
Sargent, John Singer, 130-131
Savage, Reginald, 97
Savoy Theatre, 209
Schreiner, Olive
    Story of an African Farm, The, 115-
    116, 119, 120
Scotland, 179, 232
Scotland Yard, 257
Scott, 178
Scott, C. P., 128
Scott, Sir Walter, 69
    Lay of the Last Minstrel, The, 68
    Marmion, 68
    Waverley Novels, 69
Scriptures, 29, 67, 81
Seabrooke, Elliott, 153, 272